Better Than
GOLD

Better Than GOLD

Olympian Kenny Davis and the Most Controversial Basketball Game in History

GARY P. WEST

WITH

KENNY DAVIS

Acclaim Press
MORLEY, MISSOURI

Acclaim Press
— Your Next Great Book —
P.O. Box 238
Morley, MO 63767
(573) 472-9800
www.acclaimpress.com

Book Design: Devon Burroughs
Cover Design: M. Frene Melton

Library of Congress Control Number: 2014910450
ISBN-13: 978-1-938905-68-1
ISBN-10: 1-938905-68-7

First Printing: 2014
Printed in the United States of America
10 9 8 7 6 5 4 3 2 1

Contents

Foreword

I did not know Kenny Davis very well prior to the reunion of the 1972 Olympic basketball team held in Georgetown, Kentucky in the late summer of 2012.

I, like a lot of Kentuckians, have always admired Kenny, not only as a great basketball player at Georgetown College, but for being an Olympian.

When famed sportswriter Billy Reed called me in late 2011 with an idea about putting together a 40th reunion of this team, who had refused to accept the silver medals in the controversial loss to the Russians in the championship game, I was eager to do what I could.

Kenny Davis was captain of that USA team coached by the great Hank Iba, and the fact that he was from a small NAIA school, while his teammates were all NCAA major college players, further shows the respect they all had for him.

At the reunion, Doug Collins made it clear that Kenny was not only a great player, but a leader who led with unbelievable determination.

Over the years, I've met hundreds if not thousands of great athletes, but Kenny may be the most humble great sports legend of them all. I watched him closely during the terrific reunion week and the way he treated everyone is a true testimony to his Wayne County roots.

This book by Gary West and Kenny Davis probably should have been written several years ago. The fact that it has now been done will solidify Kenny's place in sports history as one of America's most valuable citizens. His and his teammate's refusal that September day in Munich, Germany to accept a medal they felt they hadn't earned, further points to the injustice they had received in having their gold medals denied them in the most controversial basketball game ever played.

Kenny's leadership during the terrorist's tragedy that left several Israeli athletes murdered went a long way in helping to keep it all together for the American basketball team.

Tom Burleson, the big 7-3 center, became very emotional in describing the deaths of the Israelis, and talked about Kenny's leadership, calmness, and determination as team captain to win, regardless of the issues around the games.

As time goes by, Kenny's resolve in declaring to his teammates that he would never accept those silver medals instead of the gold that had been wrongly taken away from them, has now been met with unanimous consent. Those twelve silver medals still sit in storage in Switzerland residing with the International Olympic Committee, who still has hopes that someday the team will change its mind. I know for sure, however, Kenny never will.

I am pleased, as a citizen of the USA, and a proud Kentuckian to now call Kenny Davis a good friend who will never be forgotten by us.

—Jim Host
Founder and Former CEO,
Host Communications

INTRODUCTION

As difficult as it might be to explain, Kenny Davis' life might be defined by a single basketball game, a game in which he didn't score a point.

Never in his wildest dreams could he ever imagine that a game played by millions of young boys and girls would open a door wide enough for him to not only look through, but walk through and see the world. Growing up in the 1960's, Kenny's world was Monticello in Wayne County, Kentucky.

In the beginning, all he ever wanted to do was to become a Wayne County Cardinal.

Dark comes early during the winter months in Wayne County. The trees are barren and the cold of a brisk wind can reach the bones. But with little else to do after the farm chores were done, it was basketball time for Kenny.

Throughout Kentucky, many thought basketball was as close to heaven as you could get and still be on earth. And the great round ball temple that cast a giant shadow when it came to popularity and influence was in Lexington, Kentucky. That shadow extended all the way to Wayne County.

The Kentucky Wildcats were the young men many throughout the state worshipped, and they felt if you were a really good basketball player you would play for Adolph Rupp.

That was the criteria used to judge the talent of a basketball player in Kentucky. In spite of this belief there were other Kentucky colleges turning out championship teams: Ed Diddle and John Oldham at Western; Peck Hickman and Denny Crum at Louisville; Paul McBrayer at Eastern; and Cal Luther at Murray.

Kenny Davis didn't go to the University of Kentucky … couldn't play for the Wildcats. And though he only stayed 10 weeks, he did go to Western Kentucky. But then on his way to enrolling at the Air Force Academy, something strange happened. He stopped off at Georgetown College, planning only to stay there for a semester, perhaps not even playing basketball.

Suddenly, out of nowhere, his life changed.

Just as in high school, he started shooting the basketball again and again and again. His knees would flex and his legs would launch him effortlessly into the air, all the while his eyes aimed at the rim in front of him. The artistic flick of his wrist sent the ball up and out toward the basket. And more often than not the song his shot played was string music to anyone who saw it.

Coach Bob Davis saw it, and though not related, Kenny Davis, Bob Davis, and Georgetown College would forever be connected.

Three college All-American years later, against all odds, Kenny had played in the World Games, Pan American Games, playing the game he learned in Wayne County on five continents. Heady stuff for a boy who had never traveled outside of Kentucky until he went to college.

But the best was yet to come.

The crowning achievement of any American athlete would be to become an Olympian. More often than not it can define one's life. To play basketball on the world's largest stage had become a dream come true, but in the big picture of life's progression, it was no more important than when he became a Wayne County Cardinal.

From Monticello to Munich, the basics of basketball remained the same: dribble, pass, shoot, rebound and defend.

No one questioned at any level the competitiveness of Kenny Davis. Early on when it came to competition he was in a tuxedo, while everyone else was still in their pajamas. But then as he advanced, it wasn't long before other tuxedos began to appear.

Basketball became insignificant, however, when a group of terrorist slipped into Munich's Olympic Village and murdered 11 Israeli athletes, thus changing the Olympic world. Suddenly the game Kenny had played all of his life didn't seem as important as it once did. Kenny got to come home … they didn't.

The powers to be, and rightly so, declared that anything less than continuing the Games would be giving into the terrorists.

With all eyes watching, the Americans played the Russians in what became the most controversial ending to a basketball game in history.

This game helped to define who Kenny became, and he didn't score a point. Those 12 silver medals Kenny and his teammates refused to accept are today locked in a room in the Olympic Museum in Lausanne, Switzerland.

It's all in these pages, including how Kenny sold millions of tennis shoes during a 40-year career with Converse shoes.

Note: In this book, the Soviet Union will be referred to as the Russians, but in actuality its team was composed of players from 12 different states that make up Soviet Union. Many of the television, radio, newspapers and magazine reports referred to them as "the Russians." Listening to Frank Gifford do the play-by-play of that gold medal game made it sound even more confrontational when it was, "The Americans against the Russians." For marketing purposes it has always been "Here come the Russians." And so it is here.

Better Than GOLD

Olympian Kenny Davis and the Most Controversial Basketball Game in History

CHAPTER ONE

Could it be possible for a young boy from rural Kentucky to dream so big about becoming a basketball player that he actually did it? What would the odds be?

To play basketball at the highest level in the 1950's meant you usually played at the University of Kentucky for Adolph Rupp. Anything or anywhere else was considered by some to be a cut below. To hear the Wildcats on radio back then was a treat and to see them on T.V., well, it just didn't happen.

Rupp had set the standard by winning NCAA championships in 1948 and 1958, and that '48 team, made up of the so-called Fabulous Five, went on to win Olympic Gold.

Young boys in Kentucky could dream. First it was about making their high school team, and then those thoughts would turn toward Lexington, the home of the Kentucky Wildcats.

For Clyde and Zula Davis, their son Kenny, the third of six children, might just be good enough someday to make the Wayne County High School basketball team. Lord knows he worked at it enough. And besides that, he was a good kid, studied hard and most of all, stayed out of trouble. Why couldn't a boy born in Slate, Kentucky in Wayne County be a basketball player?

Kenny's teacher for the first three years at Oil Valley Elementary School was Miss Velma Alexander, a small petite woman who allowed Kenny to start school as a five-year-old, after telling his mom and dad, "As long as he doesn't cause any trouble."

"If you knew Miss Velma, getting in trouble was not going to happen," Kenny recalled.

Upon entering the fourth grade Kenny moved into another room. His teacher was Harry Roberts, a man who was as large as Miss Velma was small. "He kept things in order," says Kenny, "And he didn't take any back-talk."

Oil Valley was less than a quarter mile from the Davis home, so walking through the fields was his best and shortest route.

"I was always on time getting to class as I was afraid of Miss Velma, but there were numerous things I wanted to explore that delayed my return home. Dad, on more than one occasion, had to send my brother Ralph out to look for me, as farm chores awaited even at that early age," he said. "Our playground at school was dirt, and typical of most kids the best time during the school day was recess. If there was a basketball goal it was not something I was aware of, nor had an interest in."

But Kenny's young world as he knew it was about to change. Typical of that time period, Wayne County took several of their small aging community schools and consolidated them into one large building located in Monticello, the county seat of Wayne County.

"Oil Valley Elementary no longer existed, and I found myself as a fifth grader at Walker Elementary," he said. "Most kids, me included, were not pleased that our comfortable and secure world had changed. But that was short lived as I quickly realized that the options to distract me had increased tenfold. A larger pool of friends to choose from, especially girls, a chance to ride a school bus, and a brand new building with central heat were just a few of those options. And most of all, there was an indoor room for play regardless of inclement weather. I can't tell you the number of times recess was cancelled or altered due to bad weather at Oil Valley. Pitching rubber horse shoes was not my idea of fun.

"Little did I know that indoor play facility would mold how I would live the remainder of my life? It was a gymnasium and had regulation basketball goals on either end. It doubled as a lunchroom, but could quickly be converted back into a playing court when the lunch tables were folded back into the walls.

"I remember the first time we were allowed to use the basketball court. It was a physical education class and we were instructed to shoot layups. I had no idea what our teacher, Mr. Bill Kelly, was talking about, but followed those who did and placed myself at the back of the line.

"Next came the moment that would define who I would become. As I finished my layup, Mr. Kelly told me I was the only one who shot the ball using the correct foot. I did it naturally, right hand layup, shoot off left foot … no one taught me.

"I was hooked. I did know what I had done, but I also knew that this was fun and the affirmation from an authority figure that I did something correct was something that I knew I wanted more of."

It was a stretch, but the closest Kenny would come to getting into trouble as a small boy was his fondness for chewing gum. It wasn't just a single stick, but he would often put the whole pack in his mouth.

Clyde Davis came from a family of 12, all born and raised in Wayne County, They, too worked the land with their hands and a few mules. It was their way of life. None participated in sports, but Clyde and Zula knew quickly that Kenny was different from all of the Davis' that came before him. "He came home one day and said 'I want to play basketball,'" Clyde recalled. "He did it on his own and we didn't discourage him." He began bouncing a basketball so much that soon the family had to put up a goal.

"Dad and mom owned a small hillside farm, and with level land at a premium to grow crops and a big garden to feed a growing family, there was no way even a small portion would be allocated to use for a basketball court. But thankfully dad did not completely nix the idea. He said there was one spot we could use that was level. It measured approximately 15 x 15, which was large enough, but there was one problem we did not foresee. It was surrounded on all sides with sink holes and thorn trees.

"It was by far the worse location for a basketball court in the county, and probably the state, but that being the only option, my brother Ralph and I went to work with a fever that all Kentucky lads caught at an early age … we wanted to learn how to play this special game. We cleared stick weeds, blackberry vines and even cow paddies and cut a cedar tree for the support and bought a rim at the local Western Auto store, and we were in business.

"A court surrounded by thorn trees and sink holes was a blessing and a curse for me. The curse was it was not advisable to dribble as punctures from the thorns would quickly bring an end to my Western Auto ball. Sadly, the repair patch that worked perfectly on my bike tire was not effective on a basketball. Ralph and I went through several balls before we decided it was not a good idea to put it on the ground. But the blessing was … I learned when the ball went through the basket it diminished the chances it would wind up in a sinkhole or sustain a puncture from a nearby thorn tree. It is amazing how your concentration increases knowing that if something happens to this ball, it might be sometime before funds were available to replace it. No doubt what I learned about concentration in shooting a basketball on that crude court was foundation that would lead me to become a good shooter."

With Kenny's mom and dad now realizing that their son wanted to play basketball, they were supportive, but no one was more so than Rosa Perkins, his grandmother.

"She was mom's mother, and she was a fan," he said. "Her living with us was like having two moms. She would go to the games, and there were stories about how she would get into it with opposing fans, especially when they criticized Jack Upchurch" (a star at Wayne County several years earlier).

A family friend of the Davises', Edna Fairchild Brasier, remembers the day Kenny was born.

"Gene, Kenny's older brother and I used to walk to Greenbriar School together," she said. "We walked a mile on the main road and from Slat's Store we walked another half-mile on a gravel road. Then one day there was a lot of commotion at the Davises' house, and someone came out and said the doctor was there to deliver a baby … it was Kenny."

And then to further show the strength of Rosa Perkins, the Davis kids grandmother, Edna spoke of a time when Gene told her he was going to get a whipping the next day at school.

"Gene told his grandmother," said Edna. "And she went to school the next day and told the teacher she wasn't going to whip her grandson. She told the teacher, 'You put your pants on the same way I do, unless you hang 'em up and jump in 'em.'"

Rosa was 94 when she died.

Older brothers Gene (7 years) and Ralph (15 months) didn't play sports, but like their parents they backed Kenny. And Bruce, two years younger, later became a student manager for the high school team so he could travel to the away games. But when Kenny graduated he gave that up. Sandy, a sister is nine years younger, and another brother, Gary, who was born with Downs Syndrome, is 16 years younger.

"Probably the biggest factor in my development as a basketball player was dad and mom's decision to sell our Oil Valley farm and move to Worsham Lane," said Kenny. "In 1959 my uncle Bill Davis decided to relocate his family to a farm in Georgia, and he gave us the opportunity to buy his place which contained more level acreage and was closer to town. In the 60's, Worsham Lane was a two-mile county road located just outside Monticello city limits. A section of it was taken when a bypass was constructed around Monticello in the 90's. It was populated with small farms and residential homes. The road was narrow and carried little traffic. It was a perfect place to ride a bike and dribble a basketball. To my surprise and delight it was located only a quarter of a mile from Walker Elementary and provided me access to its playgrounds that featured factory made basketball goals and level blacktop, which provided a consistent bounce not possible on our Oil Valley court. Probably with this new surface available I should have spent more time perfecting my ball handling skills, but I continued to get more satisfaction from shooting than dribbling. Needless to say, I took advantage of every moment that became available to head to those courts.

"Two other places I spent many an hour perfecting my game was Selvedge Grocery and Bruce Phillips garage court.

"Selvedge Grocery was a thriving market located just a few blocks from downtown. The owner had two sons, Bill and Everett, who played for Monticello High School. The Selvedge boys hung a rim on the outside of the block store building and welcomed anyone who desired to stop in for pick-up games. One enormous factor that made this a desirable place to play was a security light that lit up the parking lot, and it gave us the chance to play after dark. This was a great benefit for me as dad kept my brothers and me busy on the farm during the day and to be able to play at night was a dream come true.

"Bill became a very successful doctor in the Louisville area, and Everett worked many years as a state trooper.

"Bruce Phillips was a local attorney who was dad's friend and provided all the legal work that our family required. His two sons, Hardin and Van, were avid basketball players. Both played college ball. Hardin played at Carson Newman and Van was a teammate of mine at Georgetown. They had a hoop nailed over their garage and there was a competitive game almost daily at this family home. I am sure there were times that Mr. and Mrs. Phillips and their daughter, Jane found me to be a nuisance, but that was never expressed, and I will always be grateful for their kindness."

By now Kenny was putting more miles on his red and white Western Flyer bicycle, with streamers on the handlebars and mud flaps on the fenders, one he had bought and paid for by delivering "Grit" newspapers every week.

"In most cases, youngsters do not have input as to the location where they grow up. Parents make that decision. But if I had been the one that was allowed to make that decision, my choice would have been Monticello. No one could have had a more perfect childhood than I. Wonderful parents, an amazing grandmother, special siblings, in a crime free town and able to roam free as a bird, made my childhood one that many could only dream of. I use the word "roam", which is what I did throughout the city on my bicycle."

He would ride over during the summer days to see Rita Bell, a friend and neighbor whose brother Darrell played basketball at Cumberland College. He had another friend, Peggy Dick and her brother Emerson, he would often visit, usually riding and dribbling that familiar basketball. He went very few places without it.

In the 50's and 60's, most small towns in Kentucky did not have stores that sold only sporting goods. That role, however, was often filled by the local Western Auto Store, and Kenny was a familiar face there. "There was no sporting goods store located in Monticello at that time. And the only business that carried athletic items was Western Auto," he said. "No doubt Mr. Anderson, who owned the business, grew tired of a young boy coming in day after day drooling over those items, but never buying since money was not growing on trees on the Davis farm during the 1950's. If he was annoyed he never let it show, and I still remember his kindness. I envy all those youngsters who grew up in Monticello after me as they had one of the top sporting goods stores in the state in which to shop. Later H & W Sporting Goods, owned by Ronnie Hord and Wayne Wells opened in Monticello. In a few years they sold their business to Sherman York who operated the business for years."

Even though Kenny's practicing all the time didn't bother his parents, it did strike a chord with Kenny's Uncle Lee.

"He was my oldest brother, and he told me Kenny wouldn't amount to much playing ball and all, and that he needed to get back to doing his work," Kenny's father Clyde said. "But the thing was he played ball and still did his work. He plowed tobacco with a mule and he would milk cows before he went to school. He's the only one in our family who'd do that."

Clyde says that Kenny hated hoeing weeds so much that when he'd plow the tobacco he'd also plow the weeds so he wouldn't have to hoe them.

"Kenny used to tell everyone that 'Dad made me plow with a mule and when I left home he got a tractor,'" he chuckled.

"He said the mule was getting old. But it wasn't the mule's age, it was me going away to college," said Kenny.

Chapter Two

Not just Monticello, but all of Wayne County was learning who Kenny Davis was. How could they not? Everywhere he went he had a basketball under his arm heading someplace to shoot baskets. And on several occasions they'd even see him on his bicycle, dribbling a basketball while he peddled.

Clyde Davis' mode of transportation was a green 1950 Chevy pick-up. It served him well for his farm chores, and whenever the whole family needed to go somewhere three and sometimes four would squeeze into the front seat while he drove. Anyone else who wanted to go could climb in the back.

Zula, Kenny's mom, bought some of her groceries at Abbots Grocery not far from their farm on Hwy. 92, but once a week she'd go "to town" for a larger selection at the IGA Foodline. "Town", by Wayne County lingo, meant Somerset, 14 miles away.

The Davis family farmed corn, soy beans, and a couple of acres of tobacco. Kenny says his dad was a tenant farmer most of his life, in that he contracted out to raise another 20 acres for other farmers.

"When dad got out of the Army he said if possible he'd never have another boss," Kenny said. "And he was pretty much able to do it except for my mom, of course. He was 92-years-old in January 2014, and so far he's done it his way."

Clyde Davis' property sat virtually on the city-county line, and the folks in Monticello began to realize that the little, burr headed kid who dribbled a basketball while riding his bicycle could also shoot it.

There weren't many days when Kenny didn't shoot a basketball. The weather outside was really never a factor. If snow covered his dirt court, and he couldn't find a way to get in the gym, he would shovel the white stuff off to the side and shoot.

"The city limits line came to the edge of our driveway," Kenny says. "Going into my junior year of high school at Wayne County, a survey was done on the property and I could probably have been forced to go to Monticello. But no one ever tried to get me to transfer, and I think it was the respect coaches Joe Harper (Monticello) and Ray Mills (Wayne County) had for each other."

Monticello High School, the "City" school, lays claim to Kentucky's first unofficial state basketball championship in 1914-15. There are even records that date the school's first team as far back as 1906-07. So with that said it is easy to understand that by the time the 1950's rolled around, Monticello High was considered one of the state's best programs, and under Gayle Taft in his only year of coaching, took the Monticello Trojans to the Sweet 16 with a 16-10 record. Joe Harper followed Taft, and for 23 years established a solid run, appearing in the State Tournament in 1958-59-60. The '60 team lost in the championship game to Louisville Flaget 65-56 in a state wide televised game. (Harper would later coach Wayne County High from 1980-1986). Gene Pendleton and Don Frye were both first team all-state that year. When Monticello High school merged into Wayne County in 2013, it left behind the eighth winningest basketball program in Kentucky history.

Kenny was strictly a basketball guy. Although the area had a summer Little League baseball program, it was not for him.

"I played one year and didn't care much about it," he said. "The coach put me in the outfield to hide me."

Basketball was Kenny's life. Of course he took care of his obligations on the farm. It was amazing, having a family that had never participated in organized sports, he had their full support to play basketball.

There would be times when he would watch television as a youngster, but it was certainly not one of his staples of life.

"We only got one station that I can remember, he offered. "It was WNOX and the show I do remember was a variety show of sorts, you know singers, and dancers. Its main sponsor was Cas Walker Super Market."

Kenny, though still in elementary school, would go to Wayne County High basketball games. The big star of the day was Jack Upchurch, a 6'3" rugged youngster who could score and rebound and whose family actually lived in the city limits of Monticello and the city's school district.

"I was the only one in the family who went to Wayne County High School," Upchurch recalled. "Everyone else went to Monticello. Some of the local people tried to get me to go to school in Monticello. They offered my dad a job, rent payments and spending money."

Upchurch had gained quite a bit of area attention because of his skills on the hardwood, and it wasn't just Monticello.

"Somerset offered us the same kind of deal, he continued. "But I told dad 'If I go to Monticello or Somerset, everybody in Wayne County will be mad. If I stay at Wayne County everybody will respect me.'"

Wayne County coach Lloyd Hudnall knew his star player was good, and by Upchurch's junior year he was being recruited by several colleges, including Adolph Rupp at the University of Kentucky.

"Ultimately they said I was too slow," says Upchurch. "After my senior year in 1957, I went to Wake Forest where Bones McKinney coached. I only stayed a week and then I came back and went to Eastern."

Playing basketball at Eastern Kentucky University was the primary reason Upchurch went to the Richmond, Kentucky school to play for Coach Paul McBrayer, but not the only one.

"I wanted to coach," says Upchurch, "And that's one of the reasons I went there. I saw how many Eastern grads coached in the state tournament."

Jack Upchurch graduated from Eastern after a stellar career in 1962. He stayed on to coach the freshman team before going into the Army for four years. But it didn't take him long following his discharge to put into action his goal of becoming a fulltime coach. In 1965 he landed the job at Anderson County, which culminated in 1971 with a 30-3 record. Led by Mr. Basketball, Jimmy Dan Conner, Anderson County lost to Louisville Male in the championship game of the state tournament.

The next year, Jack Upchurch was back in Wayne County. This time, one of the school's all-time great basketball players was now the head coach.

Kenny, like every small boy in every small town in Kentucky, looked at the local high school team as heroes and dreamed someday of playing basketball like they did.

As a 10-year-old he would go to the games and whenever he got a chance he would be on the court shooting wadded-up paper cups toward the basket in the high school gym. One day he hoped it would be a real basketball like the one he had at home.

What would be the odds that the little skinny grade schooler would indeed make the varsity team and even become a star?

Ray Mills had been a high school star at Clay County High School in Manchester, Kentucky, playing for legendary Wyatt "Spider" Thurman. He helped lead the Tigers to a 35-1 record in 1953, with his team's only loss coming in the quarter-finals of the State tournament to eventual champion Lexington Lafayette. Clay County had had good teams over the years, but Mills says it was his school's first trip to the Sweet 16 in Lexington.

His play that year drew the attention of Adolph Rupp, and for the next four years Mills was a Kentucky Wildcat. Years later Kenny laughed when he offered, "In addition to being an excellent player, Ray had a secondary role of being Adolph's son Herkey's protector." Along the way Mills had thought about coaching and after a short stint in the Army at Ft. Knox, he landed his first coaching job in 1958 at Wayne County High School.

Ray Mills coming to Wayne County would prove to be a defining event in the life of Kenny Davis.

Of course there had been other good coaches at Wayne County, but it was Mills who solidified Kenny's ambition to become a basketball player. How good he would be remained to be seen.

The Mills family didn't live far from the Davis', so it was somewhat convenient for Kenny to ride his bike over to Coach Mills' house to play with his sons David and Danny, several years younger.

Being in the sixth grade, 11-year-old Kenny was a boy without a team to play on.

"We didn't have a team you could play on until eighth grade," Mills recalled. "But that didn't stop Kenny. He practically lived with us. He would stay after school, watch practice, and then ride home with us. Believe it or not he did this—watching practice—for two or three years. He was like our kid to my wife, Gerry and I."

At the time Mills was the only coach at Wayne County High, so he coached all of the kids regardless of what class they were in. But it would be a couple of years before Kenny's dream of making the team at Wayne County would become a reality. However, anyone in the area who knew a basketball was pumped and not stuffed thought the youngster could overcome all odds and become a basketball player.

In time the whole county was talking about Clyde and Zula's son, Kenny. Years later Clyde would admit that the talk had indeed made them feel good. "We heard the talk … couldn't help but hear it … about how good he was. It made my wife and I feel good."

Darrell Burton had played at Wayne County with Jack Upchurch, Lloyd Hudnall and Alfred Shearer, and later had come back to teach history and be an assistant coach to Ray Mills.

"I also coached the eighth grade team," Burton said. "Kenny was a freshman and we would play our teams against the freshman during lunch break. Kenny was the difference. If he wasn't there we beat them like a drum."

"I was the 12th man on a 12-man varsity roster," says Kenny. "But playing on the B-team, if I had a bad game Coach Mills would take my varsity jersey away from me. He probably cut me from the varsity four or five times, but it was his way of pushing me to get better."

A basketball goal regardless of where it was became a lighthouse in the night in Kenny's life.

It could be the one on the side of the barn on Oil Valley Road, or the one over at Abbot's grocery, or the one his brothers carved out of the side of a hill over on East Highway 92, or the one at Coach Mill's house, or if he was lucky it was at the high school gym when he would sneak in through an unlocked window.

Mills had coached another pretty good player at Wayne County.

Ray Mills and Ralph Baker arrived at Wayne County High the same year, 1958. It was Mills' first coaching job and the 16-year-old Baker had just transferred in from nearby McCreary County where his dad worked at a fruit market in Whitley City supporting a family of six boys and two girls. When he was offered the job as a custodian at Wayne County Schools, he jumped at the chance. It didn't hurt that son Ralph was a rising basketball star and would have his junior and senior years left to play for Coach Mills.

At Wayne County Baker was the man. That first year, his junior season, his Cardinal team lost to arch rival Monticello in the finals of the district, and then in the finals of the region. Monticello was loaded. With Gene Pendelton, Don Frye, Kay Morris, Paul Frye and Junior Peyton, Monticello High was among the elite high school teams in Kentucky.

Baker had a distinguished career at Wayne County, considered among the school's all-time best, and when he graduated it was expected he would play in college. After all, three of his teammates continued to play after high school, Darrell Bell and Lou Bates went to Cumberland College and Billy Sexton to Lindsey Wilson.

It took a game between the 12th Region All-Stars and 13th Region All-Stars, in which Baker played good enough to receive a basketball scholarship offer from one of the best coaches in the nation.

"The game was in London, Kentucky," recalled Mills. "Ralph played well and Coach Diddle (Western Kentucky University) was there and offered Ralph a scholarship right after the game."

The decision to accept the offer set Baker on a course that would lead him to coaching and then a super career with the Balfour Company, a business that deals in college and high school rings, caps and gowns, announcements, and other accessories.

Baker's college career as a player was somewhat pedestrian. Playing with the likes of Darel Carrier (it was Carrier who had driven Coach Diddle from Bowling Green to London to see Baker play in the all-star game), his role was defined mostly as a rugged rebounder and defender.

For sure Kenny Davis remembered Baker, even to the point as a role model.

"I was an eighth grader and someday wanted to be like him. It was the way he conducted himself off the court and how hard he played on it," Davis recalled.

Ralph remembered Kenny, too.

"He was a little gym rat," says Baker. "A little snotty-nosed kid running around always shooting a basketball. Even as a little kid he was something."

After graduating from Western, Baker became a basketball graduate assistant for Coach John Oldham's Hilltoppers and began the process of recruiting Kenny Davis.

Ralph recalled seeing Jack Upchurch play at Wayne County, and most considered Upchurch and Baker the two best to ever play at Wayne County. By now Kenny Davis was finishing up a great career. Several schools were interested in him. Among them, the Air Force Academy in Colorado Springs. It required a congressional appointment for consideration and Congressman Tim Lee Carter had gladly made that happen. Coach Bob Davis at Georgetown College also wanted him, too. "I really considered Air Force," he said. "But Vietnam was going on and mom and dad didn't want me to go that far way to Colorado."

At 6'3", Darrell Bell had played center and forward on the Cardinals 1960 team coached by Mills. Along with teammates Ralph Baker, Billy Sexton, Lou Bates and Harold Winchester, the team was unfortunate in that it had to be in the same district as the great 1960 Monticello team. Bell was good enough to play at Cumberland College, where after his playing days he later returned as freshman coach. By then Cumberland was hoping to recruit Kenny Davis.

"I knew all about Kenny," Bell laughed. "I had seen him play and knew he was a gym rat. We had to run him out of the gym so we could practice. I think he wanted to play at Cumberland, but at the time I didn't think he'd fit in here. I had watched him grow up and told them all (at Cumberland) that he was good enough to beat us by himself. When he was at Georgetown the least he ever scored against us in all those years was 40.

"Kenny always had his game at top level even in the old-timer games. He may not have been the greatest athlete, but he outworked everyone. He got it from his dad … he was a hard worker, too."

Bell likes to tell a story he heard about current Cardinal Coach Rodney Woods.

"Coach Woods supposedly was asked by his players if those guys from the old days could play with them today? He told them no, because if they were around today you guys wouldn't even be on the team."

There's one more thing Darrell Bell will never forget about Kenny. "I was coaching at Wayne County and he stopped by the school and gave me a pair of the shoes he had worn in the Olympics."

Chapter Three

At the end of the 1962-63 season, Ray Mills resigned at Wayne County. He had officially coached Kenny Davis for only his freshman year. But it seemed longer. He had seen the little skinny neighbor boy start to grow into a taller skinny boy. At the time he knew Kenny was going to be a special player for Wayne County … he just didn't know how special.

Mills' departure was not without controversy. He told the *Louisville Courier-Journal* on February 4, 1963 his reason for leaving.

"We had lost four games in a row and I benched our leading scorer for lack of teamwork. The boy didn't show up for practice or our next game. I assumed he was off the squad.

"Superintendent Ira Bell then brought the boy to me and asked me to take him back. I told him I would take him back if the other boys wanted him back. They voted not to take him back.

"I got to thinking that I should be able to discipline my team without interference. Then I decided to quit."

And Ira Bell responded:

"Yes I asked Mills to take the boy back, but the squad voted not to and that was that. I've got no argument with Mills; he is a good coach and a good man."

Mills moved on to Ohio where he became the head coach of Hamilton High, a school noted for its basketball.

In the spring of 1963, Gerald Sinclair was hired to replace Mills. Sinclair had gone to high school at Russell County and later graduated from Eastern Kentucky University, and before coming to Wayne County his only coaching experience had been at Forkland.

He had heard about Kenny Davis, the hot-shot sophomore who was now pushing 5'11", but his team, consisting of only one senior in the starting five, finished 4-20, losing in the first game of the district.

As bad as the Cardinal's record was, that's not what Sinclair remembered most about that first year.

"We had played an away game," says Sinclair. "I don't remember where or who we even played. After the game we headed home and, as usual, we stopped to feed the team and cheerleaders. This time it was a restaurant in Somerset. I got off the bus and asked the restaurant manager if he could serve our team. He said sure.

"When our group unloaded and entered, the manager noticed that we had an African-American, Nelson Stonewall, in our group. The manager told me he would feed Nelson, but he would have to take his food and eat on the bus. I told him we all eat in the restaurant or none of us do. He said Nelson could eat with us in the restaurant, but that he would have to behave. I told him that all of our group would do that. So, we all ate together."

Kenny's sophomore year as a starter on the varsity showed few signs about his future as a basketball player. Scoring 129 points in the 19 games, he played he averaged only 6.8 points and shot an unimpressive 33% from the field.

In no way was Kenny deterred from such a lackluster season. Defying all odds, he would continue to dribble and shoot baskets whenever and wherever he could.

Most of the summer when not working on the farm or shooting baskets somewhere, he would hang out with friends at Conley Bottom, a swimming spot on Lake Cumberland a few miles from Monticello. And though he liked to have as much fun as anyone, his thoughts were never far from basketball.

The first time Kenny laid eyes on Coach Bob Davis (no relation) was the summer of 1964 at the coaches' second basketball camp at Georgetown College in Scott County. It was between Kenny's sophomore and junior year of high school.

"Our Wayne County team, five of us and Coach Sinclair rode up in one car," Kenny says.

Upon arriving, the campers were required to go to Coach Davis office on a Sunday afternoon in order to sign-in, get a t-shirt, and get their dorm room assignments.

"A counselor took us to our room in Anderson Hall, across from the gym," Kenny recalled. "It was the same dorm I lived in when I came to college. We ate in the cafeteria. I remember being pretty much overwhelmed by it all."

"Coach Davis' camps were well organized," said Kenny. "We were divided up according to the position we played—guards, forwards and centers. We were there five nights. We had games, even a tournament, and the last day they named an all-star team I made.

"I used the camps as a measuring stick to see how much I needed to improve. The camp made me realize I needed to get better. It was here that I was introduced to the art of shooting. Phil Rollins (former U of L All-American and NBA player) was there. He was a Converse rep and put on a proper shooting demonstration. And then Dickie Vories and Cecil Tuttle were there. They were seniors at Georgetown then and they were really good. Through it all Coach Davis didn't soft sell anything. He was very intense even if we were just at a camp."

Coach Sinclair would drive back from Monticello to Georgetown to retrieve his players. It was his hope the kids would be better for their time spent away from home in an effort to become better basketball players.

"I went home and practiced as much as I could," Kenny said. "You really learn to shoot on your own, and I worked on improving my form by first shooting against a wall with no basket. And then I moved to a telephone pole. If you don't hit the pole in the dead center you know what happens? You have to chase the ball right or left. Leave the goal out of it for a while. Twenty minutes a day for 30 days is what it takes."

The week he spent at the basketball camp made him realize his shortcomings and the different phases of his game he needed to turn around if he was going to elevate his game.

Jerry Cooper was one of those who had gone to Coach Bob Davis' camp in Georgetown. He had moved to Wayne County as an eighth grader, and though a year behind Kenny in school they played with and against each other during the summer break.

"During the summer he was always on his bike looking for a game," Cooper recalled. "He played a lot with the Monticello guys. We really competed against each other … lots of 3 on 3 and 4 on 4, shirts and skins games. The wildest thing we'd do back then was sneak into the gym."

Nick Humble was another classmate of Kenny's, and although he didn't play at Wayne County his junior or senior years, he still played with him during the summer.

"I first met Kenny in the fifth grade at recess on the basketball court," says Humble. "We chose up sides, and I usually played with Bobby Slagle most of the time because he always picked me first. But that day Kenny got to pick first and he picked me. From that day on we were good friends. I played at Wayne County my first two years, but I got in trouble in Algebra class and didn't play my last two years."

Humble continues:

"There was a time I was probably as good as Kenny, but he was so dedicated. I'd be out just running around town and I'd pass him and see him running or riding his bike dribbling a basketball."

Humble went on to say that Kenny became an inspiration. "I didn't pay much attention to my grades until I started running around with him in high school. Even though his parents weren't athletic, they were good people and instilled a discipline in him. If he was playing against his mother he'd play to win."

Humble, after graduation, went to work for Westinghouse in Muncie, Indiana, where he also played semi-pro baseball. He then served in the Army for two years before entering college at Lee University in Cleveland, Tennessee.

With Kenny's junior year coming around, Coach Sinclair was honest in thinking it would take a lot more than Kenny Davis to improve on a 4-20 record. He needed several other Cardinals to step up. There was 6'1" Harold Dishman who had also been a starter as a sophomore; twins Cleo and Theo Duncan, Paul Gregory, and Larry Anderson were back for their senior year.

Still the odds were against Wayne County being a 12th Region power. Kenny, by now was approaching 6-foot, but still his slight build would lead local basketball historians to think one player, especially one so small, could make such a transformation in less than a year.

The Wayne County Cardinals finished the season 15-10, but like the previous year, bowed out in the first game of the district tournament.

But now Wayne County had a new basketball star. Kenny Davis had arrived, and he was only a junior. The locals were mentioning his name in the same sentence with Jack Upchurch, Ralph Baker, Gene Pendleton and Don Frye.

What Kenny did on the basketball court had never been done in Wayne County. And though records are kept on individual player's improvement from one year to the next, it would be safe to say that not many before him had gone from scoring less than seven points one year to more than 24 the next. In 25 games he had scored 607 points. His free throw percentage went from 60% to 80%; rebounding from four per game to eight; and the field goal stat skyrocketed from 33% to 49%.

Suddenly, at this stage of his basketball life, he had defied all odds in becoming one of the best prep basketball players in a basketball crazy state.

It was at this time that Coach Sinclair was already thinking that perhaps Kenny could become even better. "Before his senior year I took him up to Eastern to let Jim Baechtold (EKU coach) watch him shoot," recalled Sinclair. "He watched and Kenny's hand would drift to the right. Baechtold told me to leave him alone."

College coaches were now once again finding their way to Monticello, this time to see a kid who had become the most prolific scorer in the state. And he still had his senior year to play.

"As time went on I saw Kenny's dedication," Sinclair says. "He played all the time, and although I wouldn't say he was fast, he was oh so quick. He could get his shot off anytime.

"No one would believe how dedicated he was … the time he put in playing the game … unbelievable. When practice was over he was never ready to quit. After practice he'd stay late after everybody else had left. Then the times I left, he'd lock up the gym."

Kenny Davis was a marked man. Now there would be no surprises for opposing teams in the 1965-66 season.

After dropping the opening game of the year 75-74 on the road at Nancy, the Cardinals reeled off 10 straight wins that included individual Kenny Davis point totals of 34, 39, 43, 28, 31, and 40.

In mid-December Wayne County had pounded Burnside 107-91 at home behind Kenny's 43 points, but then in a dramatic turn-around Burnside on February 4 won 77-64. Davis was limited to 16 points, a season low.

But if Kenny Davis caught the rest of the state by surprise, it didn't for those who knew him in Wayne County. The old saying, "If it sounds too good to be true, it probably is. No so with Kenny.

Through it all Kenny remained himself—polite, humble, and well liked, even by teammates that sometimes took exception to his shots. What was there not to like about him?

He had served notice the year before with his 24 point average, but now to prove it wasn't a fluke, he was averaging 32 points, tops in Kentucky ahead of Allen County's Jim McDaniels, Shelby County's Mike Casey (later Mr. Basketball), and Dilce Combs' Charles Minks, and Corbin's Curly Selvy. But where Kenny was equally impressive was off the court, particularly in the classroom. A straight A honor roll student and class officer, he also represented his high school in the state speech tournament in Louisville.

With Kenny well on his way to becoming one of the Cardinals all-time leading scorers, he solidified his name in the record books with a 61-point performance on January 8 against Shopville. His point total outscored the entire Shopville squad as Wayne County won 100-51.

Davis had 34 at the half. "I told a couple of my boys privately—but not Kenny— that he had a chance at our school record of 59, and if they wanted to help him break it, they could," Cardinal Coach Gerald Sinclair said at the time.

"I took him out with two minutes to play, although the fans wanted me to leave him in," Sinclair explained. "But Kenny had 55 points after the third quarter and had gotten only six in the last quarter."

Kenny had been taking about 25 shots per game, but against Shopville he put it up 38 times and connected on 24, and from the foul line he was a perfect 13 for 13. His 61 points broke the 59 point mark set in 1957 by Cardinal great Jack Upchurch.

As Wayne County rolled along, most of the attention went to Davis and anytime he got below his 30-plus average it was considered an off night. Harold Dishman, Jerry Cooper, Gary Richardson, and Danny Richardson were quick to recognize their roles as supporting cast members.

As the season wound down, Wayne County fans were set to say farewell to Davis. It was thought that they might never see the likes of Jack Upchurch and Ralph Baker, but Kenny's career put him at the top of the Cardinal all-time greats. Lily would be the final regular season game, and sporting a 16-8 record that included a win at Lily back in December, the Cardinals expected another victory.

It was not to be. Lily surprised everyone with a relatively easy 91-66 win that put a damper on a fabulous career for Kenny Davis, who scored 23 points that night.

Shortly after the loss, Kenny had been invited to be the guest of the University of Kentucky to see the Wildcats play Tennessee on February 26 in Memorial Coliseum. He met Coach Rupp and Gov. Ned Breathitt, but the highlight was shooting a few hoops on a Coliseum floor.

Wayne County had been a part of the 47th District for years and then in 1966 the Cardinals were switched to the 46th.

"The 47th district was big, 12 or 13 teams," Kenny says. "It was a struggle getting out of it. With Nancy, Shopville, Somerset, Pulaski County, Eubank and Ferguson all from Pulaski County, we could play two-thirds of our schedule in the district."

Chapter Four

For Kenny's first three years in high school, the district and regional games were played in Somerset. No local radio station in Monticello broadcast Cardinal games, so Wayne County and Monticello fans during the district and regional tournaments would drive to a vacant lot on old Hwy. 90 between Monticello and Burnside in hopes of dialing in the games on a Somerset station.

"It was actually the site of where the old mansion stood that was in the movie Raintree County," Kenny says. "It became a social event for all of the fans listening to the game on radio."

Expectations were high for the Cardinals. Coach Sinclair felt good about his starting five. Of course Kenny Davis was Mr. Big now, and he often thought back to when as a 12-year-old in 1960 how excited he and everyone else throughout the area was for the success Monticello High and Coach Joe Harper enjoyed when they reached the finals of the State Tournament. He now wanted to experience the same feeling as a player.

Rugged rebounder Harold Dishman, although only 6'1", played the pivot. Opposite Davis at the other forward was 6'3" Danny Richardson, and the guards were 5'10" Jerry Cooper, and 5'8" John Gregory. This was the core group that was expected to challenge for the 12th Region title.

Going into district play the Cardinals were 17-9, and nobody knew better than Coach Gerald Sinclair that it would take a strong showing to advance out of district play. After being switched to the 46th district, it meant that the team no longer had to travel to Somerset. The host team was the Russell County Lakers and since this was his alma mater, he had a little more incentive than usual. But, first things first. Liberty, a team Wayne County had defeated 60-58 back in December, was the opening game, and since the 46th and 47th district had been realigned, a win here would put the Cardinals into the finals against Russell County.

Crosstown rival Monticello was, according to the statewide Lit ratings, the top team in the district, and Russell County came in at number two. Both had drawn into the district's lower bracket, which meant in all probability only one of them would advance if they met in the semis. Wayne County defeated Liberty 68-62, and Russell County, after beating Casey County, knocked out Monticello to advance to the finals where they would meet Wayne County.

Basketball, being like a religion in Kentucky, often brought out the worst in fans. And if the home team was in jeopardy of losing, emotions could be revved up several notches.

The championship game turned out to be a strange one. "It was late in the fourth quarter and we had the lead," says Sinclair. "The Laker coach called timeout, but he didn't have any left. After we broke the huddle the ref started to give the Lakers the ball in front of our bench. I stood up and said we needed to shoot the technical. He told me to sit down because it was getting hot in here. We didn't get to shoot the technical and didn't get the ball. We still won 77-66, the same number of points that they had beaten us four weeks earlier."

Remember earlier about how emotions ran high among fans? Well, players at times could also feel it, too.

Following the game Sinclair took his team for a post-game meal at his step-father's restaurant in Jamestown, which is in the same county as Russell Springs.

Coach Sinclair picks it up here: "While we were waiting for our food to be served, one of the Laker players and some of his friends came in and were talking trash and said they wanted Harold Dishman because he was a dirty player. A city policeman was there and he suggested that Harold should go out the back door and get in one of our fan's cars and get back to Wayne County. After we finished eating, the rest of us got on the bus and headed home. I guess the gang wondered why they didn't see Harold get on the bus."

The headline read "The Cardinals Flew." Three words described the 77-66 46th District championship for Wayne County. Finally Kenny Davis had led his team out of the district and into the regionals. His 33 points and the strong guard play of Jerry Cooper earned both all-district honors.

With a renewed spirit and reaching the Regional Tournament for the first time in several years, the Cardinals would take on Boyle County in Danville on March 8.

Boyle County jumped to an early first quarter lead, 23-12, but Wayne County came roaring back behind Dishman and Davis, and by halftime trailed by two at 33-31. But it was all Boyle County in the second half and at the end of the third quarter led by 17. When it was over the Cardinals were out, falling 68-54.

When the season ended, both the team and Kenny had improved on the previous season. A 19-10 team record and a district title for the Cardinals had made the team competitive. And when no one thought it possible for Kenny to top his stats from the previous year, that's exactly what he did. His 32 scoring average, 82.5 % free throws, 8.5 rebound average and 50% field goals were all improvements.

Some schools were trying to use Kenny's family members to influence his college decision. One was Campbellsville College.

Sherman York grew up in Clinton County, and after graduating from there in 1963, he went on to play basketball at Campbellsville College under George Sadler.

York knew all about Kenny and his basketball ability. He also became friends with Ralph Davis, Kenny's brother, and a student at Campbellsville. Coach Sadler would use this connection to keep alive his hopes of enticing Kenny to the Taylor County college.

Although York wasn't able to attract Kenny to Campbellsville, York was attracted to Wayne County. Almost immediately after graduating from college, at the age of 22, Sherman York was hired to replace the departed Coach Sinclair as the new Cardinal coach.

"I coached there four years," York said. "And one of our best wins came in my last year when we beat Monticello for the first time in 17 years."

Eventually York became the owner of H & W Sporting Goods, a business he operated for 32 years.

"This is where I really got to know Kenny as a Converse sales rep," says York.

The finale for any high school team is its banquet, and long after the season had ended on April 15 in the high school gym, it was little surprise when Kenny left with just about every team award Coach Sinclair gave out. Along with the starters, reserves Steve DeBord, Frank Jones,

Joe Kelly, Ronnie Criswell, Gary Richardson, Lonnie Frost, managers Bruce Davis, Ronald McFarland and Darwin Keeton were recognized. And what would any team be without school spirit? Cheerleaders Betty Raines, Sue Boston, Sylvia Vire, and Janet Reagan were acknowledged for their winning efforts, too.

The guest speaker that evening was Western Kentucky University assistant basketball coach Gene Rhodes, and before the coach headed back to Bowling Green he had Kenny's and that of his parents signature on a grant-in-aid scholarship. Ralph Baker's recruiting of Kenny had finally paid off.

(A footnote to Sinclair's career was that he coached at Wayne County one more year after Kenny graduated. After several stops along the way he ended up at Logan County High School where his 1984 team won the state championship with star Fred Tisdale. "I always rated Fred and Kenny 1 and 1-A," he said. "They were both great.")

But now here was Western, all of a sudden back in the national spotlight with the likes of Clem Haskins, Dwight and Greg Smith, and Wayne Chapman, recruiting him to play for one of the best basketball programs in the country.

"We had an eye on Kenny for a long time," Baker said. "I knew him from being there. I had seen him play and knew his work ethic."

Later Baker coached high school ball at several schools across Kentucky before joining Jim Richards' staff at Western when he replaced the retired John Oldham as head coach in 1972.

Kenny Davis was now a Hilltopper. He had been passed over for some of the high profile post season all-star games in spite of being the state's leading scorer at 32 points per game. But he had landed at a school considered to be one of the best.

Kenny was disappointed at not being selected to play in the state's East-West All-Star game or the even more prestigious Kentucky-Indiana game.

"Back then players were just picked and that required some promotion since there were no tryouts," he said. "I used it as an incentive to prove to others and myself that I belonged. There were a lot of good players, and looking at the list I don't know who I would have replaced."

Kenny, despite his underwhelming physique as basketball players go, was close to slipping through the recruiting cracks. Yes, he had offers, 15 of them to be exact, but he felt he was good enough to play at the highest level, and that meant U.K. Oh, he received the usual letters, even an invitation to come to Lexington and see a game. But a scholarship offer? It never came. And probably if it hadn't been for Ralph Baker and his Wayne County connections, he might not have been recruited to Western, a power school.

Each year a list of the top high school players is set in stone. But after that, no one really knows for sure. Work ethic? Desire to be great? Both go a long way in determining a player's future. If a kid has a greater desire than one more talented, often the one with more desire wins out.

How many times has a kid been described as "too skinny to survive in the college game"; "he'll get pushed around"; "he doesn't have a true position"? And when you're a little white kid who played on a mediocre team these are the things college recruiters say about you. That's what they said about Kenny Davis.

Davis was on a freshman team that featured Charles "Curly" Selvy. Selvy was the youngest of the famous Selvy brothers from Corbin, Kentucky, and along with 6'8" Walker Banks, and Wayne Bright, lots were expected of them playing on the frosh squad (freshman were ineligible for varsity play until 1974.

Buck Sydnor, one of John Oldham's top assistant's generally was in charge of the freshman team, and most remember that the former Daviess County High School coach took a no-nonsense approach when it came to basketball. But that's the way Kenny liked it. He was all about the game, too. He didn't mind that Sydnor would get his team down in the auxiliary gym, adjacent to the main floor in Diddle Arena and work the devil out of them. Sydnor was tough, and an occasional skirmish among the teammates in the overheated gym would occur.

"He didn't mind it if some of us really went at each other," recalled Curly Selvy about that freshman year. "I can still see his glasses down on his nose and him looking over the top, with a little grin on his face."

Nevertheless, to make sure the devil stayed out of his team's life, Sydnor would pick up his players on Sunday morning and take them to church. Kenny was one of them.

There were a couple of weekends when Kenny journeyed back home to Monticello, and even without a car, finding a ride was easy.

"That's how I got to Western in the beginning," Kenny said. "There were eight to ten in my class of '66 that went to Western, and I hitched a ride with a classmate, Gary Dalton, whose father dropped us off in Bowling Green."

Kenny's time on the Hill in Bowling Green, however, didn't last long. He was there ten weeks and his career as a Hilltopper was over.

Years later John Oldham had this to say: "I'm not really sure why he left."

It seemed like one day he's here and the next day he's gone. I know Buck used to get those guys down in that hot gym and watch them scratch and claw each other. I'm not sure Kenny had ever been fussed at like that. It seemed like the next thing I knew he was playing in the Olympics."

Oldham continued:

"We missed out with Kenny. But I had a few more like that," he laughed. "I offered Dave Cowens a partial scholarship, (Cowans made All-American at Florida State and had an NBA Hall of Fame career), and we had a chance to sign Doug Collins out of Benton (Illinois) High School, but his coach, Rich Herrin, told me he wasn't sure Collins could play at this level. Like a lot of coaches, I made some mistakes."

For Kenny Davis, however, his departure from Western had nothing to do with what went on on the practice floor. He came to college to play basketball and get an education, and he knew that without basketball he would be hard pressed to even attend college.

"I knew that's what I wanted to do," Kenny said. "Mom and dad were paying for my brother Ralph, who was 15 months older, to go to college and I saw what it was costing them."

Years later Kenny talked about why he left Western, and it differed from what John Oldham recalled.

"I remember Curly Selvy telling me he had a four year scholarship guaranteed," says Kenny. "Mine was for only one year, so I went to Coach Oldham and asked him about it. He told me the school was allowed to only give a scholarship for one year at a time. I was upset about it so I called my brother Ralph to come to Bowling Green to pick me up."

It was ironic, but Ralph Baker, too, had his own personal experience with the scholarship rule while he was at Western.

Ralph Baker and Hilltopper All-American Darel Carrier had gotten into a fight during practice.

"Coach Diddle told me 'he was of good mind not to bring me back next year.' I told him he couldn't do that because I had a four-year scholarship. That's when he told me at Western there were no four year deals, only one."

Years later Ralph Davis is not sure exactly what happened, but being a supportive older brother he drove his 1959, 2-door green and white Ford from Monticello to Bowling Green as he was asked to do.

"I thought they wanted to redshirt him and he didn't want it," Ralph said. "When I got to Bowling Green he said take me to Georgetown. I dropped him off there."

Clyde, Kenny's dad, looking back on it all simply said, "We felt like things were misrepresented a little at Western, but things have a way of working out and they did."

Ralph Davis, by his own admission, was never interested in basketball. "We played a lot around the house and I helped clear off a place for a goal around an old sinkhole on the farm. But no one ever talked to me about playing."

Ralph Davis fondly recalled the days while he was still a student at Wayne County and all of the conversations about his younger brother.

"Monticello (High School) tried to get Kenny to come over there," he said. "But Ray Mills was such an influence, and so close to him that it just wasn't going to happen.

"It seemed like all Kenny did was play basketball, and I'd tell everyone that Bruce (younger brother) had to stay home and work while Kenny played basketball. But believe me Kenny worked, too."

It was common for Ralph to also be an accomplice in another of Kenny's efforts to play ball. "On snow days when school was out I'd drive him to the gym and he'd crawl through a window and shoot with no lights on until someone would come by and run him out."

There were times when he would resort to being a bit devious in finding a way into the high school gym.

"I'd put a little stone in a window or door to keep it from completely shutting so I could slip in and shoot," he said. "And we had a school janitor, Earl Edwards, who had a couple of sons that played ball, so he was forgiving when it came to me slipping in."

Chapter Five

By 1958 Bob Davis was beginning to make a name for himself. Still coaching football and basketball, he was labeled by some as a football coach coaching basketball. No one had to tell Davis good players make good coaches, and great players make great coaches. He knew that, and over a 20-year stretch he brought some great players to Georgetown.

Charlie Grote from Shelbyville, Tennessee, was the first, soon followed by former Central City great Corky Withrow, and then a pair of scoring machines Dick Vories and Cecil Tuttle. Vories and Tuttle were in the same backcourt for the Tigers in 1963-64. And to further substantiate Coach Davis' guard oriented office, the pair ended their Tiger careers as the school's one and two all-time leading scorers.

Withrow, a phenomenal two sport star in baseball and basketball, came to Georgetown in a round-about way. First signing with Kentucky after being named in 1956 to several high school All-American teams that included Jerry West, Oscar Robertson, Jackie Moreland, and "King" Kelly Coleman, he then signed a professional baseball contract with the St. Louis Cardinals.

"That made me ineligible at Kentucky because of an NCAA rule," says Withrow. "Murray then offered me, but I was ruled ineligible there. So Bullet Wilson (coach) offered me a scholarship at Kentucky Wesleyan. I was practicing with them when I was declared ineligible again."

Withrow, however still wanted to play basketball. "Austin Peay talked to me, and so did Georgetown College. I decided to get on Highway 62 and head north, so I ended up at Georgetown. Coach Davis was one of the great BS'ers of all-time," Withrow laughed. "I sat out the spring semester of 1957 and played two seasons, 1957-'58, and '58-'59."

After those two seasons in which the much-traveled Withrow was putting up numbers that made heads turn, even scoring 46 points against Hanover in 1958, but then his basketball days came to a sudden stop.

"Even though Georgetown was an NAIA school, after I had been voted Player of the Year twice, the AD's in the KIAC got together and voted me out."

Withrow left Georgetown with some great friends and great stories. One was in 1959 in Kansas City at the NAIA nationals and it involved Coach Davis, who that same year was named national Coach of the Year.

"Coach had gone to a barber shop to get a trim, and the barber cut about 4-inches up each side. He had black hair and where they cut was white as snow," laughed Withrow. Larry Phillips and I found someone to paint his scalp with black dye. Well, during the game when he started sweating and the dye started to run… ending up all over his neck and shirt."

On April 12, 1960, Davis received news that his mother, Dolly, had died back in West Virginia. It was a blow to him.

"She had Hodgkin's Disease," he said. "She held the family together. She was a tower of strength and was always there because my dad wasn't. He had some drinking issues."

That same year, 1960, Bob was selected as a coach for the NAIA Olympic Trials in Denver, and he would be working with head coach Milton Jowers of Southwest Texas State. Back then NAIA players were given a chance to showcase their talent with a chance one of them would be chosen to play in the Olympics.

An NAIA All-Star team was selected that included Jackie Moreland, Zelmo Beatty, Rudy Davalos, and Charlie Sharp. In the first round they defeated the great Ohio State team of Jerry Lucas and John Havlichek. The Phillips Oilers, an AAU team, then knocked off the NAIA boys before they fell to the NCAA All-Stars.

"They destroyed us," says Davis. "They had Lucas, Havlichek, Oscar Robertson, Darrell Imhoff, and Walt Bellamy."

Cecil Tuttle had been a star player at Hazel Green in Laurel County. Coach Bones McKinney at Wake Forest was hot after him, and had flown him to the North Carolina school to finalize his scholarship. However, when Tuttle's plane landed back at the London, Kentucky airport, there stood Bob Davis and the entire Tuttle family.

"They were all eating ice cream cones and Coach Davis had my mother worked up and crying about me going so far away from home to college," Tuttle laughed. "There was no way I was going anywhere but Georgetown."

"I made the NAIA All-Star team for the 1964 Olympic Trials," he said. "Willis Reed was a teammate, and we went to Madison Square Garden for an Olympic Trial tournament. Our NAIA team beat the NCAA All-Stars, but we ended up third. Willis and I were named Olympic team alternates."

After college Cecil Tuttle played two years with AAU's Akron Goodyear team, where he roomed with Larry Brown.

"Larry told me he was going to join Dean Smith's staff at North Carolina," Tuttle said. "I had told him about my younger brothers, Gerald and Richard. Both ended up playing there."

The second oldest to Cecil of the Tuttle brothers, Alvin, later played at Georgetown College. Cecil Tuttle ended up playing eleven years with Marathon Oil.

Coach Davis, with an aggressive personality at times, had always been smart enough to listen and take advice from those he knew he could learn from. There were opportunities along the way to learn from Rupp at U.K., Diddle at Western, Paul McBrayer at Eastern, and Peck Hickman at Louisville. But that was about basketball. He had listened when he was advised to get his master's degree. And now he had been advised to get his Ph.D.

"I was told it would help my job security along the way," he said. "It would be harder to fire me if I had my doctorate."

Davis headed for Peabody College, a small school adjacent to Vanderbilt University in Nashville, Tennessee, and after literally "locking myself in a dorm room and getting after it," in June 1963 he became Dr. Bob Davis.

That same year back at Georgetown he started what he says was the first basketball camp held on a college campus in Kentucky.

"We had 100 kids here," says Davis. "Ted Sanford was the commissioner of the Kentucky High School Athletic Association and he came over and told me our camp was illegal and all of the kids would be ineligible to play at their schools," recalled Davis. "I was mad and I told him I'd sue him and the association. These kids were not here playing as a team. They were learning basketball. Finally, they backed off. It was interesting that three years later when Lee Rose was working at Transylvania he wanted to start a camp. Ted Sanford told him to go over to Georgetown and see how they were doing it."

A year later, in 1964, what would be the odds that a little kid from Wayne County, Kentucky, would show up with the same last name as Dr. Bob's? In a round-a-bout way they would forever be linked together.

Dr. Bob's stock continued to rise. Gaining national recognition, albeit at an NAIA college, his involvement with the Olympic basketball movement didn't hurt his resume.

Davis wasn't necessarily looking to "move up" in his coaching career; after all, he was a Georgetown guy. He'd gone to school there, played sports, and spent 20 years of coaching several sports. To many, he was Mr. Georgetown College.

He had other opportunities. Sometime in the early 60's Marshall University came calling. "They were located in my hometown," Davis said. "I was willing to talk to them, so they had me there for an interview. It didn't last long, though. At the beginning the AD told me he'd be making out my schedule. I said, 'Hold it, meeting over', and I walked out. All he was doing was scheduling games with bigger and better teams for guarantees. He was all about the money, no way could a coach win there."

There were several other schools that talked to him. However, for him Georgetown was where he wanted to be.

But, what if another college, perhaps one from the Southeastern Conference, came calling? Would he even listen?

It was in February 1972, and with the season in full swing Davis received the news that his dad, known as 'Captain', died. He was buried near his mom in Spring Hill Cemetery back in Huntington, West Virginia. Now with both his mom and dad gone, Davis' life was about to take another turn.

"We had lost in the finals of the KIAC tournament to Cumberland in 1972," Davis said, "And a little later I was in Kansas City as part of the NAIA executive committee. I got a phone call from Lee Haley, the AD at Auburn. He wanted to talk to me about being their basketball coach. I told him I would be in meetings here for the next two days and it would have to be after that. He said he'd fly to Kansas City, and ask me to meet him at the airport."

Auburn had become familiar with Coach Davis through one of their former All-Americans, John Mengelt, who had played for Davis during the 1970 World Games, and when it looked like his school was going to be looking for a new coach, his influence was enough to seal the deal.

"My wife and I flew down there and they made their offer for me to be their coach," Davis said.

And how did Georgetown College react?

"I had a great relationship with our president Robert Mills," he said. "I was making $15,000 a year and Auburn's offer was $25,000, so I asked him to negotiate. I wasn't really looking to leave Georgetown, but Auburn's offer was pretty good at the time. At Georgetown I was coaching, and the department head for Health, P.E. and Athletics, working twelve months a year."

Davis took the Auburn job in the spring of 1973. He knew he had his work cut out for him.

"I had told the committee that hired me I couldn't guarantee I could get us any higher than fourth in the conference," he said. "They really wanted me to win with mostly white players back then. We had one black when I got there, so I started recruiting the best players I could. Recruiting was tough because of our location, but we started getting some pretty good players, and after two years they extended my contract."

For most of Auburn's history the school has been considered a football school, and Coach Davis quickly felt the vibes that yes it was.

Davis eventually had six black players and that's when his mail began to increase.

"I got quite a few letters about it," he said. "Some were signed, but most weren't. The thing was the football team had 10 or 12 black kids, but they wore long sleeves, and a helmet. They didn't stand out like basketball players so no one really said anything to them."

There were other issues.

"I think football had been to 10 straight bowl games before I got to Auburn," Davis continued. "And while I was there they didn't go to any. Some of the supporters were saying basketball was getting in the way of football."

Davis recalled how he would order his team's equipment and when it arrived the football team would get it.

"I looked up one day and our kids were playing with holes in their socks," he laughed. "The football team had the new ones, so I put a stop to that. I got my own equipment manager and separated everything."

After five years and a 70-60 record, Dr. Bob Davis was let go at Auburn. In the end he felt like a combination of football and his lack of successfully winning the big games did him in.

"I wouldn't trade those years for anything," he says. "My son Brad graduated from there, and my daughter Cindy went there for two years, and I made some great friends. And they paid my salary for three more years after I left. It was the big time."

Later Davis talked about the SEC coaches he competed against with fond memories. "Ray Mears at Tennessee was the best bench coach I ever faced. If I tried something unusual, he'd pick it up in no time. C.M. Newton at Alabama was great recruiter and always had strong, balanced clubs. Dale Brown at L.S.U. was a wild man, but good recruiter with rough and tumble players. Roy Skinner at Vandy was a great motivator. He took small white players and made them believe they could beat the world. Joe B. Hall at U.K. was always a great recruiter and his teams were in top physical condition. Joe and I had some great games and I was always proud I beat U.K. three times during my tenure at Auburn.

It's interesting to note that the SEC's two Alabama schools had two guys from Kentucky coaching their basketball teams, Davis at Auburn, and C.M. Newton at Alabama.

Call it what you will, but often fate can take an odd turn. Paul Lambert was coaching at Southern Illinois University, a team Auburn had defeated earlier in the season, and when Davis was terminated, Lambert was hired to take his place.

"I had scheduled several speaking engagements with Auburn alumni, and one of those was in Columbus, Georgia," Davis said. "It was usually a big turn out there, so I would spend the night. Paul took my hotel reservation at the Holiday Inn there."

Davis went on to say that in June of 1978 a fire swept through the hotel and tragically Coach Paul Lambert died, without ever coaching a game at Auburn. Sonny Smith was then hired.

Bob Davis was out of a job, but once again fate stepped in.

After selling Omelet Shoppe franchises to Auburn alumni and friends he had met along the way, the Davis family moved to Birmingham for a while.

"I had interest in several of the Omelet Shoppes," said Davis. "But by the fall of 1979, I sold it all off."

It was back to Georgetown, Kentucky for Davis in November 1979, and soon after he went to work with Jim Host Communications with their sight on establishing a Southeastern Conference Network.

"Jim already had the U.K. Network and I had all of the contacts in the conference," he said. "But in July 1980 Jim lost the U.K. bid and our plans went down the drain."

It was a sudden broken tooth that sent Dr. Bob Davis' life in a completely different direction.

"I had to have a cap on it," he said. "I decided to call Bill Collins, a dentist in Versailles. He had played football for me at Georgetown College. We talked and I told him I was leaving Host and really didn't want to stay in athletics."

Bill's wife was Martha Layne Collins, Lt. Governor of Kentucky. Bill set up a meeting between his wife and his old Georgetown coach, and on November 15, 1980, Dr. Bob Davis became the chief administrative officer for the Lt. Governor.

In 1982 Collins decided to run for Governor, and Davis was right there. Running against Dr. Harvey Sloane and Dr. Grady Stumbo in the Democratic primary, she narrowly won and then beat baseball Hall of Famer Jim Bunning in the general election by a wide margin, to become Kentucky's first woman governor.

Dr. Bob Davis was now a politician. Well, sort of. He worked in the administration of Governor Collins, Governor Wallace Wilkinson, and Governor Brereton Jones, and by his own admission enjoyed a 20-year stint in Kentucky state government as a second career.

CHAPTER SIX

Kenny didn't return to his home in Monticello when he decided to leave Western.

"I was embarrassed that I had left," he said. "I felt like I had let some people down. It just wasn't a good situation for me at that time. But I still knew I could play. I knew it for sure when practice started at Georgetown and right off I was better than most."

Davis had withdrawn from his classes at Western with passing grades, and with education and getting a college degree a priority with him, he hit the classroom as hard as he hit the hardwood.

"Kenny left at night," recalled former Western team manager Lloyd Gardner, who later coached Louisville Fairdale to the high school state championship. "I had no idea he was leaving. It was my job to get the freshmen up every morning at 7 a.m., so I had the keys to all the rooms. His room was across from mine in Barnes-Campbell Hall, so I went into his room and found a note on his desk that said, 'Lloyd please turn in my books.'"

Few people knew at the time what was churning in Kenny's head. The truth of the matter was he didn't initially transfer to Georgetown to play basketball at all. He was going there for the sole purpose of being Kenny Davis the student.

When he decided to leave Western he immediately contacted Bob Spear, the head basketball coach at the Air Force Academy in Colorado Springs about transferring there. After all, that originally had been his second choice after Western.

"I found out they didn't take second semester students," Kenny said. "The way all of the academics were set up if you did not enroll with the fall class you had to wait until the following year. So Coach Spear suggested I go to Georgetown and take classes to obtain some hours that I could transfer."

Upon arrival at Georgetown, quickly Kenny realized a military career may not be in the cards after all.

"Almost immediately I realized the guard orientated offense that Coach Davis employed was the perfect fit for me," he said.

This was how close Kenny came to not becoming a college All-American and Hall of Famer, as well as the all-time leading scorer among colleges in Kentucky. Important, too, was that at the Air Force Academy he may not have been in position to make the Olympic team.

Unknowingly, Kenny would later become a bit of a Western trivia question: Who were the four consecutive state high school scoring champions signed by the Hilltoppers from 1965 thru 1968? Answer: 1965-Rich Hendrick, Bristow, 42 point average; 1966-Kenny Davis, Wayne County, 32 point average; 1967-Jim McDaniels, Allen County, 34 point average; and 1968-Terry Davis (no relation) Shelby County, 35 point average.

It may have been an emotional setback for Kenny when he left Bowling Green, but all was not in vain. He practiced daily with some great players like Clem Haskins, Dwight Smith, Wayne Chapman, and freshman teammate Curly Selvy. He had gotten a taste of college life and college coaching, and not to be overlooked, Western was where team manager Lloyd Gardner taught Kenny the technique of tying a necktie. Later in life this would prove to be an art he would become known for.

"I was in basketball heaven, playing pick-up games with those great players," he said. "I also tried to learn as much as possible from Rich Hendrick, the scoring machine from Bristow, who could fill it up."

Kenny had only known Coach Davis through two summer basketball camps that catered to young high school kids. It was hardly enough time to determine if he would be a coach Kenny would like to play for in college, especially four years.

The truth of the matter when he was at that camp, playing basketball in college was the furthest thing from his mind. After all he was only 15, and just becoming a good player on the Wayne County varsity was his major goal.

Coach Bob Davis was all about fundamentals.

"He was hands on at those camps," Kenny recalled. "But now here I was at Georgetown and I quickly saw that Coach Davis ran all of his offense through his guards, and there had been a lot of them here before me (Charlie Grote, Dickie Vories, and Cecil Tuttle), and they had scored a lot of points. Plus, I had no place else to go. It was stay here or go back home."

In 1969, Dr. Bob Davis decided to put what he practiced into written words with the publication of a book. In typical Bob Davis form the title cut through the chase.

"Aggressive Basketball" was the title, a surprise to no one who had ever played for him or even saw Georgetown College play. On page one of his book the tone is set when he writes "aggressive basketball means winning basketball."

His book is full of advice and experiences to coaches that have happened throughout his life.

He wrote:

> "It's not a popularity contest (being a coach)...the players have to respect him, but not like him as a pal. Never brag about his players until after they graduate, and then talk about them constantly, have deep affection for them."
>
> Davis writes that he has turned lambs into tigers, and every move a coach makes must be for the good of the player. "He drives them with only one thing in mind...to make them better men. An overwhelming desire to win is the American way of life. To do only what is expected implies there is no such thing as progress."
>
> Davis, the coach, admits in his book to being tough. After losing a game he says his team practiced the following day from 4:30 a.m. to 7:30 a.m., 3 p.m. to 6 p.m., and then again from 8 p.m. to 9:30 p.m. He even admits that with his team trailing at halftime to kicking over some lockers anchored to concrete. He broke his toe. But the good thing, he wrote, was his team came back and won.

The book continued:

> "Don't show any mercy on the basketball court. If you have an urge to be kind to your fellow man, join the Peace Corps."
>
> Davis had rules, too.

"No drinking…reduced smoking during season, and never in public. If you have already acquired a smoking (habit), only in your room."

And then his book listed several drills he put his team through.

"Every drill should be given a name that encourages aggressive play."

1. Blood & Guts Drill — rebounding
2. Wampass Cat Drill — loose balls
3. No Man's Land — keyhole (area of court)

There was one more of Davis' drills that over the years has remained a source of humorous conversation, although probably not at the time.

The Pink Panty Drill was the name given to one of the exercises in rebounding. Here's how it was described:

"The entire squad is allowed to choose a position under the basket. The coach or a student manager shoots. As each player gets two rebounds he sits down. The last player left standing (without two rebounds) are asked to wear pink ladies bloomers for the entire day."

Does anyone really think Coach Davis "asked his" players to wear them? Would "told" be more accurate?

Years later, some of Coach Davis former players wanted to recognize their old coach who was now back living in Georgetown. Mike Calhoun took it upon himself to help spearhead the event. Calhoun had been an outstanding player for the Tigers during the Kenny Davis-Jimmy Reid era, and had firsthand experiences of enduring a labor of love career. And now here he was, at the time coaching basketball at Eastern Kentucky University in Richmond, wanting to pay homage to a man who had made life miserable for him and his teammates.

"I went to Georgetown's president and suggested a roast," says Calhoun. "We had a crowd. I was the MC, and we were able to get some of the ex-players like Charlie Grote, Kenny and Larry Phillips. There were quite a few more, too. Gov. (Martha Layne) Collins showed up and Kenny had a letter from C.M. Newton. We filled the gym for Coach Davis."

Just to make sure that Coach Davis didn't think they had forgotten all of those drills, Calhoun went out and bought a size 50 pair of pink panties to present that night.

"I had them framed and we presented Coach with them," laughed Calhoun. That roast turned into the kickoff of the Hall of Fame at the college."

It was easy to see why Mike Calhoun was a good MC that night. Most importantly he knew the subject matter and then like most coaches who are asked to make speaking tours, he is full of good one liners.

"My first impression of Kenny Davis when I saw him was he had one shoe on and one off. Did you lose a shoe," I asked him. 'No, I just found one,'" he said.

Bob Davis had built a career on getting good transfers to Georgetown, and Calhoun was no exception. He had come in from the University of Cincinnati in 1968, and says he really wasn't prepared for what he saw and experienced during some of those first practice sessions.

"My high school coach, Ray Ross, was a 1958 Georgetown graduate and I couldn't believe he sent me down there," Calhoun offered. "I can still vividly see those loose ball drills, rough and tumble, fighting, scratching and all the yelling".

The mental toughness and physical challenges were all a part of Coach Bob Davis' style. For sure he was an aggressive taskmaster.

Calhoun had watched Kenny and Reid pair-up at guards, and then when he was a junior he teamed up with Davis in the backcourt after Reid had graduated.

"He wasn't selfish," says Calhoun of Kenny. "He had a role and did it well, and was so knowledgeable of the game he knew how to support everybody else's role, too."

Calhoun continued his accolades, but with a bit of sarcasm mixed with humor.

"Kenny's definition of a bad shot was if someone else shot it. And we had one game where Coach, after a timeout, told us to slow the game down. Kenny said he'd just arch the ball a little more."

On a more serious note Calhoun said Kenny never received the credit he deserved as a good defensive player.

"He was a complete player at both ends," he said. "I'll tell you this about him at practice. His first shot in practice looked like the last shot in practice. And that's the way he did his job at Converse for 40 years."

Mike Calhoun says, "At the end of the day we knew Coach Davis would take care of us, but he expected us (players) to hold up our end. Every job I've ever had was Coach Davis and Kenny Davis driven."

CHAPTER SEVEN

In the beginning the only thing that Kenny Davis and Bob Davis had in common was their last names. As their relationship evolved, however, it became difficult to mention one without the other.

On the surface they were nothing alike. Kenny's emotions were more often than not kept on the inside. His actions as a basketball player spoke much louder than his words. Coach Davis, on the other hand, wore his emotions on his sleeve. They were there for everyone to see and hear. His fiery and sometimes unpredictable personality became his calling card.

Long before he became Dr. Bob Davis, or even Coach Davis, he had a good sense of where he wanted to go in life.

From his father, William, he got his spirit of which allowed him to occasionally live on the edge of his professional life.

"My dad was called Captain," Bob Davis says. "He got his name because he was a rebel, and the black sheep of the family. When he was 15 he ran away from home and joined the Army...went to Mexico to fight Poncho Villa in the Mexican uprising of 1910-1914."

Captain found out he didn't like the Army, and because of his age was allowed to come home. But when World War I rolled around he was back in and on the first ship heading overseas.

"His commanding officer was General Pershing," Davis continued. "And in 1935, Captain got one of the largest (military) bonuses ever given in Virginia."

Davis says his dad could never stay in one place for very long. From farming in Virginia, to coal mining in McDowell, West Virginia. He was on the move, that is, until he met Dolly Wilson, a school teacher in Huntington, West Virginia.

Captain and Dolly married and moved to the 400-acre Davis farm in Virginia. However, it didn't take Bob's mother long to realize her family would be much better off with a better quality of life and more educational opportunities if they moved back to West Virginia. And so they did.

It was from his mother, Dolly, that Bob Davis got his ability to see a project thru. The desire for an education came with it.

After graduating from Vinson High School in Huntington in 1944, Bob joined the Navy, and just as he had done in high school, he participated in lots of sports when he had time, even taking up boxing.

Upon leaving the Navy in 1946, Davis passed on a basketball scholarship to Marshall College, and instead, because one of his high school coaches had gone to Georgetown College in Georgetown, Kentucky, decided to enroll there.

At Georgetown Bob played football and ran on the track team.

"My weight would go up and down," he recalled. "I had to weigh 180 for football and 160 for track."

By now Davis' reputation as a competitor was well established. His teammates and those he played against had seen it up close and personal.

"All I wanted to do was compete," he said. "I loved football, but track was my best sport, the mile and two mile. I didn't have much of a social life and certainly didn't have time to date."

He did find time to pledge the Kappa Alpha social fraternity, but there was little doubt that its importance was far behind athletics and his classroom work.

For most of Davis' playing days, Georgetown College was a member of the Kentucky Intercollegiate Athletic Conference (KIAC). From 1930 to 1949 league members were Louisville, Western, Eastern, Murray, and Morehead, but then the state supported schools (Western, Eastern, Murray and Morehead) broke away to hook up with several Tennessee schools to form the Ohio Valley Conference. The KIAC then now consisted of Georgetown, Transylvania, Union, Berea, Centre, and Kentucky Wesleyan. Bellarmine joined in 1953, and the following year Villa Madonna.

In basketball, from 1945 to 1953, Georgetown had only two winning seasons, but little did the school know, things would soon get better.

Bob Davis' life took a different turn that would forever change his life, when during his senior year in 1950, he met a pretty freshman girl from Ft. Thomas, Kentucky. And it happened on Valentine Day.

Joyce Huddleston was just who he needed in life to give him a different perspective. All out consumed with athletics, he now found out there was another world out there. Still, he never lost focus on what he wanted to do. But now it included Joyce, and that made him even more driven to be a success.

When C.Q. Smith came to him shortly after graduation and asked him to become an assistant coach at High Point College in North Carolina, it didn't take him long to reach a decision.

"Here was a chance for me at such a young age to actually become a college coach," Davis said. "Heck yes, I did it! I was an assistant coach in basketball and football. I lived in the gym and ate with the team in the school cafeteria. How much better could it be?"

A short time later he became the head basketball coach at High Point, making him one of the youngest head coaches in the nation.

"We were an NAIA school (National Association of Intercollegiate Athletes)," he said. "There were 550 schools, most of them real small in this category, and back then the majority of the big NCAA schools weren't recruiting the black players. Can you imagine the talent?"

As much as Davis was into his job at High Point, his thoughts were never far from Joyce back in Georgetown, and in 1952, the two were married in Ft. Thomas, Kentucky.

At High Point he had begun to think about getting his master's degree. He had enough foresight to know that he wanted to coach for a long time, and in order to do so he would have to further his education. He never forgot the lessons he learned from his old high school coach, Homer "Kid" McCoy, back at Vinson High in West Virginia. He also appreciated Cam Henderson, the inventor of the zone defense at Marshall University. If he was to continue his climb up the coaching ladder, Davis knew he would have to utilize the knowledge of every coach he had come in contact with and those were two he had learned from.

It didn't take long. In 1953, Georgetown's director of athletics called Davis to see if he wanted to "come home" and be the school's baseball coach.

"I'd never played the sport," Davis said. "But at High Point I had a couple of students who were into baseball and for two years they taught me the sport."

Bobby Terrell had been one of Corbin High School's best basketball players ever, good enough to play for Peck Hickman's Louisville Cardinals after graduation. But Bob's first love was baseball. Though he also played baseball at Louisville, following a baseball game between the Cardinals and Tigers, a conversation with Georgetown baseball coach Humsey Yessin convinced Terrell to somewhat alter his educational plans.

"Humsey told me I should think about transferring to Georgetown and play baseball," Terrell says. "I thought about it and hitchhiked to Georgetown at the end of the semester. I played a semester of basketball there and decided to focus on baseball and later signed a minor league contract."

By the time Terrell arrived at Georgetown, however, Yessin had been called into the Army and Bob Davis was now the baseball coach.

"He didn't know much about baseball," said Terrell, who is a member of the Tiger Hall of Fame, "And he admitted it. But he was a great leader. He didn't do to us what he did in basketball, and he would even ask us for our ideas. But I will say this, we were in shape."

In 1954, Terrell and teammates Kenny Cox, Jim Jenkins, John Lykins, Billy Sykes, Bill McBee, Al Peffer, Tuss Loving, and Pete Gill won the KIAC championship with a 10-2 record. The aces of the pitching staff that year were lefthander Roy Bowling, who became one of the all-time great girls high school coaches at Laurel County, and Martin 'Bones' Carr, a right hander. (Davis' career coaching record at Georgetown was 25-13).

Not only was Bob Davis now married, but his coaching life was moving at an accelerated pace. And don't forget the importance of academics were never far from his thoughts.

Georgetown College President Leo Eddleman named Davis an assistant professor "while I worked on my masters at U.K."

By now there weren't enough hours in a day for him. He was involved in coaching not only baseball, but basketball and football, in addition to teaching 12 hours of classes a week. And on top of all that he worked at a campus restaurant whenever he could. He was making $3,600 a year.

"Looking back on it, I was lucky to have had a lot of energy and good health," he said.

When Davis became the head basketball coach at Georgetown in 1953, there were those who described him as a "football guy coaching basketball."

It was evident for those who ever saw a Bob Davis team practice that some of the drills did indeed resemble something that might be seen on the football field. And from the beginning, anyone who played for him checked their ego at the door. This style of coaching would serve Kenny Davis well a few years later when he met Coach Henry Iba.

Some of the biggest names in Kentucky sports history had been students and athletes at Georgetown College.

Blanton Collier, who had a notable career at the University of Kentucky in the 50's and 60's, coaching football and later winning a world championship with the Cleveland Browns, played football and basketball at Georgetown.

Collier, a Millersburg, Kentucky native, to this day has the distinction of being the last Kentucky football coach to depart with a winning record. As unbelievable as that sounds, his 41-36-3 mark means that it has been well over half a century since the University of Kentucky has had a winning football coach.

Another Georgetown connection to U.K. was Harry Lancaster, who would become a trusty assistant basketball coach to Adolph Rupp and later the director of athletics.

Coaching in the shadows of Rupp and his Wildcat team, Bob Davis never blinked. He knew his role and he knew what he had been hired to do: win basketball games.

Because of Lancaster's connection to Georgetown College, the Tigers were invited to several pre-season scrimmages with the Kentucky Wildcats.

"Coach Rupp was such a presence," Davis recalled. "And his teams were so strong and quick that we could only keep up not much past the first half."

There was one of these scrimmages in Georgetown that Davis will never forget.

"Both of our teams had run several fast breaks, and repeatedly thrown the ball away," said Davis. "Coach Rupp jumped off the bench and screamed, 'Throw me the ball.' His player immediately threw him the ball. He said, 'Okay, you stumble bums run up and down the floor. You don't need the ball.' His team and all of my players started sprinting up and down the floor. After five minutes they were almost fatigued. Coach Rupp called his players over to talk, and my players came over to me. I asked them why they were running, because I hadn't said for them to run. They all answered that when Coach Rupp said run they were going to run. That's how powerful Coach Rupp was."

Though affiliated with the Baptist Church, Georgetown College and Davis in particular had no aspirations of turning the coaches' strategies into a hardwood ministry. He would be preaching alright, but from a different book. One of those books was titled "Aggressive Basketball," one he penned in 1969.

While Davis was coaching football, several of his players quit the team and declared they had decided to become ministerial students. This caused Dr. Romie Judd, the school's interim president at the time to say that "Coach Davis has sent more men into the ministry than several churches he knew about."

The promise of money to support Davis and his recruiting efforts was made by the college's President Eddleman. Although never enough, it was better than it had been, and it showed the school's commitment to showcase a winning basketball team. The college administration realized that sports, especially if they won, could lead to increased donations, not just to athletics, but to the entire college.

Bob Davis knew that in spite of the successes at U.K., U of L, Western, Eastern and Murray, there was still some room in a basketball crazy state.

After all, Kentucky State in nearby Frankfort had found a way to squeeze in. Coached by Lucias Mitchell, and featuring future pros Elmore Smith and Travis "Machine Gun" Grant, this was a team that won NAIA national titles. It was also a team Bob Davis felt could have won at any level of the college game.

"They were loaded," he said. "We played them several times when they had those good teams…they were big, fast and could shoot."

Before long Davis was being described as colorful, not only in his relationship with his players, but also by friends and alumni, and for sure he knew how to keep the school's name in the media, even outside of Georgetown. With Rupp at Kentucky and Ed Diddle at Western, Bob Davis had his work cut out for him, and the easiest way to make headlines was to win games. That meant he had to recruit good players.

His future players had no idea what was in store when they arrived on campus. He, of course, tried to evaluate players that would fit his style. With limited resources and staff, he had to make every scholarship count. He could ill afford many mistakes. When his recruits showed up in the fall to begin classes, they were also going to enroll in another class—basketball, Bob Davis style.

Some, especially the kids from Kentucky, had attended Davis' summer basketball camp, and were at least familiar with the location of the gym. But let it be known that a summer basketball camp, however, did give Coach Davis an opportunity to see kids shoot, run, jump and even listen. He would take these elements and process them enough to determine if they could play basketball at Georgetown, and even more importantly play for him.

Davis never intended to lose a player once he arrived on campus. If he did, it meant that he had possibly misjudged a recruit. He accepted some of the blame. He didn't like surprises, and if there were he wanted it to be the kind where a player was actually better than he hoped. More often than not he was able to bring this out of his boys. Today, it is referred to as "up-coaching", something he had been doing for a long time.

It was some of those practices that Bob Davis relished. He seemed to find excitement in creating situational practice sessions, intermingled with lessons in life his players never knew existed this side of hell.

In the beginning the younger players went through their paces in bewilderment, questioning themselves why they were here and silently wondering if their coach was a bit deranged. But more often than not they mustered an inner strength that they had made the right decision.

Practice sessions lasted several hours with an emphasis on fundamentals and physical conditioning. Davis knew, like most successful coaches, that winning came down to which team made the fewest mistakes. If mistakes were going to be made, he wanted them made on the practice floor and not in the game.

Chapter Eight

It didn't take Kenny long for his Georgetown teammates to hang the nickname "Little Bob" on the new arrival. Though their last names were the same, they were not related, but over the years, long after college, there were those that thought Kenny was Coach Davis' son. Later, even Kenny's Marathon Oil teammates picked up on the name.

When Kenny arrived at Georgetown in November 1966, he moved into the Alumni Gym where Coach Davis had arranged his living quarters. His first semester there he took 18 hours of studies, and when he wasn't in class he could be found in the gym shooting and shooting.

"I didn't go home (back to Wayne County)," he says. "I wore shorts under my jeans, and after class I went straight to the gym."

Kenny did not have enough transferable hours from Western to be eligible for the Georgetown team in the spring semester of 1967, so he had to wait until the fall of 1967 before he could play. He would then be ready for his freshman year of college.

Basketball and books, just as in high school, were once again his life. And just as in high school, any romance would have to wait.

High school coach Gerald Sinclair recalled that there were several girls who wanted to date Kenny, but he just didn't have time.

"He had his priorities," Sinclair laughed, "And dating wasn't one of them. Some of his teammates would kid him about all the girls that wanted to date him. He told them by the time he studied and practiced basketball he didn't have time for girls."

Nothing had changed at Georgetown. At least not yet.

By church doctrine, Georgetown College was classified as a private Baptist College. But that didn't mean its students didn't like to have fun. An enrollment of 1,200 included a mix of Bible Belt southerners, Midwesterners, and kids from the eastern seaboard. While many were content for a date night downtown at Fava's Restaurant after a movie at the Bluegrass Drive-In, there were others who quickly found their way to Lexington, 15 minutes away.

Local sports writer Bill Mingus picked up on Kenny Davis' arrival to Georgetown.

"He's a conscientious boy, off the court as well as on, belying the "jock" stereotype," he wrote.

Mingus went on to write that there would be an occasional report of a soft drink machine punched in the side in an attempt to get two for the price of one. Or if they hit the jackpot it might be a bunch of them.

Soon after his arrival, he began to hear the stories among some of the Tigers' returning players about the practice sessions they endured under Coach Davis. There would be some who would leave the team at the end of the season, deciding they didn't want to play basketball after all. Was Kenny having second thoughts? Perhaps the Air Force Academy was still an option.

"I was set on staying here," he said. "I knew I could play, and the offense Coach Davis ran was built around guards, so I really was in paradise."

As wild and crazy the stories were about Coach Davis and his methods to make his team better, there were players who had stayed the course and withstood the "stuff" that had been dished out. They had cussed their coaches' mere existence, but later after they had graduated, they admired and appreciated what he had done, not only for them, but to them.

When Kenny finally got his college career underway, most were waiting to see if this so-called high school scoring machine could do the same at Georgetown. There had been some fabulous players here before he came along, and there were some who thought the hype on Kenny Davis might be a little exaggerated. The odds were against him putting up scoring numbers like Charlie Grote, Corky Withrow, Cecil Tuttle and Dick Vories. Kenny was well aware of them, and had met Tuttle and Vories at the Bob Davis Basketball Camp he had attended a few years earlier.

Vories was the school's all-time point leader with 2,968, and Tuttle was not far behind with 2,340, as well as holding the single game mark with 47. As confident as Kenny was about his own abilities, even he never dreamed he would or could put up those kinds of numbers. And no one else did either.

Kenny was in the starting lineup for the opening game of the season, and wound up being a starter in 16 of the 26 games. He showed flashes of greatness, mixed with ho-hum games that sent him to the bench. The Tigers finished the 1967-68 season with a record of 20-7, and Kenny scored at 11.6 points per game. Certainly it wasn't a disappointing year for the kid from Wayne County, but it wasn't hall of fame numbers either. Senior Larry Banfield, a 6'5" forward proved to be, at least statistically, the Tigers best player, averaging just under 20 points per game, and 14 rebounds.

A thumbnail overview before the 1968-69 season put out by Georgetown's sports information office wrote that it sure would be nice if Kenny could get his average up to 15.

Cecil Tuttle saw Kenny that freshman season, and he knew the sky was the limit. "What body control he had with the ball," Tuttle said. "He could get around defenders like they weren't even there. I knew then he was going to be good…really good."

The Kenny Davis fans saw away from the hardwood was not the same Kenny Davis they saw when he was on it. Polite, soft spoken, well-mannered, and even sometime unassuming, he had the look of a choirboy. But on the court he took on an entirely different image. He became the choir boy assassin. His game could be described as controlled violence. Those steely eyes, clenched teeth and set jaw were focused on only one thing—victory. He was a rare athlete, indeed. He could flip a switch and become a different person altogether.

This was the Kenny Davis that was ready for his sophomore year. And what a season it was. In 35 games he scored under 20 points three times, and had several 30 plus outings, including 48 against Kentucky State to break Tuttle's one game mark, and then when the season had ended he owned the single season record as well with a total of 965 points compared to Vories record of 861.

Davis' shots came from soft jumpers from the outside, mixed with dribble-drive assaults on the basket, long before the term became popular. By contrast, Vories got many of his points by often shooting off the wrong foot. It would baffle the defender. He would dribble toward the basket and plant one foot, fall back and shoot. The defender would buckle, still thinking Vories was going to take another step. Kenny's game was completely different.

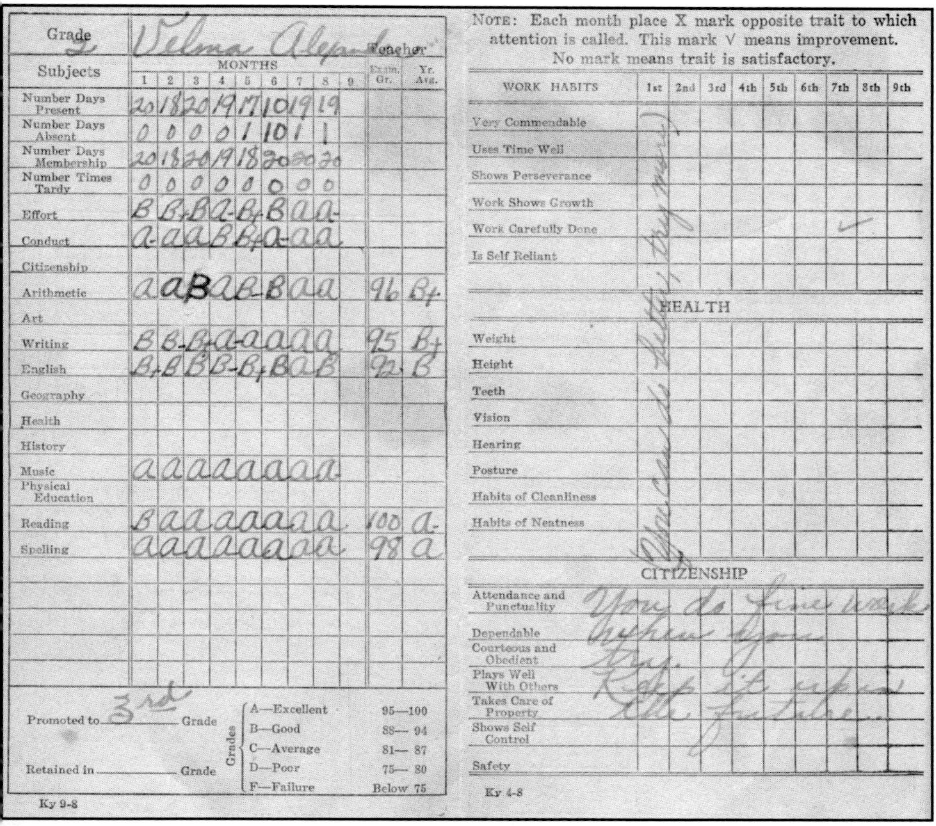

Grade 2	Velma Alexander Teacher										
Subjects	MONTHS 1	2	3	4	5	6	7	8	9	Exam. Gr.	Yr. Avg.
Number Days Present	20	18	20	19	17	10	19	19			
Number Days Absent	0	0	0	0	1	10	1	1			
Number Days Membership	20	18	20	19	18	20	20	20			
Number Times Tardy	0	0	0	0	0	0	0	0			
Effort	B	B+	B	A-	B+	B	A	A-			
Conduct	A-	A	A	B	B+	A-	A	A			
Citizenship											
Arithmetic	A	A	B	A	B-	B	A	A		96	B+
Art											
Writing	B	B-	B+	A-	A	A	A	A		95	B+
English	B+	B	B	B-	B+	B	A	B		92	B
Geography											
Health											
History											
Music	A	A	A	A	A	A	A	A-			
Physical Education											
Reading	B	A	A	A	A	A	A	A		100	A-
Spelling	A	A	A	A	A	A	A	A		98	A

Promoted to 3rd Grade

Retained in ______ Grade

Grades: A—Excellent 95—100; B—Good 88—94; C—Average 81—87; D—Poor 75—80; F—Failure Below 75

Ky 9-8

NOTE: Each month place X mark opposite trait to which attention is called. This mark √ means improvement. No mark means trait is satisfactory.

WORK HABITS	1st	2nd	3rd	4th	5th	6th	7th	8th	9th
Very Commendable									
Uses Time Well									
Shows Perseverance									
Work Shows Growth									
Work Carefully Done							√		
Is Self Reliant									
HEALTH									
Weight									
Height									
Teeth									
Vision									
Hearing									
Posture									
Habits of Cleanliness									
Habits of Neatness									
CITIZENSHIP									
Attendance and Punctuality									
Dependable									
Courteous and Obedient									
Plays Well With Others									
Takes Care of Property									
Shows Self Control									
Safety									

You do fine work when you try. Keep it up in the future.

Ky 4-8

Kenny's second grade report card, Oil Valley School, April 1956.

Kenny Davis, 6th grade, Walker Elementary, 1960.

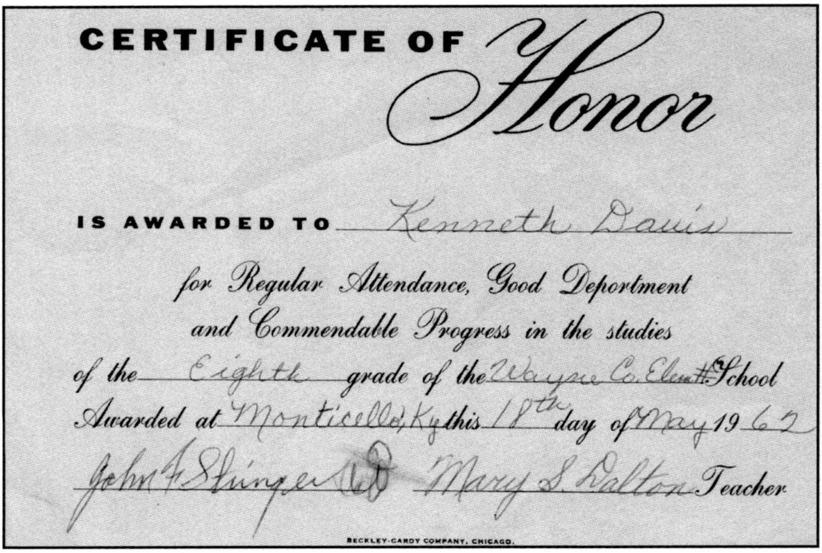

CERTIFICATE OF *Honor*

IS AWARDED TO Kenneth Davis

for Regular Attendance, Good Deportment and Commendable Progress in the studies of the Eighth *grade of the* Wayne Co. Elem. *School*

Awarded at Monticello, Ky *this* 18th *day of* May *19*62

John F. Stringer Mary S. Dalton *Teacher*

BECKLEY-CARDY COMPANY, CHICAGO.

1963-64 Wayne Co. Team. Back row: Nelson Stonewall, Tommy Sexton, Paul Gregory, Cleo Duncan, Harold Dishm Donnie Frost, Wayne Huchinson, Theo Duncan, Glen Correll, Kenny Davis, Ralph Reagan, Jerry Cooper. Front Managers: Ray Chesney, George Corder, Donald Criswell.

2005 DAWAHARES/KHSAA
Hall of Fame Induction Celebration

RAY MILLS

Ray Mills was a basketball standout at Clay County. He was a two-year starter for the Tigers in 1952 and 1953. As a senior, coached by "Spider" Thurman, Mills led the Tigers to one of the best seasons in the schools' early history. That year, the team swept through the regular season, winning 29 consecutive games and earned the school's first Regional Championship and trip to the State Basketball Tournament. The team ended the season with a quarterfinal finish in the State Tournament and at one point had won 35 consecutive games. During that memorable year, Mills and the Tigers set many records as he set the Southeastern Kentucky Conference single-game scoring mark with 45 points. His honors included All-District three times, All-Region twice and the top selection for All-State his senior year. Mills went on to play for legendary coach Adolph Rupp at the University of Kentucky and led the freshman team in scoring and rebounding his first year. He and his wife Gerry, have four children JoAnne, David, Danny and Belinda and four grandchildren Morgan, Dylan, Matthew and Carmen.

MEDAL PRESENTATION
BY
"SPIDER" THURMAN

SPONSORED BY
DEDICATED CARRIERS

13

Ray Mills was the basketball coach for Wayne Co. High School during Kenny's Freshman year. He was inducted to the KHSAA Hall of Fame in 2005.

Kenny follows through after a shot pictured in the 1964 Wayne County yearbook.

First Row: Bruce Davis, Larry Anderson, Bobby Slagle, Johnny Gregory, Carter Gregory, Jerry Cooper, Ralph Ragan, George Corder. Second Row: Coach Sinclair, Kenny Davis, Harold Dishman, Paul Gregory, Theo Duncan, Carter Blevins, Donnie Frost.

Kenny's senior high school yearbook photo, 1966.

Kenny presents the 1966 District Championship trophy to Wayne County principal, A.J. Lloyd.

Kenny and Betty Raines, voted Best Athletes of Wayne County High School, 1966.

Kenny shooting free throws during a game in his senior year at Wayne County High School, 1966.

1965-66 Wayne County High School basketball team. Front row, l-r: Gary Richardson, Manager Bruce Davis, Ronald McFarland, Darwin Keeton, Lonnie Frost. Second row: Kenny Davis, Jerry Cooper, John Gregory, Harold Dishman, Danny Richardson. Third row: Steve DeBord, Donald Humble, Frank Jones, Joe Kelly, Ronnie Criswell, Coach Gerald Sinclair.

1964-65 Wayne County High School cheerleaders. Pictured top-bottom: DeAnna Hardwick, Betty Raines, Sue Slagle, Sylvia Vire, and Lyla Jones.

Wayne County High School cheerleaders, 1965-66. Pictured l-r: Sylvia Vine, Betty Raines, Lyla Jones, Sue Boston, and Janet Reagan.

Cheerleaders: (l-r) Nancy Juett, Sally Zartman, Linda Moss, Cindy Hopkins, Mary Sue Burton, Nancy Smith, Marie Covington, and Michelle Amin.

Shirley Upchurch, head majorette, and Ruth Ann DeBord, drum majorette, Wayne County High School, 1966.

Kenny Davis and Rita Bell at Wayne County High School graduation, May 1966.

Mr. and Mrs. Earl Edwards, Wayne County High School custodians. Mr. Edwards would let Kenny in the gym to shoot.

1966-67 Western Kentucky University Scholarship freshmen. l-r: Curly Selvy, Walker Banks, Wayne Bright, Charles Starbuck and Kenny Davis.

Georgetown College's three Davis boys talk things over in preparation for the NAIA District 24 basketball playoffs March 3-4 at Carson-Newman. John (left) is a senior forward from Durham, N.C. Kenny (right), a sophomore guard from Wayne County, leads Kentucky's collegiate scorers. Dr. Bob is in his 18th year as head coach and has had at least 20 wins 12 times, including this season. Kenny scored 25 in a 90-72 win over Northwood last night.

Grant And Davi Named To NAI A-A First Team

KANSAS CITY (AP) — Travis Grant, a me of Kentucky State's championship squad, was nam the All-American basketball team announced Thur by the National Association of Intercollegiate Athl

The 6-foot-7 guard also carried off the NAIA scoring crown with 1,098 points in 31 games for an average of 35.4 that helped his team wrap up the association title.

Kenny Davis, a 6-foot guard from Georgetown, Ky., College, landed a spot on the 10-man honor club.

James Silas, Stephen F. Austin's 6-2 guard, a sophomore like Grant, was picked along with Jake Ford of Maryland State, Greg Hyder of Eastern New Mexico and Fred Davis of Howard Payne, the last three being repeaters from the 1969 club.

Rounding out the squad were Bob Mabry of Rio Grande, the leading rebounder in collegiate basketball history with 2,265; Paul Adams, Central Washington; Rob St. Pierre of Hanover, Ind., and Doug Williams of St. Mary's of Texas.

Elmore Smith of Kentucky State was placed on the second team.

Grant's drive for the scoring honor started with a 75-point outburst against Northwood, Ind. on Feb. 5. He scored 91 points in two NAIA district games and paced all players in the NAIA title tournament here with 137 points in five games.

Leroy Jenkins of Detroit College finished second in production with an avera 33.4.

Kenny Davis All-American

GEORGETOWN ALL-AMERICAN–Georgetown's junior guard Kenny Davis (a former Wayne County High star) has been named to the First Team National Association of Intercollegiate Athletics All American selections. The 6'0" Monticello native averaged 29.2 points per game this season, hitting 48 percent from the field and 80 percent from the strip. He totalled 847 points during the season and holds the single game and season scoring records at Georgetown. Last year as a sophomore Davis was named to the Second Team Selections.

WANTED

All-American Notices For

Kentucky's No. 1 Sharpshooter

KENNY DAVIS - Georgetown College
6' 0'' Sophomore Guard

1968-69 Kentucky College scoring leader, 27.4 average.

Single-game college scoring record of 48 points against Kentucky State.

With seven games left to play and 685 points, he should break the season record of 861.

Scored 30 or more in 23 of 25 games.

Held below 20 points only twice since becoming a starter.

Sparkplug and team leader of the GRRRRReat TIGERS.

If you see a blank All-American ballot, insert the name KENNY DAVIS in the proper blank and you will have the reward of having made a good choice.

2-6-69

Kenny drives against Cumberland College in the NAIA District 24 Championship game, 1969.

Kenny Davis headed for another basket, 1969 yearbook.

Bradley gives Davis some blocking. Georgetown College 1969 yearbook.

Most Athletic, Jim Reid, Georgetown College 1969 yearbook.

Kenny Davis - Senior Guard Captain-1970-71 Tigers N.A.I.A First Team All American, 1969-70

1969 yearbook. Front Row: Mike Wilson, Joe Ogletree, Jim Reid, Kenny Davis, Geo Lockwood, Jim Gibbs. Seecond Row: Mick Kennedy (coach), Steve Moore, Craig Tschudi, Jerry Osborne, John Davis, Barry Zwick, Frank Kemplin (Manager). Third Row: Gary Moore, Jerry Bradley, Jim Dickerson, Lenny Myers, Jim Bailey, Dan Cook.

1970 World University Team. Front Row l-r: Bob Davis, Head Coach (Georgetown College), Bill Wall, Team Manager; John Mengelt (Auburn University), Jim Cleamons (Ohio State), Jake Jones (Assumption College), Brian Wilson (Alternate), Kenny Davis (Georgetown College), Ed Badger Assistant Coach, Oscar Smuckler, Referee. Back Row L to R: David Smith (Guilford College), Cliff Meely (U. of Colorado), David Robish (U. of Kansas), Jim McDaniels (Western Kentucky University), Dana Lewis (Tulsa University), George McGinnis (Indiana University), Bob Ford (Perdue University), Tom Parker (U. of Kentucky).

Kenny Davis was voted "Most Athletic" at Georgetown College, 1970.

The Tiger offense is triggered by co-captain Kenny Davis. As a sophomore Davis averaged 27.6 points a game hitting 45% from the field. He was selected on the N.A.I.A. All-American Team and looks forward to two more productive seasons. Georgetown College 1970 yearbook.

Kenny Davis was also selected for the U.S.A. College All-Star team, which represented America in France, Italy, Austria, Turkey, Africa, Belgium, Germany, Yugoslavia, and other countries. While on the tour, Davis started every game and averaged fourteen points. Georgetown College 1970 Yearbook.

Senior co-captain Jim Reid from Beaver Dam, Kentucky, provides the all-around play and leadership vital to a championship team. His 16 point average was second only to Davis. Georgetown College 1970 yearbook.

Fourth runner-up Sandy Butler; Third runner up Rita Renfro; Miss Belle of the Blue Sharon Caldwell; First runner up Nancye Hatfield; Second runner-up Liz Zimmerman. Georgetown College 1970 yearbook.

Rita Renfro performs during the Georgetown College Miss Belle of the Blue pageant.

1970 Yearbook. Kneeling l-r: Joe Ogletree, Jim Reid, Barry Zwick, Mike Calhoun, Kenny Davis. Back Row L to R: Jerry Osborne, Gary Moore, Jim Bailey, Lenny Myers, Tom Stewart, Wayne Wilson, Willie Day.

1970-71 Georgetown College Tigers. Seated, center, David Moore, Manager. (First Row l-r): Assistant Coach Jim Reid, Conley, Conatser, Ogletree, Fritsch, Lockwood, Davis, and Head Coach Bob Davis. (Second Row l-r): Zwick, White, Owen, Calhoun, Phillips, Moore, Graduate Assistant Tim Somerville. (Third Row l-r.): Wikinson, Allen, Miller, Vance, Proud, Stewart, and Flint.

1971 College All Star Basketball Game. Played at U. of Dayton April 7, 1971. Seated l-r Kenny Davis (Georgetown College), Bill Smith (Syracuse), Artis Gilmore (Jacksonville U.), Coach Dutch Louborg, Jim McDaniels (Western KY U.), Jim Day (Morehead State), John Roche (U. of South Carolina). Back Row l-r Jim Cleamons (Ohio St. U.), Austin Carr (Notre Dame), George Jackson (U. of Dayton), Rich Yunkus (Georgia Tech), Charlie Yelverton (Fordham), Charlie Davis (Wake Forest).

Georgetown College 1970-71 Basketball program.

DR. ROBERT DAVIS – Coach

JIM REID – Asst. Coach

COACHES

BOB DAVIS, basketball coach since 1953, is also chairman of the Department of Physical Education and Athletics.

After his graduation from Georgetown College in 1950, he served as assistant coach of High Point College at High Point, North Carolina. The next year he was elevated to head coach and led his squad to a 20 won, 10 lost record, and was runner-up in the North State Conference. In 1952-53, High Point won the Conference Championship.

Over 17 seasons his Georgetown teams have rolled up a 354-159 won-lost record, placing him among the top 12 coaches in America. Eight of his charges have been selected to N.A.I.A. All-American teams.

During his 17 year period he was called upon to coach football when Georgetown revived that sport after a two-year layoff, and to head the baseball nine. In between seasons he has somehow managed to complete the requirements toward a doctorate at Peabody College. Officially he is now Dr. Davis.

He brought home the K.I.A.C. Tourney five times and placed second three times during the 11 years his teams belonged to that Conference. Georgetown has represented District 24 in the National Association of Intercollegiate Athletics at Kansas City eight times during that period, placing fourth in 1958 and second in 1961.

Named "N.A.I.A. Coach of the Year" in 1959 he was assistant coach of the N.A.I.A. All-Star team that defeated the Lucas-led Ohio State aggregation in 1959 Olympic playoffs at Denver. Currently he is on the executive committee of the N.A.I.A. and is vice-chairman of the U.S. Olympic Selection Committee.

Bob is also very much in demand as a speaker and instructor for regional and national basketball clinics. In addition he has recently published a book. As you might expect the title of his book is *Aggressive Basketball.*

In the summer of 1965 Bob took the Tigers to Israel, at the invitation of the Israeli government and the Sports for Israel organization. For his efforts he returned to Kentucky with the first international trophy Georgetown College had ever won.

Two years ago Davis was business manager and assistant coach of the "Little Men's" team that won the World's Championship in Spain with a 6-1 record. No player could exceed 5'11" so this was quite an unusual team for Davis to coach.

Then, the Israelis decided to invite Bob back again, so in early September he took a group of A.A.U. stars, including Georgetown players Dick Vories, Tom Tripman, Leonard Myers and John Davis, for his second visit. Here he played against the No. 2 and No. 3 Israeli National teams plus other selected squads and wound up with a 4-2 record and a trophy for the best won-lost record.

This past summer Dr. Davis took a team of U.S. College roundballers on a playing tour behind the Iron Curtain to compete in the World University Games. Georgetown's N.A.I.A. All American Kenny Davis was the leading scorer on the American squad which lost only two of twenty games.

JIM REID is Assistant Coach this year, replacing Larry Phillips as Davis' right hand man. Reid is a '70 Georgetown graduate and was for four years one of the Tigers' most dependable performers. Last year as a senior he was awarded the L. R. Cooke Trophy as the outstanding Georgetown athlete, based on scholarship and character as well as athletic prowess.

3

Coaches pictured in the Georgetown College 1970-71 Basketball program.

e state department sponsored a college all-star tour
ainst the Czech Republic, July 1969.

Program cover for the Czech Republic tour.

Billy Keller of Purdue University (left) and Kenny Davis of Georgetown College, from the College All-Star program for the Czech Republic tour.

Seattle SuperSonics

158 THOMAS STREET • SEATTLE, WASHINGTON 98109 • MAin 4-3404

November 23, 1970

Dear Kenny:

We have enclosed a Personal Questionnaire for you to complete at your earliest convenience and return to the Seattle SuperSonics.

This questionnaire will assist in making our final determination in the evaluation of future prospects for our organization.

For your information, there WILL NOT be a common collegiate draft in 1971 between the National Basketball Association and the American Basketball Association.

We would suggest that you wait until both the National Basketball Association and American Basketball Association drafts are completed and you have been contacted by both leagues before making a final decision.

Also, if you have an agent, attorney, or advisor who will be representing you during contract negotiations, we would appreciate his name, address and phone number; please list below.**

We have enclosed a business reply envelope for your convenience.

Best of luck to you and your team in the 1970-71 season.

Sincerely,

Henry Akin

Henry Akin
Head Scout
Seattle SuperSonics

HA:sf

Mr. Kenny Davis
Athletic Dept.
Georgetown College
College St.
Georgetown, Ky. 40324

'71 Pan Am Team. Henry Wilmore, Brian Taylor, Kenny Davis, Don Buse, Paul Westphal, Bob McAdoo, Luke Witte, Jim Chones, Jim Forbes. Dwight Jones, Chuck Terry, Bob Ford.

Kenny at his desk in Frankfort in the fall of 1971.

NEW YORK PITTSBURGH ATLANTA ST. LOUIS BALTIMORE

MARTY BLAKE AND ASSOCIATES
Sports Consultants

312 Camelot Drive Pittsburgh, Pa. 15220 AC 412 531-9396

February 10, 1971

Dr. Robert M. Davis
Head Basketball Coach
Georgetown College
Georgetown, Kentucky

Dear Bob:

I have severed my relationship as President of the Pittsburgh Condors of the ABA and plan to enter business for myself in the field of player management and as a consultant to sports organizations - both amateur and professional.

I have already help draft for three ABA clubs and will do the same for several NBA teams. I am interested in offering my services to represent Ken Davis if he is not already represented.

I have never contacted a player directly and do not intend to - which may make me unique in this field but I have too many friends in the coaching ranks. I can offer a two-fold program - getting a young man drafted high and getting him a good contract. As you may know, I have trained most of the general managers in both leagues.

I can supply more than 100 recommendations from coaches and executives in spobts. I plan to move back to Atlanta june 15 and open offices there, in New York and in St. Louis.

Through Ed Mosler, I plan to offer my services free to the United States Olympic Committee.

If I can be of any service to you...or to Ken, please do not hesitate contacting me.

Sincerely,
MARTY BLAKE AND ASSOCIATES.

Marty Blake

MB/lk

Olympic Basketball Trial, Air Force Academy, 1972. Pictured l-r: Coach Bob Davis; John Tolmie, Navy; Jim Forbes, Texas, El Paso; Henry Steele, Northeast Louisiana; Bill Newton, Louisiana State University; Ed Ratleff, Long Beach; Tom Kelzelko, Toledo; Kenny Davis, Georgetown; and Bill Vining, Asst. Coach.

72 Olympic Trials Camp, Air Force Academy, Colorado, June 12-25, 1972. Row One: Herb Mols, Asst. Mgr., Olympic ım; Bill Summers, Camp Administrator and Mgr., Olympic Team; Henry P. Iba, Olympic Coach; Don Haskins, ;t. Coach, Olympic Team; John Bach, Asst. Coach, Olympic Team; Dr. Irving Dardick, Camp Physician. Row Two: :. "Whitey" Gwynne, Trainer, Olympic Team; Byron Bird, Trainer; Ed Badger, Coach; Tom Kivisto; Bob Lauriski; nald Richard; Tom Burleson; Mike Green; Kevin Joyce; Bob Wilson; Marshall Emery, Manager; Bobby Scott, Of- ial; Charles Welty, Trainer. Row Three: Naz Servidio, Official; Joe Cipriano, Coach; Tom Henderson; Bob Cremins; ne Kirk; Dwight Jones; Cliff Parsons Jr.; Tom McMillen; Doug Collins; Tynes Hildebrand, Mgr.; Norman Van Ar- ılen, Official. Row Four: Jim Bain, Official; Joe B. Hall, Coach; George Karl; Marv Schmitt; Dick Harris; James ɛwer; Luke Witte; Kermit Washington; Don Crenshaw; Art Wilmore; Jim Reid, Mgr.; Frank Cutko, Official. Row e: John Daneker, Official; Robert Knight, Coach; Barry Parkhill; Jackie Young; Michael Stewart; Swen Nater; Bob ɛes; Charles Kozak; Gregg Popovich; Capt. Jack Herron, Mgr.; Ben Dreith, Official. Row Six: Steve Honzo, Official; ı Halsten, Coach; Marvin Barnes; Larry Pounds; Bernard Hardin; Len Kosmalski; Jim Retseck; Mike Casey; Bob rsen; Billy Shepherd; Ed Van Winkle, Mgr. Row Seven: Reggie Minton, Coach; Allan Hornyak; Tony Miller; Billie ıires; Larry Kenon; Jim Lister; Harry Rogers; Kevin Kunnert; Bill Nietman. Row Eight: Robert Davis, Coach; Kenny vis; Tom Kozelko; Ed Ratleff; Bill Newton; Henry Steele; James Forbes; John Tolmie; Bill Vining, Coach. Row Nine: an Nicholson, Coach; Chuck Terry; Mike Bantom; Dan Traylor; Elmer Austin; John Brown; Mike D'Antoni; Scott ırtin; Pete Humanik, Mgr.; John Russell, Official.

The marriage of Miss Rita Renfro, daughter of Mr. and Mrs. Dallas Renfro of Paint Lick and Kenny Davis, son of Mr. and Mrs. Clyde Davis of Monticello was solemnized on May 16 at the bride's home in the presence of the couple's families. The double ring ceremony was performed by the groom's uncle, Orville Perkins. Rita's only attendant was her college roomate, Miss Yvonne Robinson of Covington. Kenny's Big Brother in the Kappa Alpha Fraternity, Jimmy Porter of Danville, served as best man. After a short wedding trip, the couple are living at 702B Warrendale Ct., Georgetown College, where they plan to resume their studies.

FLIGHT TIME FOR OLYMPIANS - Three members of the U.S. Olympic basketball team examine a model of a jet plane before boarding a larger version at Chicago's O'Hare Field. From left are Kenny Davis of Georgetown (Ky.), Doug Collins of Illinois State and Bob Jones of North Carolina. The Olympic squad flies from San Francisco to Hawaii later this week for three weeks of intensive practice in preparation for the Munich Games.

CHARTER TICKET AND BAGGAGE CHECK
Issued By
Pan American World Airways, Inc.

No: 026 - CH **0156416**

Subject to the Conditions of Contract appearing on page 2 and in conjunction with

Ticket Number 026 430 013 70 10 Issued to U. S. OLYMPIC COMMITTEE
Name of Charterer

The holder hereof and his baggage will be carried:

From:	To:	Charter No:	Date
Washington	Munich	C 950	8/19/72
Munich	Washington	C 950	9/09/72

Date and Place of Issue
NYC
09 August 1972
PAA
Agent

9253-1558G Not Refundable and Not Transferable

Pictured is Kenny Davis of Georgetown College who recently competed at the Olympic Development Camp held at the Air Force Academy in Colorado. The 44 athletes who participated in the camp were trained in International Rules under the direction of Mr. Henry Iba, head coach of the Olympics. Davis was the leading scorer at the camp with an average of 23 PPG for the six exhibition games that were played. He is presently on tour with an all-star team which is touring Europe.

OLYMPIC TEAM USA
1972 U.S. Olympic Team Ring
Champions Select Josten's
The World's Finest Custom Jewelry
by
Josten's

Sears is proud to be a part of the American Team
Providing easy-care fashions that keep pace with active athletes is an honor we've had twice before. The previous occasions were the 1971 Pan American Games in Cali, Colombia and the 1972 Winter Olympic Games in Sapporo, Japan.
The complete wardrobe is an all-out effort involving numerous people—from Sears personnel to members of the United States Olympics Apparel Committee, who made modifications and final design decisions. Completely contemporary in styling, this wardrobe was specifically designed to complement the trim, athletic build. Total worktime and manpower is inestimable: everyone involved worked hard and long to provide you with the finest in practical yet fashionable outfits.
As wardrobe supplier, Sears will provide uniforms for more than 600 men and women. Coordination of these wardrobes was no small task, considering that weights alone varied from 95 pounds to 400 pounds — and shoe sizes from 5½E to 16D.
Your efforts will be telecast to 50 million U.S. homes
From August 26th to September 10th the eyes of the world will focus on the drama of competition unfolding at the Summer Games. ABC-TV will beam tape and live color coverage to the States via satellite to an estimated 50 million American homes . . . that's over 125 million people!
Sears would like to congratulate you on being selected to represent the United States at the 1972 Summer Olympics. We would like to take this opportunity to wish you the best of luck in Munich.
SEARS, ROEBUCK AND CO.

The Longines Olympic watch
To members of the 1972 U.S. Olympic Teams:
We congratulate you on being United States Representatives in the 1972 Olympics. Your performances were outstanding and the honor is one which will remain with you for a lifetime.
As a compelling reminder of your unforgettable achievements, the United States Olympic Committee is making available a fine Longines Man's and Lady's watch. The dial of these watches will bear the easy-to-read, easy-to-see legend, "U.S. OLYMPIC TEAM, 1972."
These Longines watches are practical and particularly useful mementos of your Olympic participation, an hourly reminder and identification of your role in the world's greatest sports event.
The watches are handsomely styled with convenient calendar dials - Man's watch with automatic movement. Worthy timepieces commemorating your participation in the Olympics.

You go on parade at the 1972 Summe
Parade Dress Outfits Shown at left are the outfits you'll be wearing during the opening and closing ceremonies of the 1972 Summer Olympics. They will be pre-shipped to Munich and distributed to you upon arrival.
Women's Outfit: Red knit blazer. White pleated skirt. Long sleeve navy and white polka dot blouse. Navy shoulder bag. White crinkle patent leather moccasins and panty hose. Alternate item: White leather belt.
Men's Outfit: White knit blazer. Short sleeve navy shirt. Red, white and navy tie (half Windsor knot). Red, white and navy leather belt. Red flare-leg knit slacks. White crinkle patent leather demi-boots and white dress socks.

THE WHITE HOUSE

WASHINGTON

TO THE MEMBERS OF THE UNITED STATES OLYMPIC TEAM

The first of the milers to break the four minute barrier, Roger Bannister, has written, "There is a need to feel our bodies have a skill and energy of their own, apart from the man-made machines they may drive. There is the desire to find in sport a companionship with kindred people. I have found all these."

The time is near when each of you – the finest athletes of this good land – will match these skills and energies against competitors from across the world. You have emerged from the fires of countless testings as champions in your own right. You have persevered and endured, striving not only to win but to excel. Like Bannister, you have driven yourselves unsparingly and all Americans join as one in saluting you.

We are deeply proud of our Olympic Team, not simply because you will carry our colors with honor, but also because you have had the courage to be yourselves. You have proven the surpassing value of individual effort and determination. Now, once again, you will be tested as individuals, called upon to give that extra measure which sets Olympians apart from all others.

Your countrymen look forward to honoring you for the victories you will doubtless earn. But, as we know, the ultimate goal of the Olympic Games is not victory. It is, rather, the element of participation in one of this earth's worthy endeavors to bring its inhabitants together – "the companionship of kindred people" in a mutual pursuit of excellence. Centuries ago, a wise Roman remarked that "in great attempts, it is glorious even to fail." The XXth Olympiad is one of those attempts, and whatever the measure of your success during the Games, you will have brought honor to your country and to yourself.

You are America, and her traditions, aspirations, and indomitable spirit go with you on your journey. Good luck and Godspeed.

Olympic practice in Hawaii prior to Jim Forbes joining the team. Note John Brown (second from right) is still on the team in this photo.

World is 'gaining'

#84

'We can't continue'—Iba

By EARL COX

Courier-Journal and Times Executive Sports Editor

MUNICH — The United States has never lost a game since basketball was introduced as an Olympic sport 36 years ago in Berlin.

The current American team tripled the score on Japan 99-33 yesterday to finish its preliminary round with a perfect 7-0 record. Only two more victories and the U.S. will be Olympic champion for the eighth time.

But Hank Iba, the veteran coach of the U.S. team, warned yesterday that the rest of the world is catching up and "we must do something different. We can't continue—it's over after this year."

Americans have contributed greatly to teaching other countries the fundamentals of basketball, Iba said, pointing out that, among many other coaches, UK's Adolph Rupp has made several trips abroad to conduct clinics. Another U.S. coach, Memphis State's Gene Bartow, is coaching the Puerto Rican team in the current Olympics.

"And what I can't understand is the many Americans who have given up their citizenship so they can play for foreign teams," Iba said. Two members of Spain's team are former U.S. citizens—Cliff Luyk, who played at Florida, and Wayne Brabender, who played at Minnesota-Morris. It isn't uncommon for just average U.S. players to be paid between $20,000 and $30,000 to come to Europe to play "amateur" ball.

"Americans need to go back to fundamentals," said Iba. "Look at our team. Sometimes we play what I call county fair or playground basketball. Then look at Russia. They do things the way they're supposed to be done."

The U.S. will play Italy, Yugoslavia or Puerto Rico in a semi-final game Wednesday. Russia, which finished preliminary play with a 7-0 record also, will meet Cuba or Brazil in the other semi-final game Wednesday. The two winners will play for the championship Friday.

Iba was asked if he thought his team would be as good as it is.

"I hoped so," he said. "I thought we had a chance. The one thing we lack is leadership and we lack that because of youth. That's why we spread the captaincy around. In 1968 we had Mike Silliman to provide the leadership. He was a captain in the Army, had been to Korea and was intelligent," said Iba of the former St. Xavier star.

Should the NCAA championship team be picked to provide the nucleus of the U.S. Olympic team?

"That won't win it," said Iba quickly. Then he hedged a bit about last season's UCLA team, but he added, "It just won't win the Olympics year-in and year-out."

UNITED STATES 99				JAPAN 33			
Player	FG	FT	TP	Player	FG	FT	TP
D. Jones	6	2-4	14	Toriguchi	0	0-0	0
Forbes	0	0-2	0	Sugita	0	0-0	0
Brewer	3	4-4	10	Yokoyama	1	2-2	4
Joyce	2	0-0	4	Abe	1	3-4	5
Henderson	4	2-2	10	Hattori	4	0-0	8
Davis	1	0-0	2	Yoshikawa	2	0-0	4
Collins	3	4-4	10	Chicusa	0	0-0	0
Bantom	9	0-2	18	Mori	4	1-4	9
R. Jones	5	0-0	10	Somatomo	0	0-0	0
Burleson	2	1-2	5	Numata	0	3-4	3
McMillen	5	4-4	14				
Ratleff	1	0-0	2				
Totals	41	17-24	99	Totals	12	9-14	33

Halftime: U.S. 51-18.

U.S. played best against Japan, says Davis

Editor's note: Kentuckian Kenny Davis, a member of the U.S. Olympic basketball team, talked with Earl Cox, executive sports editor of The Courier-Journal and Times, in Munich yesterday. Here's what Davis said:

Just think, here we are the unbeaten champions of our group in the Olympic games basketball tournament and the people back home in Kentucky aren't even up yet. As you know, our game started at 4 a.m. Sunday. That's Louisville and Georgetown time, but even 9 a.m. German time is pretty early to be playing basketball.

We played probably our best game against Japan, but . . . well, they're not much better than Egypt. We beat Japan 99-33 and Egypt 96-31. Overall it was probably our best game. Our defense was much better; it had to be because Japan was so quick.

Dwight Jones, our center, really came back with a good game. He got 14 points and nine rebounds. To tell you the truth, Dwight sulks a little. But he looked okay against Japan and he'll be the key for us from now on.

We have the work behind us now and just two more games to go.

Somebody asked me if it hurt us because we really don't have what can be considered a first team. I don't think so because you can't play just five people in international ball. As a rule you have to have eight good players and we have them. That's why Coach Iba plays so many different people. I'll admit it doesn't help team unity.

I played 8 minutes and 54 seconds against Japan and scored two points. I missed five other easy shots because I'm so tight. I just need a chance to play a little more.

Associated Press

Bantom bounce

MICHAEL BANTOM (7) of the U.S. tips in a basket against Japan in the Olympic game yesterday in Munich. The Yanks won 99-33 in the first round final.

Sports on the air

Television

8 p.m.—Yankees-Orioles, NBC, Channel 3.

8 p.m.—Olympics (track and field, boxing, diving, swimming) ABC, Channel 32.

Radio

11:30 a.m.—Southern 500 auto race at Darlington, S.C., WTMT (620).

7:45 p.m.—Reds-Dodgers, WLW (700), WHAS (840).

7:50 p.m.—Colonels-Toledo, WKLO-FM (99.7).

8:15 p.m.—Braves-Astros, WSM (650).

11:10 p.m.—Louisville Downs race, WHAS (840).

Rita – Thought you'd like this. Flem 6:22pm Monday

Olympic Basketball Team coverage, *The Courier-Journal*, September 4, 1972.

U.S. Team marching into Olympic Stadium.

Kenny in his room at Olympic Village in Munich, looking at his new Kodak camera given to every Olympic athlete.

Russ cage gold upheld; silver refused by U.S.

Today's Olympic Edition

- Yanks sweep archery gold P. 28
- U.S. swimmer awarded bronze P. 26
- Olympic Medal standings P. 27
- U.S.A. great, long jump champ says P. 25

By JACK ELLIS, Sports Editor

MUNICH (S&S) — Well it's final now. What just about everybody figured would happen did. An appeals jury did not uphold the American protest of the Russian victory in the basketball finale late Saturday night, and the score stands, Russia 51, U.S. 50.

The upset was the first defeat ever for the Americans in Olympic history and broke skein of 63 straight triumphs.

The American representativ[e] at the Sunday press conferenc[e] M.K. Summers, U.S. Olymp[ic] basketball chairman, a[n]nounced after the ruling th[at] the United States, althoug[h] complimenting the Russians o[n] their victory, could not accep[t]

(Cont. on Page 27, Col. 1)

The STARS and STRIPES
AUTHORIZED UNOFFICIAL PUBLICATION FOR THE U.S. ARMED FORCES
Vol. 31, No. 146 10¢ Daily and Sunday
Monday, September 11, 1972 C 1F 21855 A

Monday, September 11, 1972 THE STARS AND STRIPES C Page 27

Silver, no

U.S. cagers refuse medal after jury upholds Russ win

(Continued from Page 1)

the decision. Later, the American team refused to accept the silver medal of to appear at the victory ceremony scheduled in the main stadium. The latter was rained out anyway.

In a sometimes stormy press conference, it was plainly established that the officials were in error in giving the Russians three "overtime" seconds.

The official scorer, Hans Penchert, who appeared at the meeting, stated that no scorer or timer said there were three seconds left, that there was legally only one second left to play and that the game was officially ended with the U.S. leading 50-49.

The president of the appeals jury, Hungarian Ferenc Hepp, admitted that the referee signaled three seconds left after conferring at the table, even though the FIBA (International Amateur Federation of Basketball) delegate, Edmond Bigot, signaled one second left. But Bigot did not attempt to correct the referee, Rento Reghetto.

Bigot was the only official at the table who had the authority, but he did nothing to halt play and confer with the referee over the discrepancy in the time.

There also was some confusion in just what Reghetto did signal. Reghetto, a Brazilian, told the press earlier that he signaled one, not three seconds. Hepp said Reghetto told the jury that he did signal three seconds.

But the question arises why Bigot didn't correct the erroneous time set by the referee. No answer was forthcoming on this question except that the referee has the authority to adjust the time if he thinks it is in error. The clock, however, was actually set for three seconds — time enough for the Russians to sink the winning goal.

The official explanation given the press was that the referee and FIBA delegate ordered the three seconds, but conflicting statements cast a great deal of doubt on whether either one gave the three-second ruling. Reference was made to the FIBA secretary general, Dr. William Robert Jones, of England, who was seen by the press at the scorer's table. Holding up three fingers as if to signal three seconds.

The appeals jury, consisting, besides Hepp, of delegates from Puerto Rico, Cuba and Poland, thus took it upon themselves — after numerous conferences and a 14-hour delay — to believe what they said the referee told them and uphold the score of 51-50 for the Russians, even though it was admitted the officials were in error in alloting the extra time.

Thus ended the proud reign of the U.S. in Olympic basketball. It had won seven straight gold medals, starting at Berlin in 1936, and had never lost a game in Olympic competition.

Russia's winning basket was scored on a two-handed layup shot by Aleksander Belov on a floor-length pass from Ivan Edeshko. The play followed two free throws by Doug Collins, which had put the U.S. ahead, 50-49, for the first time in the game.

Belov eluded Kevin Joyce and Jim Forbes to take the pass with a leaping catch. He came down, then jumped agair to bank in the ball.

Decisive play

The decisive play came after the game had ended, claimed the furious American head coach, Hank Iba.

"I cannot fathom anything so incomprehensible," he said after the game.

The dispute raged over Russia being given two inbound plays in what was supposed to be the final three seconds.

Toss in a questionable Russian timeout and a floor mob scene with one second left and you've really got the makings of a controversy.

In any case, Iba said, there wasn't enough time left in the game for all the action that transpired, leaving the Russians on top.

The coach also said that it was a "mighty funny call" on Belov's bucket. He said that Joyce and Forbes were knocked down by Belov — "they certainly didn't trip themselves."

Iba was asked why he let his players return to the floor to resume play on what he considered an extra chance for the Russians and the coach replied, "The official told me there was what the circumstances. We had them puzzled from the start since we used a different lineup to confuse them at the beginning."

Russia led at halftime, 26-21.

Until Collins's clutch free throws it looked as if the Russians were going to snap Uncle Sam's string without the aid of a clock. They jumped off to a quick 4-0 lead and upped it to 10 points halfway through the period as they outrebounded, outshot and outdefensed the Americans.

But Collins, Tommy Henderson and Tom McMillan hit for goals late in the period to bring the Yanks back to within five points, 26-21, at the half.

The second half was almost a repeat of the first. The Russians opened a 10-point gap with less than 10 minutes remaining and the Yanks seemed out of it.

But Ed Ratleff, Jim Brewer and Mike Bantom brought it back to 44-38 and the big American cheering section came alive.

Then Joyce got it really hopping when he connected for two quick fielders and it was 44-42 with four minutes left.

The Russians got three quick foul shots before Joyce hit another fielder and Collins netted two free throws to move within one point.

The Russians got it back to

Box score

UNITED STATES	G	F	T	RUSSIA	G	F	T
Brewer	3	3-4	9	ABelov	3	2-4	8
Hendrsn	4	1-2	9	Sankoze	2	4-8	8
RJones	0	0-0	0	Korkia	1	2-2	4
DJones	2	2-4	6	Sharmdov	1	2-4	4
Ratleff	3	0-0	6	SBelov	8	4-6	20
Bantom	1	0-2	2	Edeshko	0	0-0	0
Burleson	0	0-0	0	Paulkas	0	3-4	3
Collins	1	6-6	8	Volnov	0	0-0	0
Davis	0	0-0	0	Polivoda	0	0-0	0
Forbes	1	0-0	2	Dvorni	0	0-0	0
Joyce	3	0-0	6	Kovalnke	0	0-0	0
McMilln	1	0-0	2	Boloshev	2	0-0	4
Totals	19	12-16	50	Totals	17	17-28	51

United States .... 21 29—50
Russia .... 26 25—51

Fouled out—United States, Bantom; Russia, None.

Total fouls—United States 26, Russia 25.

FEDERATION INTERNATIONALE DE BASKETBALL AMATEUR
INTERNATIONAL AMATEUR BASKETBALL FEDERATION
F. I. B. A.

19, Rugendas Strasse
München-Solln
Allemagne

1972 C- 1578

LICENCE DE JOUEUR INTERNATIONAL:
Nom Kenneth DAVIS
Pays ETATS - UNIS
Jones
Secrétaire général

Kenny's official F.I.B.A. ID card, 1972.

Front Row: M. K. Summers, Coach John Bach, Coach Henry Iba, Don Haskins, Whitey Gwynne, Herb Mols 2nd Row: John Mclendon, Kenny Davis, Kevin Joyce, Tom Henderson, Doug Collins, Ed Ratleff. Back Row: Bobby Jones, Jim Brewer, Tom McMillen, Tom Burleson, Dwight Jones, Mike Bantom, Jim Forbes.

USA versus Japan, Kenny Davis #4 and Doug Collins #5.

Kenny sitting outside his Olympic Village room in Munich, not long after the terrorist attack.

Steve Prefontaine of the Olympic track team talks with Kenny at Olympic Village.

1972 Olympic patch

U.S. Olympic Basketball team member, Kenny Davis of Monticello, Ky., is fitted with official uniform by Sears, Roebuck and Co. tailor. Hundreds of athletes and officials are in Washington, D.C. for processing prior to departure for the Olympic Games to be held in Munich August 26 to September 10.

Kenny and his father.

WASHINGTON

September 12, 1972

Dear Mr. Davis:

I know how disappointed you must be after the final game last Saturday, but you may be certain your fellow citizens still think of you as champions. You played with outstanding skill, and on behalf of all Americans, I want to congratulate you for a splendid come-from-behind performance.

With my best wishes,

Sincerely,

Richard Nixon

Mr. Kenneth Davis
702-B Warrendale Court
Georgetown, Kentucky 40324

Yank jubilation comes too soon

U.S. basketball players Mike Bantom (back to camera) and Tom McMillan celebrate a U.S. basketball "victory" Saturday but were interrupted by a ruling on the hectic finish of the Olympic championship game Saturday night. The U.S. appeared to win, 50-49, in the closing seconds but a timing snafu was revealed and the Russians given time for one last play. It worked and the Soviets won, 51-50, to take the gold medal, although the verdict wasn't official until Sunday afternoon after a lengthy protest hearing at which the videotapes were rerun It was the first time in Olympic history that the U.S. didn't win the gold medal. —S&S, Grandy

Clock, smock . . .

Veteran United States basketball coach H filing an official protest over a timing gold medal clash between the U.S. and

Shorter w marathon

From press dispatch

MUNICH — American thinclads won two of nine gold medals up for grabs in the final day of track and field competition at he 20th Olympic Games here Sunday in what must go down as the most frustrating 11 days in U.S. track history.

Frank Shorter became the first American since 1908 to win the grueling marathon when he ran the 26-mile race in 2 hours, 12 minutes, 19.7 seconds, the fastest-ever Olympic time. Ken

Moore fourth.

And meter Larry Gerald Eddie record- gold m

The good f mond, the wo an eve

(Co

WINTER '72

the basketball bulletin

THE NATIONAL ASSOCIATION OF BASKETBALL COACHES OF THE UNITED STATES

William Edward "Ed" Ratleff

Shooting guard / Small forward
6' 6" | 195 pounds

Hometown: Bellefontaine, Ohio

College: California State University, Long Beach

College Achievements: Two-time All-American, two-time Big West Conference Player of the Year, inducted into CSULB Hall of Fame

Olympic Stat Line: Nine games, averaged 6.4 points and 3.1 rebounds per game

Professional Experience: Sixth overall pick in the 1973 Draft to the Houston Rockets, where he remained until 1978

Professional Stats: 2,813 points, 1,363 rebounds and 896 assists

Life After Basketball: Coached college basketball at Long Beach State for six years; now lives in Long Beach, and has worked as a State Farm agent since 1986

Family: Two children, Paige and Dillon, also reside in Long Beach, California

Kevin Joyce

Guard
6' 3" | 190 pounds

Hometown: Bayside, N.Y.

College: University of South Carolina

College Achievements: Scored over 1,400 points in three years, and averaged 20.4 points per game his senior year; 42-inch vertical jump; helped take USC to the 1971 ACC Tournament title game, where 6' 3" Joyce famously out-jumped UNC's 6'10" Lee Dedmon with four seconds remaining, helping to secure a win for the Gamecocks

Olympic Stat Line: Nine games, averaged 5.3 points and 1.2 rebounds per game

Professional Experience: Selected eleventh overall pick in the 1973 NBA Draft by the Golden State Warriors, but chose the American Basketball Association instead; played professionally for the Indiana Pacers, San Diego Sails and Kentucky Colonels.

Life After Basketball: Currently an equity salesman with NavPoint LLC in New York

Family: Joyce and his wife, Ginna, reside in Long Beach, N.Y., with their three children – twins Mary and Kevin, and daughter Sally

Charles Thomas "Tom" McMillen

Power forward / Center
6' 11" | 215 pounds

Hometown: Elmira, N.Y.

College: University of Maryland

College Achievements: 1973 Consensus NCAA All-American Second Team, Rhodes Scholar

Olympic Stat Line: Nine games, averaged 6.8 points and 4.3 rebounds per game

Professional Experience: Ninth overall pick of 1974 NBA Draft to the Buffalo Braves, and also played for the New York Knicks, Atlanta Hawks and Washington Bullets

Life After Basketball: Retired in 1986 in pursuit of politics; elected to the U.S. Congress from 1987-1993 as a Democrat to represent Maryland's 4th district; was a Presidential appointee from 1993-1997; currently serves as Chairman and CEO of an investment firm and Chairman of the National Foundation on Fitness, Sports and Nutrition

Family: McMillen and his wife, Judy, currently reside in Maryland

Interesting Facts: Known to be the tallest U.S. Congressman in history

James Turner "Jim" Brewer

Power forward
6' 9" | 210 pounds

Hometown: Maywood, Ill.

College: University of Minnesota

Olympic Stat Line: Nine games, averaged 7.6 points and 7.1 rebounds per game

Professional Experience: Selected first round, second pick, of the 1973 NBA Draft by the Cleveland Cavaliers; continued for the Detroit Pistons, the Portland Trail Blazers and the Los Angeles Lakers; played in Italy for three years before retiring from basketball in 1985

Life After Basketball: Brewer was an assistant coach in the NBA for 17 years with the Minnesota Timberwolves, Los Angeles Clippers, Toronto Raptors and Boston Celtics. He was also director of player personnel during his time with the Timberwolves. Brewer now serves on the Drug Education Foundation "Truth About Drugs" board of directors, which educates youth on the effects of drugs through seminars.

Family: Brewer and wife, Patsy, have two children, Pherah and Jimmy, currently residing in Los Angeles, Calif.

Interesting Facts: While playing for the Cleveland Cavaliers, his fans would cheer "Two for the Brew!" when he scored during home games

Tommy Burleson

Center
7′ 2″ | 225 pounds

Hometown: Crossnore, N.C.

College: North Carolina State University

College Achievements: 1974 NCAA Champion, three-time All-ACC (1972-1974), two-time All-American (1973-1974), two-time Everett Case Award (1973-1974), ACC Tournament MVP, 1974 Eastern Regional co-MVP, NCAA All Final Four Team 1974, College of Agriculture LS/BS, Gamma Sigma Delta Honor's Society, John Speaks Award

College Stats: Averaged 20 points and 12 rebounds per game

Olympic Stat Line: Seven games, averaged 3.9 points and 2.1 rebounds per game

Professional Experience: Seven-year NBA career began when he was selected as the third overall pick of the 1974 NBA Draft by the Seattle SuperSonics; also played for the Kansas City Kings and the Atlanta Hawks; earned NBA All-Rookie First Team in 1975 and ACC 50th Anniversary men's basketball team in 2002, which honors the fifty greatest players in Atlantic Coast Conference history

Life After Basketball: Burleson has won the North Carolina 4-H Lifetime Achievement Award, and was inducted into the NC Sports Hall of Fame in 1996. He's run the Tommy Burleson Basketball Camp for 27 years, and currently works as the director of planning and inspections for Avery County, N.C. Burleson is very active in community service, and his volunteer projects includes workshops with special needs individuals, working with a battered women's shelter and promoting cancer research. Tommy Burleson Ministries supports a hospital, school and orphanage in Malawi, Africa.

Family: Burleson and his wife, Denise, have three sons, Robert, 29, David, 27, and Quentin, 22.

12

James Ricardo "Jim" Forbes

Forward
6′ 8″ | 201 pounds

Hometown: El Paso, Texas

College: University of Texas at El Paso

College Achievements: 1971 Pan American team

Olympic Stat Line: Nine games, averaged 5.1 points and 3.1 rebounds per game

Life After Basketball: Returned to UTEP as an assistant coach, then left this position 28 years ago to use his knowledge and experience obtained as both a player and a coach at UTEP to develop and coach successful high school programs in Texas

Dwight Jones

Power forward / Center
6′ 10″ | 210 pounds

Hometown: Houston, Texas

College: University of Houston

Olympic Stat Line: Nine games, averaged 9.2 points and 5.7 rebounds per game

Professional Experience: Ninth overall pick of the 1973 NBA Draft to the Atlanta Hawks; 10–year NBA career playing for the Houston Rockets, Chicago Bulls and Los Angeles Lakers; played for Bic Trieste in Italy for one year after the NBA

Professional Achievements: Made 6,230 points, 4,513 rebounds and 911 assists during NBA career

Life After Basketball: basketball camps for underprivileged kids and working in the car business since 1987 in different positions from salesman to general sales manager

Family: Married to Felicia Jones with six kids; Keesha, Meika, Dwight II, Dawhn, Krystal, and Emanuel, and four grandkids; Jackie, Corey, Kera, and Dwight III

Doug Collins

Shooting guard / small forward
6′ 6″ | 180 pounds

Hometown: Christopher, Ill.

College: Illinois State University

Olympic Stat Line: Nine games, averaged 7.3 points and 2.3 rebounds per game

Professional Experience: Selected first overall pick of the 1973 NBA Draft by the Philadelphia 76ers, where he stayed until 1981 when an injury forced him to forgo his athletic career

Professional Achievements: NBA All-Star team for four consecutive years; career totals of 7,427 points, grabbed 1,339 rebounds and passed 1,368 assists

Coaching: Since 1986, he's coached the Chicago Bulls, the Detroit Pistons and the Washington Wizards. Collins has been coaching the 76ers since 2010, having the unique honor of running one of the teams he played for; coached Michael Jordan, Scottie Pippen, Horace Grant, Theo Ratliff, Allan Houston, Richard Hamilton and many other notable athletes

Coaching Achievements: NBA Coach of the Year

Family: Doug and his wife Kathy, currently reside in Delaware Valley. They have two children, Chris and Kelly, who share their father's passion for basketball

Robert Clyde "Bobby" Jones

Small forward
6' 9" | 210 pounds

Hometown: Charlotte, N.C.

College: University of North Carolina

College Achievements: 1974 NCAA All-America Second Team; bachelor's degree in psychology

Olympic Stat Line: Eight games, averaged 4.6 points and 3.1 rebounds per game

Professional Experience: Twelve-year professional career began with fifth overall pick in the 1974 NBA Draft by the Houston Rockets; also played for the Denver Nuggets and the Philadelphia 76ers

Professional Achievements: Four-time NBA All-Star, eight-time NBA All-Defensive First Team, 1983 NBA Champion, 1976 ABA All-Star, 1983 NBA Sixth Man of the Year, 1985 NBA All-Defensive Second Team, 1976 All-ABA Second Team and two-time ABA All-Defensive First Team, 1975 ABA All-Rookie First Team

Life After Basketball: moved back to Charlotte, where he cofounded a religiously affiliated nonprofit that supports underprivileged children through sports, and coaches a Christian middle school's boys basketball team

Family: Married to Tess West Jones for 38 years, has three children; Eric, Matt and Meredith, and three grandchildren; Elliott, Isabelle and Benjamin

Mike Bantom

Power forward / Center
6' 9" | 200 pounds

Hometown: Philadelphia, Pa.

College: Saint Joseph's University

Olympic Stat Line: Nine games, averaged 7.7 points and 4.9 rebounds per game

Professional Experience: Selected by the Phoenix Suns with the eighth pick of the 1973 NBA Draft; played in the NBA for nine years for the Seattle SuperSonics, the New York Nets, the Indiana Pacers and the Philadelphia 76ers; played in Italy from 1982 to 1989 after leaving the NBA

NBA Stats: 8,568 points, 4,517 rebounds and 1,623 assists

Life After Basketball: Served as the Licensing Manager for NBA International and NBA International Director of Marketing, and currently holds the position of NBA Senior Vice President of Player Development

Family: Four children; Robbie, Misha, Brenda and Alan

Edward Thomas "Tom" Henderson

Shooting guard
6' 3" | 190 lbs

Hometown: Newberry, S.C.

College: San Jacinto Junior College, then transferred to the University of Hawaii

College Achievements: Averaged more than 30 points per game at SJJC; first team All-American in 1974

Olympic Stat Line: Nine games, averaged 9.2 points and 2.0 rebounds per game

Professional Experience: Picked seventh overall in the NBA Draft by the Atlanta Hawks; 9-year NBA career with the Washington Bullets and the Houston Rockets

Professional Achievements: 1978 NBA Champion; 6,008 points and 3,136 assists

Life After Basketball: Administrator at a Houston-area juvenile facility

Kenneth "Kenny" Davis

Shooting guard
6' 1" | 165 pounds

Hometown: Monticello, Ky.

College: Georgetown College

College Achievements: Three-time All-American and three-time AAU All-American; one of only two players in Kentucky basketball history to score more than 3,000 point; holds both single season and career records at Georgetown College; inducted into Georgetown College Hall of Fame; 1970 World University team; 1971 Pan American team; traveled to five continents and 26 countries

Olympic Stat Line: Six games, averaged 2.3 points and 0.7 rebounds per game

Life After Basketball: Sales executive at Converse since 1972, and works part-time as a motivational speaker; has a written provision in his will that neither his wife nor his children shall accept the silver medal after he passes away

Family: lives with wife Rita, in Paint Lick, Kentucky

History

"Each time that I feel sorry for myself that we don't have that gold medal, I think about those Israeli kids that they took out of there in caskets."

– Kenny Davis, captain, 1972 U.S. Olympic basketball team

years they've lived in a limbo of their own making, neither winners nor losers but men of respect just ne, and – mostly, objects of curiosity for having the courage of their convictions in a world that has increasingly ambivalent since that August day in 1972 when they said "no, never," to the silver medal nat is still the most controversial basketball game ever.

coaches and players from both America and the now-defunct Soviet Union, that game pretty much the rest of their lives. Everywhere they've gone, from that day to this, people want to talk about it, ask t, give their opinion about it. It was undoubtedly the biggest story of the Olympic Games in Munich of course, for the horror in which masked criminals with assault weapons kidnapped 11 Israelis and ced the civilized world to terrorism.

lnapping occurred he U.S. basketball team rching inexorably to a edal showdown with iet Union. The players naware of it until rumors running through the ic village where all the ate, slept, and socialized. e rest of the world, they d around TV sets to mesmerized as the tragedy ed. By the time of the edal game, the hostages ead, murdered in cold and the Olympic world never be quite the same.

into the gold-medal game, everybody knew that, for the first time since basketball became an Olympic 1948, the U.S. was vulnerable. In those days, the team consisted of college players and one representative om the armed forces, the junior-college tanks, and the AAU. But in 1972, some of the best college players, otably Bill Walton of UCLA, declined to try out for personal reasons, an ominous turn of events for the a time when the rest of the world was beginning to close the talent gap in basketball.

History

Still, the U.S. took a 63-0 Olympic record into the gold-medal game in Munich. It was unthinkable that the Americans could get beaten in the game they invented. And with gifted players such as Doug Collins of Illinois State, Tom McMillen of Maryland, Tom Burleson of N.C. State, Bobby Jones of North Carolina, and Ed Ratleff of Long Beach State, it wasn't as if the U.S. team was bereft of talent. Olympic Coach Henry Iba of Oklahoma State had every reason to be confident that his final game would end with a victory.

This was to be the final game of a storied coaching career in which Iba won back-to-back NCAA titles at Oklahoma A&M (now Oklahoma State) with 7-footer Bob "Foothills" Kurland in 1945-'46. But while basketball had changed in the 1960s, moving to an up-tempo style that produced prodigious scorers like Pete Maravich of LSU, Dan Issel of Kentucky, and Austin Carr of Notre Dame, Iba remained true to his trademark slowdown motion offense.

That was just fine with the rest of the world, which then played the more plodding style that might be expected of teams just learning the game. Heading into the gold-medal game, the Americans were convinced, almost to a man, that they could run the Soviets out of the arena if Iba would turn them loose.

Instead, the old coach gave them one more burden to carry: He suspended the 7-4 Burleson, the team's tallest player and one of its best defenders, for having allowed his fiancée to visit his room in the Olympic Village. Despite Burleson's impassioned pleas to play against the Soviets, Iba stuck to his Oklahoma State six-shooters.

With the U.S. trailing 49-48 and three seconds remaining, Collins, now the coach of the Philadelphia 76ers, was driving to the basket when he was fouled hard by Zurab Sakandelidze and knocked into the basket stanchion. A 6-foot-6 shooting guard from Illinois State, Collins was just the player Iba wanted shooting with the game on the line. When there was some question whether Collins was too woozy to shoot, Iba said he would not lobby for a substitute shooter as long as Collins could stand up and see.

Although his vision was blurred, Collins sank his first shot to tie the game. But just as Collins lifted the ball to begin his second free throw, the horn from the scorer's table sounded, beginning an incredible chain of events that confused and outraged fair-minded basketball fans around the globe.

After Collins made his second free throw, (with the ball then being "live" under the rules at the time), the Soviets inbounded the ball and began dribbling upcourt. But a referee stopped play with one second remaining and the Soviets still in backcourt because Soviet assistant coach Sergein Bashkin had charged out of the team's designated bench area to protest that head coach Vladimir Kondrashin had called a timeout prior to Collins' second free throw – even though it was illegal to call a timeout when the official had placed the ball in the shooter's hand, just as it was illegal for a coach to come on the floor during play.

History

The jury included three members from Soviet-bloc nations, so it wasn't surprising that the U.S. appeal was denied. In announcing the decision, jury foreman Ferenc Hepp of Hungary acknowledged only that the vote was not unanimous. The U.S. players did not accept the verdict, declined to accept their silver medals, and did not participate in the presentation ceremony.

Before leaving Munich, the U.S. players made a pact that nobody would ever accept his silver medal unless they all did. To this day, the medals are supposedly locked away in an International Olympic Committee vault in Switzerland. Davis even had it written into his will that after his death, none of his descendants would ever be able to accept the silver medal.

So by their own choice, the players don't have any tokens to show for their experience in Munich. All they have is the frustration of knowing they were never truly defeated on the court. Over the last 40 years, the players often have been sought out for interviews, including once in 1992 when Sports Illustrated did a long story to observe the 20th anniversary. Some were called for quotes when the Soviet Belov died and was buried with his gold medal around his neck.

None have allowed their lives to be defined soley by not having the gold. A few – Collins and Jones, most notably – went on to standout careers in the NBA. McMillen gave up basketball for politics, and was elected to several terms in the U.S. House of Representatives from his district in Maryland. Mike Bantom became one of NBA commissioner David Stern's top aides. The others went into careers in business, education, and other non-basketball fields.

Since leaving Munich 40 years ago, the team has never had an official reunion. But tonight – Aug. 25, 2012 – that long-overdue event is finally happening. The reunion is being held in Lexington and Georgetown because team captain Davis lives in nearby Paint Lick and graduated from Georgetown College. The reunion will be conducted under the auspices of Courage in Munich, which received seed money from the Converse Shoe Company, maker of the iconic Chuck Taylor All-Star sneakers and Davis' employer since the Munich Olympics.

Even now, the 1972 gold-medal game and the U.S. team's decision to not accept the silver medal remains a topic of debate not only by basketball historians, but by others who are fascinated by the role sports played in international politics during those days. The Soviets and their allies saw victory in sports as a validation of their way of life. It was particularly important, from a propaganda standpoint, that they defeat the U.S. in basketball, the sport Americans had invented and dominated. A well-researched series in the Bloomberg Report supported the Americans' suspicions, as did a recently-published book by Chicago attorney, David "Taps" Gallagher. Fittingly, the book's title is "Stolen Glory."

No banquet can restore the glory stolen from the American team that day 40 years ago in Munich. Yet it's not too late to thank the players publicly, for the first time, for having the courage of their convictions. By refusing the pieces of silver, by standing up for justice and fairness, the players demonstrated that victory without honor is hollow, indeed.

"The players are really excited about the reunion," Davis said. "It will be great to be together again for the first time in 40 years. We were cheated out of the ultimate thrill in sports – standing on the victory stand and accepting the gold medal while the national anthem is played. We can't get that back, but at least we have the satisfaction of knowing we did the right thing."

After several minutes in which it became clear that both the game officials and the German scorekeepers were either woefully inept or downright biased against the U.S., a man named William Jones, who then headed the Federation of International Basketball Association (FIBA), came out of the stands and ordered that the last three seconds be replayed. In so doing, he overruled the game officials, who ruled that one second remained. Although Jones later admitted that he had no authority over a game in progress, he also ordered that no technical fouls be levied against the Soviets.

Finally, the players took their places on the court for a second inbounds play. But the referees, failing to notice that the scorer's table still was working on resetting the clock to three seconds, gave the ball to Soviet inbounder Ivan Edeshko. With the clock inexplicably showing 50 seconds and the 6-foot-11 McMillen hounding him, Edeshko made a short inbounds pass to Modestas Paulauskas, who then threw a long pass as the horn sounded. The pass was tipped off the backboard and the Americans, thinking the game was over and they had won, rushed on the court to celebrate.

"The feeling was incredible," said team captain Kenny Davis, the all-time leading scorer in Georgetown College history who had made the team as an AAU player representing Marathon Oil. "We had won the gold medal! But then all that changed. We were totally confused."

At William Jones' insistence, the officials ordered the court to be cleared and again brought the players back into position for a third inbounds play. Iba briefly considered taking his team off the court but didn't because he was afraid the officials would forfeit the game to the Soviets. As he told his coaching staff, "I don't want to lose this game later tonight, sitting on my butt."

As McMillen again prepared to harass Edesko on the inbounds play, official Artenik Arabadjian gestured to McMillen to back several feet away from Edeshko. Although there was no rule requiring him to do so, McMillen did as he was told, giving Edeshko a clear and unobstructed opportunity to throw a full-court pass to Aleksandr Belov standing under the Soviet goal.

With the team's two best big defenders – Burleson and Bobby Jones sitting on the bench and watching helplessly, Belov and two U.S. players, Kevin Joyce and James Forbes, went up for the ball. As Belov caught the ball and came down, Joyce's momentum carried him out of bounds and Forbes fell down, allowing Belov to gather himself and put in the layup that gave the Soviet Union a 51-50 victory.

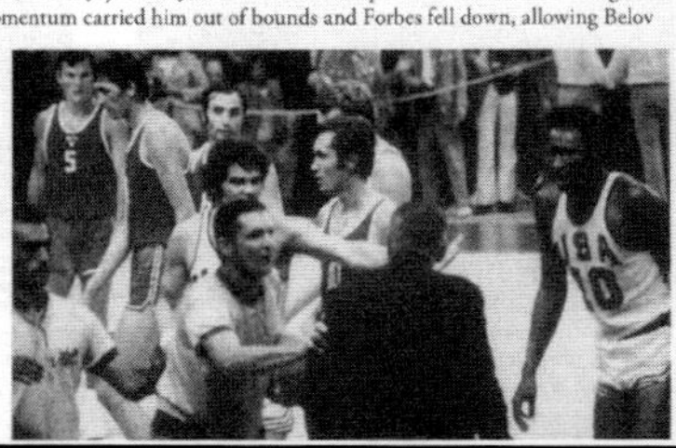

In the crazy aftermath, Iba had his pocket picked and lost his wallet with $600 in it. But that robbery was nothing to what had just happened on the floor. Referee Renato Righetto refused to sign the official scorebook and the U.S. team immediately fired a protest, which was heard on the spot by FIBA's five-man jury of appeal.

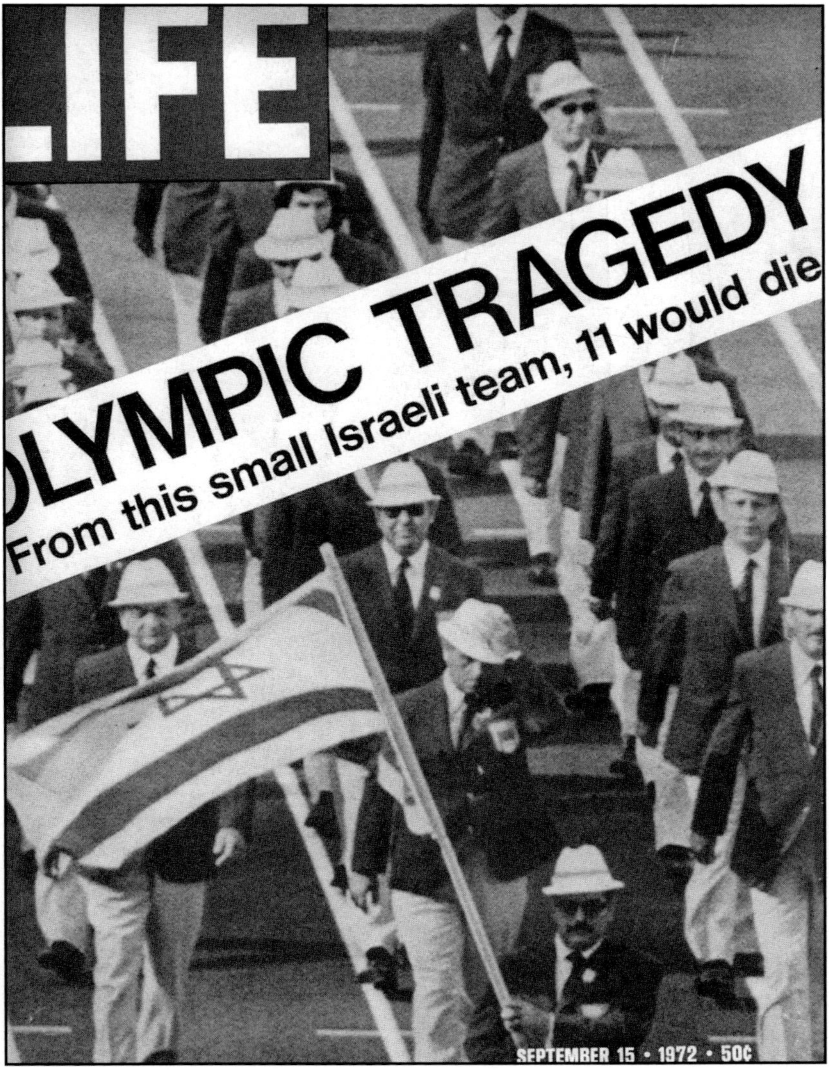

Sadly, the 1972 Olympic Games will be remembered for the act of terrorism which resulted in the killing of hostages from the Israeli team. A terrorist (right) discusses terms in the Olympic village with Herr Hans-Dietrich Genscher (centre), the West German Minister of the Interior, and other officials.

Building 31 at the Olympic Village in Munich. Note: the actual bullet holes may be seen from where law enforcement officials stormed the building.

OLYMPICS TRAGEDY: 20 YEARS LATER

Today's tight security is legacy

By Steve Woodward
USA TODAY

The apartment building at 31 Connollystrasse bears little resemblance to a place forever linked with the darkest hours in Olympic Games history.

There are no signs in Munich that lead visitors to the site, but those who find it are quickly taken back to Sept. 5, 1972 — the day terrorists would permanently alter the magnitude of the Games and strip the event of its supposed innocence.

Twenty years later, athletes have just returned from the Summer Olympics in Barcelona, where police and military personnel, bomb-sniffing dogs, armored tanks and machine guns were as much a part of the daily landscape as the flags of participating nations.

Every Olympic host city of the past two decades has been guided by the harsh lessons of Munich. Barcelona enlisted nearly 50,000 trained experts into its security force at a cost approaching $300 million.

Most of the measures taken by today's Olympic security planners are precautionary, driven by the memory of a Munich Olympic Village that was "guarded" by unarmed patrols uniformed in pastel blue. At the time, officials believed strongly that passive security would prove to the world that Germany had emerged as a new, progressive nation.

Eight terrorists had something else to prove, however.

For the families and friends of the 11 Israeli athletes who were killed after being taken hostage by the Arab intruders, there is no consolation in knowing that the sequence of events leading to the Munich tragedy almost certainly will never be duplicated.

In today's high-tech, high-security Olympic Villages, terrorists would be identified by electronic surveillance and likely apprehended, if not killed.

Even if a group managed to penetrate the security net and reach the vicinity of an apartment building, it would never get close enough to place a key in the door.

Just after 4 a.m. on the 11th day of the Munich Games, the sound of a key in the door at 31 Connollystrasse sent the Israeli athletes dashing for the rear exits of their apartments. Some were lucky enough to escape. Within 24 hours, two Israelis were killed on the premises and nine more would be murdered.

Harold Zimman, a member of the U.S. Olympic Committee's Board of Directors, attended the Munich Games and had dined with the president of the Israeli Olympic Committee only hours before the hostages were taken.

"It was sadness I felt more than anger," Zimman says now. "All you could think about were these young, innocent people, many only one generation (removed) from the Holocaust."

On Saturday, as they have for many years, a few residents might pause before the small gray monument in front of No. 31 and leave a flower. The monument lists the 11 names and is accompanied by an inscription: "Honor their memory".

Anduk Spitzer, a newborn infant in 1972 when her father Andre Spitzer was killed in Munich, was troubled by her visit.

"I wanted so much to knock on the door and ask, 'Do you know what happened here?' " Spitzer told NBC-TV for its Munich documentary last month. "The biggest thing of my life happened here and nobody knows."

How Munich terror unfolded

Twenty years ago Saturday, terrorists climbed a fence into an Olympic Village in Munich and shattered the peaceful world of international competition.

▶ **4:30 a.m.** — Five Arab terrorists climb a 6-foot, 6-inch fence surrounding the Olympic Village. They were not apprehended because they appeared to be athletes. They wore sweatsuits and carried weapons in athletic bags.

▶ **4:55 a.m.** — Terrorists knock on the door of Israeli wrestling coach Moshe Weinberg at 31 Connollystrasse. He opens the door, realizes the danger and yells to countrymen to escape. Some escape while Weinberg and weightlifter Joseph Romano are killed by Arab gunfire.

▶ **5:45 a.m.** — The Arabs gather nine Israeli hostages from the second and third floors.

▶ **9:30 a.m.** — Terrorists identify themselves as Palestinians and call for the release of 200 Arab prisoners in Israel.

▶ **Late afternoon** — Arabs agree to German plan to take terrorists and hostages to a NATO air base 15 miles west of Munich by helicopter.

▶ **10 p.m.** — Hostages, bound and blindfolded, are led by terrorists to bus. They are driven to three helicopters in a field outside Olympic Village.

▶ **10:15 p.m.-12:45 a.m.** — Helicopters reach air base; bungled sniper attack by German sharpshooters leads to bloody shootout; all nine hostages are killed, five terrorists killed, three captured; German policeman killed.

OLYMPICS' DARKEST DAY: A terrorist stands on the balcony at 31 ... 1972, during the attack that left 11 Israeli athletes dead.

Killings forever changed sense

The hosts of the 1972 Munich Olympics had promised an atmosphere of serenity. As the Games rolled into their final week, everyone was convinced Munich would deliver.

In an instant, serenity was gone. ABC's Jim McKay vividly remembers how initial reports of a hostage crisis were met with disbelief.

"We had put the possibility out of our minds," McKay says. McKay and others who covered the '72 Games had quickly grown to appreciate the easy access to the Munich athletes' village, access that ceased to exist at future Games.

"I'd walk over to the village every day," says NBC Sports executive producer Terry O'Neill, an ABC researcher in Munich. "There was nobody to stop you."

That is precisely why 11 Israeli athletes were taken hostage.

Although McKay was able to tell a U.S. TV audience about the violent conclusion of the seige — it was over just after

The desperate final gamble

The Germans finally agreed to have a plane waiting to take the Arabs and their hostages to Cairo. The helicopter above, hovering at the Olympic Village, was one of three which airlifted them to the airport. But authorities felt that a trip to Cairo would have been "certain death" for the Israelis. In a desperate gamble at the airport, sharpshooters opened up on the Arabs in the midnight darkness, and the day's tension exploded in small-arms fire and detonating hand grenades. At right, one shattered helicopter stands on the field. The final toll: all the hostages, five commandos and one policeman dead; three commandos captured.

8

SHADOW OF DEATH AT MUNICH

The Arab commando, masked figure of doom, keeps watch from the balcony of the Israeli Olympic team's quarters. Inside, two Israelis are already dead, gunned down by the Arabs as they forced their way into the building. Nine other Israelis are being held hostage. Through a long day the hair-trigger negotiations go on. Late in the evening, captors and hostages are lifted by helicopter to an airport 20 miles away. There, the most terrible event in Olympic history ends.

LIFE

The Haywire Olympics

Can they be fixed by '76?

Frank Shorter, first American to win the marathon in 64 years, was a happy exception for the battered U.S. team

SEPTEMBER 22 • 1972 • 50¢

We won! We won!

"With all that happened to the other Americans," said a player on the never-defeated U.S. basketball team, "we figured there was just no way it could happen to us too." But it did, as these photographs by Rich Clarkson show. After a bruising defensive game in which the U.S. trailed until the final three seconds, time apparently ran out with the score U.S. 50, Russia 49. The U.S. team erupted with joy (above) but the celebration was frustratingly premature. The top official present ordered the three seconds replayed. This time the Soviets scored (opposite page) and the final jubilation was theirs. The dazed U.S. faces at right reflect the impact of the turnabout. The U.S. appealed, but a five-man international jury upheld the Russian victory. The U.S. players, still convinced they had won, refused to accept their silver medals.

No we didn't...

...the Russians did

In the three extra seconds of play, Russia's Aleksandr Belov elbowed U.S. defenders to the floor and scored (sequence at top), touching off the bear-hugging above. Films of the final seconds showed at least two Soviet rule violations that were not called.

THE OLYMPICS IN REVIEW . . .

The Road To Munich

Date	Score	Opponent	High Scorer
July 21	80-46	Hawaii All Stars	Dwight Jones 16
July 26	79-41	Hawaii All Stars	Tom Henderson 14 Jim Brewer 14
July 29	95-42	Kaneohe MAS	Henderson 16
Aug. 2	89-57	Kaneohe MAS	Mike Bantom-17
Aug. 10	65-52	Ex-Olympians (Dayton)	D. Jones 18
Aug. 11	84-71	Pro-All Stars (Louisville)	Ed Ratleff 15
Aug. 13	65-63	Pro All Stars (Los Angeles)	Henderson 17
Aug. 15	82-76	ABA All Stars (Greensboro)	Doug Collins 32
Aug. 16	76-65	Pro All Stars (Buffalo)	D. Jones 21
Aug. 27	66-35	Czechoslovakia	Henderson 16
Aug. 28	81-55	Australia	Ratleff 18
Aug. 29	67-48	Cuba	D. Jones 18
Aug. 30	61-54	Brazil	Henderson 12
Sept. 1	96-31	Egypt	Bantom 17
Sept. 2	72-56	Spain	Bantom 11
Sept. 3	99-33	Japan	Bantom 18
Sept. 7	68-38	Italy	Jim Forbes 14
Sept. 9	50-51°	U.S.S.R.	Brewer-Henderson 9

°Under I.O.C. Review as Protest.

1972 Olympic Basketball Team

No.	Player	Position	Age	Hgt.	Wt.	Home	School (Graduation)
4	Kenny Davis	G	23	6'1	179	Georgetown, Ky.	Marathon Oil (Georgetown 1971)
5	Doug Collins	G	20	6'6	170	Benton, Ill.	Illinois State 1973
6	Tom Henderson	G	20	6'3	190	Bronx, N. Y.	San Jacinto J. C. 1972 (Hawaii 1974)
7	Mike Bantom	F	20	6'8	205	Philadelphia, Pa.	St. Josephs 1973
8	Bob Jones	F	20	6'9	210	Charlotte, N. C.	North Carolina 1974
9	Dwight Jones	C	20	6'9	210	Houston, Texas	Houston 1974
10*	John Brown	F	20	6'8	220	Dixon, Missouri	Missouri 1973
11	Jim Brewer	C-F	20	6'7	215	Maywood, Ill.	Minnesota 1973
12	Tom Burleson	C	20	7'4	230	Newland, N. C.	North Carolina State 1974
13	Tom McMillen	C-F	20	6'11	210	Mansfield, Pa.	Maryland 1974
14	Kevin Joyce	G	21	6'2	190	Merrick, L. I., N.Y.	South Carolina 1973
15	Ed Ratleff	G-F	22	6'6	195	Columbus, Ohio	Long Beach State 1973

*Due to a broken foot, Brown was replaced by Jim Forbes, 6'7; from the Univ. of Texas (El Paso)

COACH: Henry P. Iba, Oklahoma State U.

Assistant Coach: Don Haskins, U. of Texas-ElPaso.

Assistant Coach: John Bach, Penn State U.

Manager: M. K. "Bill" Summers, Brownstown, Indiana.
Chairman, 1972 U.S. Olympic Basketball Committee.

Assistant Manager: Herbert J. Mols, Park School, Amherst, N. Y.

Trainer: Albert C. "Whitey" Gwynne, West Virginia U.

Game Officials: Naz Servido, Erie, Pa., Jim Bain, Decatur, Ill. Selected to work Olympic games in Munich.

Olympic Results

GROUP A

66 USA	Czechoslovakia 35
105 Cuba	Egypt 64
110 Brazil	Japan 55
79 Spain	Australia 74
81 USA	Australia 55
110 Brazil	Egypt 84
74 Cuba	Spain 53
74 Czechoslovakia	Japan 61
67 USA	Cuba 48
72 Brazil	Spain 69
78 Japan	Egypt 73
69 Czechoslovakia	Australia 68
61 USA	Brazil 54
72 Spain	Egypt 58
92 Australia	Japan 76
77 Cuba	Czechoslovakia 65
96 USA	Egypt 31
84 Cuba	Australia 70
87 Spain	Japan 76
83 Brazil	Czechoslovakia 82
72 USA	Spain 56
94 Czechoslovakia	Egypt 64
75 Australia	Brazil 69
108 Cuba	Japan 63
99 USA	Japan 33
74 Czechoslovakia	Spain 70
89 Australia	Egypt 66
64 Cuba	Brazil 63

GROUP B

94 Russia	Senegal 52
85 Yugoslavia	Italy 78
81 Puerto Rico	West Germany 74
90 Poland	Phillipines 75
87 Russia	West Germany 63
92 Puerto Rico	Phillipines 72
85 Yugoslavia	Poland 64
92 Italy	Senegal 56
95 Poland	Senegal 59
79 Russia	Italy 66
79 Puerto Rico	Yugoslavia 74
93 West Germany	Phillipines 74
94 Russia	Poland 64
68 Italy	West Germany 57
117 Yugoslavia	Phillipines 76
92 Puerto Rico	Senegal 57
81 Yugoslavia	West Germany 56
68 Phillipines	Senegal 62
71 Italy	Poland 59
100 Russia	Puerto Rico 87
73 Yugoslavia	Senegal 57
67 West Germany	Poland 65
111 Russia	Phillipines 80
71 Italy	Puerto Rico 54
85 Puerto Rico	Poland 83
74 Russia	Yugoslavia 67
101 Italy	Phillipines 81
72 West Germany	Senegal 62

SEMI-FINALS

68 USA	Italy 38
67 Russia	Cuba 61
66 Yugoslavia	Czechoslovakia 63
87 Puerto Rico	Brazil 83

GROUP STANDINGS

GROUP A

	W	L
United States	7	0
Cuba	6	1
Brazil	4	3
Czechoslovakia	4	3
Australia	3	4
Spain	3	4
Japan	1	6
Egypt	0	7

GROUP B

	W	L
Russia	7	0
Italy	5	2
Yugoslavia	5	2
Puerto Rico	5	2
West Germany	3	4
Poland	2	5
Phillipines	1	6
Senegal	0	7

USA SCORING—ALL GAMES

	G	FG	F	Pts.
Dwight Jones	9	34	18	86
Mike Banton	9	31	13	75
Tom Henderson	9	35	3	73
Doug Collins	9	24	17	65
Tom McMillen	9	25	10	60
Jim Brewer	9	21	18	60
Ed Ratleff	9	27	5	59
Jim Forbes	9	29	0	58
Bob Jones	8	15	11	41
Kevin Joyce	9	17	6	40
Tom Burleson	8	10	10	30
Ken Davis	7	5	4	14
USA Totals	9	273	115	661
Opponents Total	9	161	92	414

FINAL STANDINGS

(15) 2 Senegal	Egypt 0
(13) 82 Phillipines	Japan 73
(11) 84 Spain	West Germany 83
(9) 91 Australia	Poland 83
(7) 87 Brazil	Czechoslovakia 69
(5) 86 Yugoslovaia	Puerto Rico 70
(3) 66 Cuba	Italy 65
(1) 51 Russia	U.S.A. 50

CHAMPIONSHIP GAME

Russia (51)

	G	FT	Pts.
Polivoda	0	0-0	0
Paulauskas	0	3-4	3
Skakandidz	2	4-8	8
Sharm'edov	1	2-4	4
Boloshev	2	0-0	4
Edeshko	0	0-0	0
S. Belov	8	4-6	20
Korkia	1	2-2	4
Dvorni	0	0-0	0
Volnov	0	0-0	0
A. Belov	3	2-4	8
Kovalenko	0	0-0	0
Totals	17	17-28	51

United States (50)

	G	FT	Pts.
Davis	0	0-0	0
Collins	1	6-6	8
Henderson	4	1-2	9
Bantom	1	0-2	2
R. Jones	0	0-0	0
D. Jones	2	2-4	6
Forbes	1	0-0	2
Brewer	3	3-4	9
Burleson	0	0-0	0
McMillen	1	0-0	2
Joyce	3	0-0	6
Ratleff	3	0-0	6
Total	19	12-18	50

Russia	26	25	—51
U.S.A.	21	29	—50

Total fouls—Russia 25, U.S.A. 26 Attendance—6500

1. The USA is protesting the extra three seconds granted because the game according to FIBA rules was over

2. The USA was shooting the second of a two shot foul. this free throw was made. at the point the free throw was made, there were three seconds remaining.

3. at this point according to fiba rules....neither team can call a time out. the official score sheet does not show a time out in the last three seconds.

4. the opponents played the ball and ran off two seconds. according to fiba rules this was the only official way to continue the game.

5. with one second remaining spectators ran onto the playing court the referees stopped the game at this time. at this point with one second remaining according to fiba rules they acted correctly.

6. when the spectators were removed, the game was started with one second to go.

7. the one second was played and the horn sounded, officially ending the game...the official score was u.s.a. 50, ...urs 49

8. according to fiba rules the game is officially over.

M. K. Summers
U.S.A. Basketball Chairman

U.S. loses its appeal of Olympics basketball

By WILLIAM GILDEA
© L.A. Times-Washington Post Service

MUNICH—In a decision marked with political overtones, the International Amateur Basketball Federation (FIBA) yesterday disallowed a United States protest that Russia had scored the winning goal in the Olympic championship basketball game after time had expired.

The decision was handed down by a five-member FIBA jury of appeals, consisting of representatives from Hungary, Poland, Cuba, Italy and Puerto Rico. The vote was believed to have been 3-2, the United States apparently the victim of a Communist bloc vote.

After the futile protest that the clock had illegally been set back to three seconds remaining, just enough time for the Russians to hand the Americans their first defeat ever in Olympic basketball competition after 63 victories, U.S. basketball chairman M. K. Summers of Brownstown, Ind., declared that the players would not accept the silver medals.

Russia's basketball team accepted the Olympic gold medal with broad grins and triumphant waves last night while the U.S. team boycotted the ceremony.

The United States voted unanimously to refuse the silver medal and asked for a review by the International Olympic Committee.

The executive board of the IOC agreed to take up the protest at a meeting this morning. However, the medal ceremony was not put off, and the IOC has never been known to intervene in technical aspects of running sports events.

The medal presentation was held at the end of the final team handball game in the Olympics' crowded Sportshalle.

When it was announced that Dr. R. William Jones, FIBA's secretary-general, would take part in the presentation, there was mild applause and a few scattered boos. It was Jones who had decided at the end of the game that the Russians must be given another three seconds

See AMERICANS
Back page, col. 4, this section

Russians top medals totals as Olympic Games near end

Associated Press

MUNICH — With only one equestrian event remaining this morning before tonight's closing ceremonies of the 20th Olympiad, Americans began the return home after one of the United States' most disappointing showings in the history of these international games.

The Americans picked up a total of five gold medals, one silver and three bronzes in yesterday's final full day of events, but the traditionally dominant Yanks also saw the imposing Russian team, with its hammer and sickle emblems, walk off with the team honors.

The Soviets took 51 gold medals and a total of 99 medals overall to 33 golds and 93 total for the United States. East Germany was third with 66 medals, 20 of them gold.

The American track and field team won only six gold medals—including yesterday's marathon victory by Frank Shorter and 400-meter relay triumph by the team of Larry Black, Robert Taylor, Gerald Tinker and Eddie Hart—the worst of all time. However, the U.S. total of 22 topped Russia's 18.

Other Americans to win gold medals on what would have been the final day of the Games had it not been for the slaying of 11 Israeli team members by Arab guerillas last week, were:

- Ray Seales, who outpointed Bulgarian Anghel Anghelov for the light welterweight boxing first place;
- John Williams of Cranesville, Pa., and Doreen Wilber of Jefferson, Iowa, who won the men's and women's archery championships.

The silver medal was won by the women's 1,600-meter relay team of Mabel Fergerson, Madeline Manning Jackson, Cheryl Toussaint and Kathy Hammond, while three bronzes went to American boxers, Ricardo Carreras, Marvin Johnson and Jesse Valdez.

The other bronze medal was awarded to Tom McBreen of San Mateo, Calif., who had finished fourth in the controversial 400-meter freestyle swimming final Sept. 1.

It was the race won by 16-year-old Rick DeMont of San Rafael, Calif., who later was stripped of his gold medal when dope tests showed he had used a banned medication to ease an asthmatic condition.

When he was disqualified, officials vacillated on moving up other finishers and re-awarding the medals. Yesterday's action completed the official finish of the event.

The bitterest and most embarrassing blow to the Americans in the most bizarre Olympics ever came when a special jury denied an American protest of the last-gasp 51-50 loss in basketball to the Russians Saturday.

The Americans apparently had won the game 50-49 before the last three seconds of the game were played over in violation of the international rules, the Americans maintained. Russia scored the winning basket on a controversial play during those seconds.

Mother's cheers help

Seales, a 20-year-old southpaw from Tacoma, Wash., got vocal assistance from his mother in winning his bout with the Bulgarian, which averted America's first gold shutout in boxing in 24 years.

"Hit him, hit him!" Seales' mother, Belencita, shouted from a ringside seat in the press section with a voice that carried above the cheers of the crowd. "That's it . . . do it again!"

It was almost as if Seales had to battle for the fans' attention. "I'm always aware my mother's out there," the young fighter said. "I can always hear her voice." So could just about everyone else.

Seales' father, a fire chief in the Virgin Islands, was also at the fight—but Ray said he couldn't hear his dad's voice.

Seales got votes of 59-58 from British, Korean and Panamanian judges. Polish and Cuban judges, who initially scored it a draw, gave their votes to Anghelov under Olympic rules which require a judge giving a draw to make a decision for one fighter.

Seales, who said he plans to give the gold medal to his mother, brought a few extra cheers during the awards ceremony when he pulled an artificial red-white-and-blue rose from his robe and waved it to the crowd.

In other finals yesterday, East Europe swept the gold medals in all 10 weight classes of Greco-Roman wrestling, Russia heading the list with four.

West Germany won its first-ever gold medal in field hockey, beating favored Pakistan 1-0, and Poland beat defending champion Hungary 2-1 in the soccer final. Yugoslavia won the gold medal in team handball, beating Czechoslovakia 21-16.

Associated Press

Here's the basket that did it!

RUSSIA'S Alexander Belov leaps high to score his extra-chance basket in the final Olympic game, giving his team a 51-50 victory over the United States. A U.S. protest was turned down yesterday.

The Courier-Journal, September 11, 1972.

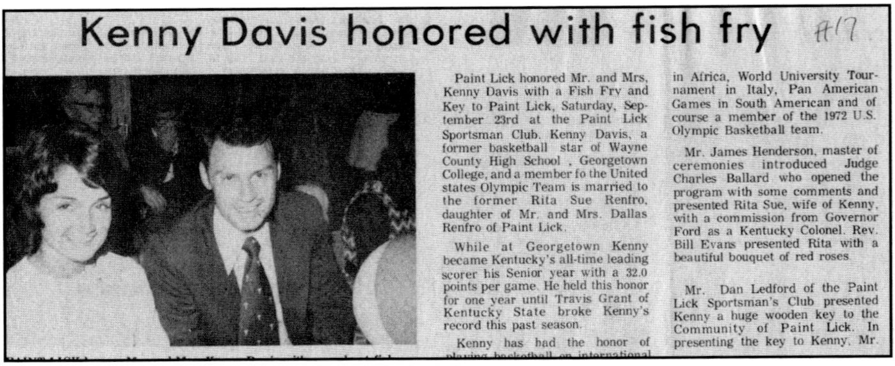

Kenny Davis honored with fish fry

Paint Lick honored Mr. and Mrs. Kenny Davis with a Fish Fry and Key to Paint Lick, Saturday, September 23rd at the Paint Lick Sportsman Club. Kenny Davis, a former basketball star of Wayne County High School , Georgetown College, and a member fo the United states Olympic Team is married to the former Rita Sue Renfro, daughter of Mr. and Mrs. Dallas Renfro of Paint Lick.

While at Georgetown Kenny became Kentucky's all-time leading scorer his Senior year with a 32.0 points per game. He held this honor for one year until Travis Grant of Kentucky State broke Kenny's record this past season.

Kenny has had the honor of playing basketball on international in Africa, World University Tournament in Italy, Pan American Games in South American and of course a member of the 1972 U.S. Olympic Basketball team.

Mr. James Henderson, master of ceremonies introduced Judge Charles Ballard who opened the program with some comments and presented Rita Sue, wife of Kenny, with a commission from Governor Ford as a Kentucky Colonel. Rev. Bill Evans presented Rita with a beautiful bouquet of red roses.

Mr. Dan Ledford of the Paint Lick Sportsman's Club presented Kenny a huge wooden key to the Community of Paint Lick. In presenting the key to Kenny, Mr.

Kenny and Rita at Kenny Davis Day, Monticello, September 1972.

Kenny and Rita, Kenny Davis Day, October 1972.

Rita and Kenny pause after a fish fry honoring Kenny, with members of his family of Monticello, Kentucky. Left to Right, Ralph Davis and wife, Carolyn, Kenny Davis. and wife, Rita Sue, Mr. Clyde Davis and wife, Zula.

Kenny Davis Day set for Sept. 16

KEN DAVIS DAY, scheduled for Saturday, September 16th, will begin with a parade at 1:30 p.m. The parade will assemble on Kendrick Avenue and march to the Wayne Co. School. Weather permitting the ceremonies will take place at the Wayne County Football Stadium, and if weather forbids the ceremonies will be held in the Wayne County Field House.

Plans now include the following speakers: County Judge, the Honorable Wilson Shearer; Mayor of Monticello, the honorable Carl C. Shearer; Superintendent, Clarence Bates of the Wayne County Schools; former principal, A.J. Lloyd; present principal, George O. Horton, along with out of town guests. The tenative principal speaker will be Coach Davis of Georgetown College.

Each citizen of Wayne County is given a cordial invitation to attend these services, and to honor KENNY DAVIS for his contribution to the summer Olympics held in Munich, Germany.

H 79

Clyde and Zula Davis, Kenny Davis Day, Monticello, October 1972.

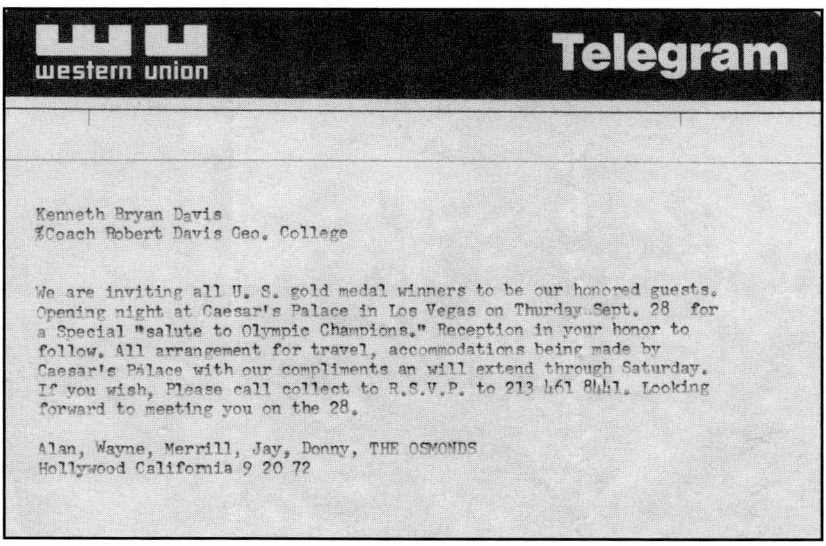

western union Telegram

Kenneth Bryan Davis
%Coach Robert Davis Geo. College

We are inviting all U. S. gold medal winners to be our honored guests. Opening night at Caesar's Palace in Los Vegas on Thurday Sept. 28 for a Special "salute to Olympic Champions." Reception in your honor to follow. All arrangement for travel, accommodations being made by Caesar's Palace with our compliments an will extend through Saturday. If you wish, Please call collect to R.S.V.P. to 213 461 8441. Looking forward to meeting you on the 28.

Alan, Wayne, Merrill, Jay, Donny, THE OSMONDS
Hollywood California 9 20 72

Telegram from The Osmonds inviting Kenny to a salute to Olympic champions, 1972.

Missouri State as basketball coach in 1946 and served until 1961. He has been associated with Central Missouri State College athletic teams for the past 26 years as coach of basketball, football, tennis, and golf, and has also served as Athletic Director during this period. (Keth passed away last April 16.)

James Miller is one of the ten players selected for the All-Time, All-Tournament team in 1971. Miller appeared in the NAIA finals three years while playing for East Texas State in 1953, 1954, and 1955.

Miller was selected as a member of the All-Tournament team all three years, and in 1955, when he led East Texas State to the national title, he was voted the Most Valuable Player Award. In 13 tournament games, Miller averaged 19 points per game, good enough for 15th place on the All-Time Tournament scoring chart.

The East Texas standout was a three-year letterman and member of the Dean's Honor Roll in addition to his athletic prowess.

Official News Release

National Association of Intercollegiate Athletics

1205 Baltimore, Kansas City, Missouri 64105

KANSAS CITY, Mo.—The National Association of Intercollegiate Athletics (NAIA) Executive Committee, meeting in its Annual Convention, today released the following resolution:

"Any National Association of Intercollegiate Athletics (NAIA) member institution which has a team, coach, or spectators involved in incidents of a violent nature at athletic contests in which the institution's team is competing will be subject to immiedate investigation by the National Office of the NAIA. This investigation will be conducted by the Executive Secretary of the NAIA.

After a complete investigation, the President of NAYA, the Chairman of the National Committee on Conduct of Athletics, and the Executive Secretary will be responsible for taking such action as is deemed necessary as a result of the investigation.

The NAIA intends to fulfill its obligation as a National Organization to all member institutions and to the public they serve in not ignoring, condoning, or tolerating conduct detrimental to intercollegiate athletics."

It was a happy occasion as John Norlander (left) and Jo-Jo Dean (right) presented the annual Converse Rubber Company award to outgoing NAIA Basketball Coaches Association President, Jim Gudger (center) of East Texas State.

29

Joe Dean, pictured at right, hired Kenny to join the Converse Shoe Co. two weeks after the Olympics.

RITA SUE DAVIS

Mrs. Davis speaks at conference

Highlights of the afternoon session of Wilderness trail FHA District Leradership Conference was the talk given by Mrs. Kenny Davis. She spoke on "Decisions that count."

Rita, a former graduate of Garrard County High, Garrard County Chapter Officer and during her FHA days held two district offices, District Recreational Leader and District president. She also received her State Homemaker Degree. A graduate of Georgetown College, at present Mrs. Davis is a commercial teacher at Scott County High. +

GOLD MEDAL WINNERS — These are some of the members of Marathon Oil's team who were part of the U.S. basketball unit which recently won the Intercontinental Cup in Brazil. In front are Scotty Baesler (left) and coach Pat Doyle. Standing (from left) are Kenny David, Gene Kirk, Cecil Tuttle and Phil Argento. (Staff Photo).

Marathon Players Lifted U.S. To International Title

The sixth Intercontinental Cub basketball championship belongs to the United States and a large share of the credit belongs to Lexington's outstanding amateur team, Marathon Oil.

It was a team comprised of Marathon and five other players from the National Amateur Basketball League, of which Marathon is a member, that captured the tournament held last week in San Paulo, Brazil.

The title came at the expense of Olympic teams from Russia, Brazil and Poland.

Marathon lost just one of three games, that in its opener to the Soviet Union 77-67.

The championship was unexpected because, since the 1968 Olympics, the United States has been taking its lumps in international competition. With the exception of military games, the U.S. had not won any tournament titles.

The victory also strengthened the chances of Phil Argento and Kenny Davis, both Marathon players, of making the U.S. Olympic squad for the summer games in Munich this year.

A look at each game . . .

RUSSIA 77, U.S. 67 — Using a man-to-man defense, the Americans were unable to stop Russia which rushed to a 31-14 advantage. Switching to a zone, the U.S. sliced the deficit to 10 points at halftime.

The U.S was able to cut that to four points in the second half but the loss of four big men who fouled out killed its chances.

Jim Day, the 6-7 Marathon standout, was also injured and Russia's front line, consisting of players 7-4, 6-9 and 6-8, took advantage of it.

U.S. 83, BRAZIL 61 — With a crowd of 20,000 and bongo drums urging them on, host Brazil appeared to be a tough club to beat. This was the same Brazil team which won the Pan American Games title in Columbia last summer.

It started out like a Brazil runaway. The hosts quickly jumped to a 12-point lead but the U.S, behind the shooting of Argento and Bill DeHere, closed the gap to five points at the half.

Marathon players Argento, Davis and Cecil Tuttle personally silenced the bongo drums after intermission. Five successful fielders by Tuttle and four each from Argento and Davis led a U.S. blitz which accounted for a 47-20 second half advantage.

U.S. 80, POLAND 76 — A tired American team repeatedly ran up leads of 10-12 points but watched them vanish.

It was up to Tuttle to decide things as he hit four consecutive field goals for an eight-point lead which withstood a late Polish rally.

Brazil edged Russia 65-64 to hand the Soviets their second loss in the round robin tournament and clinch the title for the Americans.

Davis was the leading U.S. scorer for the event, finishing with 48. Argento added 4[illegible]. Leading rebounders were DeHere and Gene Kirk with 1[illegible] each.

Despite a size disadvantage against every opponent, the Americans outrebounded their foes in all three games.

Marvin (Bo-Bo) Renfro, a senior at Garrard County High, brother to Mrs. Kenny Davis, talks over the game of basketball with Mr. Earl Combs, a member of the Baseball Hall of Fame. Bo-Bo is discussing with Mr. Combs how to cut down on errors and Mr. Combs quickly answers, "son, it takes many, many hours of hard practice." Bo-Bo plays shortstop for Garrard County High.

Associated Press

POLICEMEN from all over West Germany attended the funeral in Munich yesterday of 32-year-old Munich police officer Anton Fliegerbauer, who was shot and killed during the Tuesday night airport gun battle in which nine Israelis and five Palestinian guerrillas also were slain.

Secret burial in Germany is ordered for 5 guerrillas; 3 survivors charged

Associated Press

MUNICH — West German authorities yesterday ordered a secret burial for the five Arab guerrillas killed in the Olympics' day of terror and charged their three surviving comrades with murder and kidnaping.

With the five dead men still unidentified, the Munich district attorney's office said the location and time of burial would not be made public, for security reasons. He added that burial would take place in West Germany.

Formal arrest warrants were issued against the three surviving Arabs, charging them with the kidnaping and murder of 12 persons. The victims were 11 Israeli Olympians and a West German policeman.

The three—Al Abed al Kadir Dnawy, 21; Abdullah Mohamed Somer, 22, and Ibrahim Masoud Badran, 20—were captured early Wednesday after a shootout with police at Fuerstenfeldbruck Air Base. Nine of the Israeli Olympians were slain there, as were the five Arabs and the German policeman. Two Israelis were killed earlier by the Arabs.

No death penalty in Germany

Under West German law, the three Arabs can be held indefinitely, subject to regular review by a judge, until formally indicted and tried. There is no death penalty in West Germany; life imprisonment is the maximum sentence.

The trio will have three months to select defense attorneys before a court assigns them lawyers. The Bavarian Interior Ministry said yesterday that they had not yet requested legal counsel.

The Arabs and their prisoners had been ferried by German air force helicopter from the Olympic Village to Fuerstenfeldbruck, where they believed they would be transferred to a waiting Lufthansa Boeing 727 for a flight to Cairo.

When two of the Arabs went to inspect

Arab hand grenade and the others in a second copter raked by gunfire.

An Egyptian government spokesman charged Thursday that the Israeli hostages were killed by "German bullets" during the battle. Munich Police President Manfred Schreiber conceded yesterday it was not yet known exactly how the nine Israelis died, that the matter is still being investigated.

But the arrest warrants against the three Arabs, charging them with 12 murders, indicated an official view that all the nine tied and blindfolded hostages found dead in the two helicopters had been slain by the terrorists.

West German authorities confirmed the expulsion of 14 Arabs flown to Rome yesterday, but said this was a routine

Munich massacre.

A spokesman for the North Rhine-Westphalian state said in Duesseldorf that Arabs and other foreigners are regularly expelled from West Germany for such offenses as illegal entry, expired residence permits or after conviction on criminal charges.

In Zurich, Switzerland, meanwhile, Interpol, the international police organization, warned the Swiss government that Arab terrorists might try to blow up fuel storage tanks and commit other sabotage in Switzerland.

All police and border guards were alerted. Officials said special vigilance was ordered in the northeast along the German border. There was no indication why neutral Switzerland might be a

Spitz has No. 7; mov

Associated Press

Mark Spitz: world's most popular gold miner

INSIDE and outside the natatorium, Mark Spitz is the man of the hour. Above, he receives the accolades of teammates after accepting his 7th gold medal of the Olympic Games for the 400 medley swim and, below, he is mobbed by autograph seekers near his quarters at Olympic Village.

News that swimmer Mark Spitz wins his seventh gold medal, The Courier-Journal, September 5, 1972.

Kenny looked forward to visiting Freedom Hall, and playing against the Louisville Cardinals. For Louisville fans, and probably their players, the game was considered a "warm-up" or even pre-season. But this year might be a bit different, at least that was Georgetown's thinking.

Not only was Kenny playing good, but the Tiger's other guard, Jim Reid, who had played high school ball at Beaver Dam, could put up numbers right alongside of Kenny's.

At halftime the Tigers trailed the Cards 44-42, and Reid had 19 points.

The Cardinals eventually won 90-82. Reid fouled out with 4:55 left, but finished with a game high 27, while Davis had 26. The crowd of 8,131 in Freedom Hall that night was not happy and they let their home team know it. For Louisville, Jerry King had 24, and Butch Beard and Mike Grosso had 12 each.

"All four years I was at Georgetown we were their opening game," says Kenny. "And I had a wonderful experience playing there. That was a generous offer on their part (U of L's) as the guarantee (money) we received from those games funded the remainder of our season. But we were never able to pull the upset and leave there with a victory.

"Looking back, that was probably for the best as no doubt a win would have ended the series, and finding another cash cow that was that generous would have proved difficult."

Kenny was having a head-turning sophomore season, but make no mistake about it, he had some strong support from teammates. Reid, teaming with Davis in the Tiger backcourt, made for lots of comparison with Vories and Tuttle, and then when you add forwards Lenny Myers and Jerry Osborne, it made it difficult for the opposition to defend just one player.

Meyers could be a rebounding machine as he was in a game against Union College when he gathered 31. John Davis, a 6'3" leaper could get up, too. In the game against Kentucky State, John Davis had 20 boards to support Kenny's 48 points. It turned out to be an individual shootout between Kenny and Kentucky State's All-American Travis "Machine Gun" Grant, who tallied 36.

The Tigers finished the regular season 22-10 and then had to travel to Jefferson City, Tennessee to play Cumberland College for the NAIA District 24 title and a trip to the 32-team nationals in Kansas City. The Tigers won 67-65 in a bazaar ending. Lenny Meyers scored the winning basket on a goal tending call against Cumberland College as the game ended. With emotions high, a Cumberland fan slugged Jimmy Reid as Georgetown was cutting the nets down. For the game Kenny had 20 points, and John Davis matched his 20 to go along with 17 rebounds.

The Tigers advanced to Kansas City where they fell to Eastern Michigan in the first round 87-85. The Tigers placed five players in double figures, led by Kenny's 28, Reid 18, John Davis 15, Myers 12, and Osborne 10. However, it was their 21 turnovers that eventually did them in.

Along the way 6'8" Lenny Myers had broken the school rebounding record held by Bob Jones (later coached at Kentucky Wesleyan and the father of Jeff Jones later an All-ACC player at Virginia). And Kenny? Well, he set all kinds of records at Georgetown, made the NAIA All-Tournament team, and then Little All-American. He had had quite a sophomore season, averaging more than 27 points a game, which among all college divisions ranked him third behind LSU's Pete Maravich and Purdue's Rick Mount.

If someone only looked at the box score they might think he was a gunner. But was he? His coach Bob Davis didn't think so.

"If you're not careful he won't take many shots," his coach said. "If somebody else is hitting, Kenny won't shoot, he'll pass off. This is good, but on the other hand when you have a boy who can shoot like him, you want to cash in on his talents."

After the season Kenny was named to a Collegiate All-Star team that played a 20 game tour of Africa, Asia, and Europe.

It was here that Kenny encountered one of the best guards he had ever seen, much less played on the same team with. Billy Keller had been a Mr. Basketball out of Indiana before playing at Purdue, and "When I realized I wasn't going to beat him out, I was fortunate to be the other starting guard with him on that team," Kenny said.

Jim Gudger, of East Texas State, coached the team and Kenny and the coach's path would cross a couple of years later.

Though the team suffered only two losses, those games became less important to Kenny compared to the experiences and memories he collected for a lifetime. What he saw and experienced in this newly opened world was difficult to explain to friends and family back in Georgetown and Monticello. After all, he had never been out of the state of Kentucky until he went to college. Even at the age of 20 he realized he was seeing something very few Americans would ever do. It was indeed another world to him, though quite often wishing someway, somehow, he could be eating a hamburger at the Pool Hall on the square in Monticello or sandwich from Fava's in downtown Georgetown. Yes, a chili dog from the Lake View Restaurant in Burnside would have tasted pretty good, too.

With Kenny at Georgetown and the rest of his family back in Monticello, they, too, had been caught up in the excitement of their son's basketball success.

Clyde and Zula decided early on they were going to see as many games as possible—the good Lord willing. Georgetown from Monticello was a three-hour trip each way, and because darkness would come early during the winter, Clyde could get his milking done early and they'd pile in his 1968 Chevy pickup and head to Georgetown.

"Mom said if the truck broke down driving home she would be okay," laughed Kenny. "But not if it happened on the way."

The Davis family also made some of Georgetown's games on the road that were actually closer to Monticello than Georgetown. Carson-Newman in Jefferson City, Tennessee, Union College in Barbourville, Campbellsville, and Lindsey Wilson in Columbia were drivable "road" games."

Ralph Davis, the second oldest of Kenny's brothers, also pitched in and drove his parents to games.

"I drove them quite a bit," he said. "And we took James Lee Bell with us, too. He helped us around the farm, and we all called him Lee Jack. He and Kenny thought so much of each other, there'd always be a carload."

Sometimes little sister Sandy would make the trip to see her older brother play. And so would Gene Davis, the oldest of Clyde and Zula's children.

"I was nine years younger than Kenny," offered Sandy. "I remember going to some of the games, but mostly I stayed home with my handicapped brother, Gary, and my grandmother."

Sandy continues:

"After four boys, my mother was glad to finally have a girl. I didn't have to do some of the things they did, and all four brothers thought they were in charge, but we're close now."

Gene Davis recalled going "just about anywhere within a 100 miles" to see his brother play."

Gene admits not ever being interested in sports, but he did follow Kenny.

"I was sort of the rambler of the family," he laughed. "I've been everywhere, and I lived in San Diego for a while working in the car business.

"I heard all the stories about Kenny playing basketball, and he would dribble a ball everywhere," he said. "Mom said he'd fall asleep with a basketball in bed. Heck, I used to tell everyone Kenny played basketball and I checked out the cheerleaders."

It became routine when the Davis family went to Georgetown they would all go out to eat after the game. But those games that ended in a Georgetown loss put their post-game outings in jeopardy.

"I remember when they got beat one night, Coach Davis held the gym door open for the fans to leave as quickly as possible," Ralph Davis recalled. "He told the team, 'when the clock strikes midnight, don't even look up…just keep running.' It made my mother mad. We didn't get to visit with Kenny and go out to eat."

Chapter Nine

One of the knocks against Georgetown and Coach Davis in particular was the rough and tumble play of his team; in other words, aggressive basketball. And to add a little fuel to the fire, there were several road games where some of the Tiger football players would go along to lend not only their vocal support but physical support. They would whoop it and create an electric atmosphere that would sometime create a home game feeling for the traveling Tigers.

One fan of a Georgetown opponent remarked that "If you beat Georgetown, then you have to fight them."

A writer from Barbourville (Union College) wrote: "He (Coach Bob Davis) is so persistent that when everything is going against him that he makes a human spectacle of himself, causing fans to dislike his attitude at every turn. The Tigers always draw well when they come to Barbourville, but they simply can't play without roughing it up on the floor and in the stands."

Expectations were high as usual for the Tigers, and in an odd sort of way the schedule for the 1969-70 season revealed that only 12 games would be played in Alumni Gym, while 17 would be on the road. It was, in Coach Davis' words, necessary to play more road games because "that's where they play the tournament."

Why shouldn't everyone in Georgetown be excited? With a back court returning that averaged 47 points a game and an inside game that featured one of the school's all-time top rebounders, a return trip to the nationals in Kansas City seemed like a good bet.

Kenny Davis and Jim Reid averaged 29.2 and 16.5 points respectively to lead the Tigers, who returned four starters' from last year's 24-11 team. Rugged rebounder Lenny Myers was back with his 14.1 boards per outing. Seniors Jerry Osborne, a double figure scorer, and Willie Day returned, too. Depth would come from sophomore Mike

Calhoun, a transfer from the University of Cincinnati, Joe Oglethorpe, freshman Tom Stewart from Danville, Barry Zwick, and Tony Vance.

But the season didn't go exactly as planned.

"I put myself out on a limb and got it sawed off," Bob Davis told anyone who listened as the season wound down. "I told all the newspaper boys at the beginning of the season how tough we were going to be, but it hasn't worked out that way. By golly, it did look like we were going to be tough. We had four seniors, plus Kenny Davis, a junior ready to play, but then things started to happen.

"I had six boys to replace John Davis, the only starter we lost. In fact, I pinned my whole recruiting campaign on this one need. You know what happened? Four left school, one's ineligible, and the other one isn't playing."

Star freshman-to-be Tom Stewart did not become eligible at mid-year. "We would have been tough as nails with Stewart in there," said Davis.

And then the real hammer came down on the Tigers when 6'8" center Lenny Myers, the team's top rebounder, quit school.

"He'd had some personal problems," Davis added. "So I had a powerful talk with him. It must have been so powerful he decided to drop out of school."

Throughout the season Kenny Davis had some big games, twice scoring 42, but there were also games where he couldn't "throw it in the ocean." One of those nights was against Tennessee Wesleyan when he was held to 17. And then the unbelievable happened. It was against St. Benedict's, and with no time on the clock, Kenny Davis stood at the foul line with his Georgetown team trailing 68-67. Hit the first and the worst the Tigers can do is overtime. Hit both and they win. An 85% free throw shooter, he had already hit 10 of 11 for the night and scored a total of 28 points. But the unthinkable happened. He missed, and the Tigers lost.

Jimmy Reid had been an explosive scorer, too. He had scored at least 20 points in 18 games that included 36 and 27 against Thomas More and 27 against Campbellsville.

With no post-season games on the horizon that year, Coach Davis began to plan and experiment some for the next year.

While the Tigers were going 17-13 for the year, nearby Kentucky State laid claim to their first-ever NAIA national title behind All-Americans Travis Grant and Elmore Smith.

As for the annual U of L-Georgetown game, played this time in late February, the Tigers in a declining state fell 107-85. Mike Grosso scored a career high 33 points, while Georgetown was led by Reid's 22, Osborne's 21, and Davis' 19.

With the season over, Jimmy Reid had closed out a brilliant career with 1,369 points and despite a not so great year for the team, he would go down as one of the school's best, averaging 21 his senior year. He had captained the team for two years.

Soon after graduating, Reid became an assistant coach for the Tigers, and in 1973 when Coach Davis left to become the basketball coach at Auburn, he became the head coach at Georgetown College at the age of 25.

And what a coach he was. Implementing what he had learned from the legendary Davis, Reid developed his own style and over his 23-year coaching career he became the winningest basketball coach in Georgetown history with 529-199 record. His last six squads averaged 30 wins a season and his 1996 team was national NAIA runner-up.

Jimmy Reid, a NAIA Hall of Fame member, died of cancer in 1996.

"Jimmy and I played and roomed together for three years and remained close for the next 26 years until his passing," Kenny says. "Smokey Jones, a referee, told me once that if Jim Reid protested a call…he probably missed the call.

"He had a remarkable ability to relate to his players. I never saw Jimmy take a player out of the game without that player's expression being one of that's exactly what should have happened. Hating to come out of a game myself, I know how much coaching talent it takes to convince a player of that mindset."

Georgetown College has a history of hanging on to basketball coaches, and it all started with Bob Davis. His 20 years produced a 415-182. The Tigers didn't miss a beat when Reid's assistant, Happy Osborne followed with a 456-84 mark in 16 seasons.

Even though the basketball season at Georgetown could not end soon enough, it didn't mean it had ended for the two Davis'—Dr. Bob and Kenny.

Coach Davis had been selected to coach the USA team in the World University Games in Turin, Italy.

But before Kenny could even think about making the World Games, he was invited to the Olympic Development Camp the first three weeks in July at the Air Force Academy in Colorado. It was a must for him. Some of the top amateur basketball players in the nation were there representing the Armed Services, American Athletic Association and NAIA.

Rest was out of the question. What were the odds of the kid from Wayne County Kentucky poised once again to represent his country on the world stage of basketball?

By his own admission Kenny dated only one girl in high school, choosing to concentrate on his studies and basketball, and at Georgetown little had changed until one June Sunday afternoon in 1968. That's when Kenny added a third element to his priorities in life.

"The freshmen were arriving for summer school and Gene Witt, a KA (Kappa Alpha) fraternity brother and myself decided to walk over to the girls dorm where the new freshmen would be living for their summer classes," says Kenny. "We had a two-hour window for them to arrive, so we parked ourselves on a park bench and waited for the show to begin."

It wasn't long before cars with license plates from different locations began to pull up in front of the dorm, and just as Kenny and Gene had expected, out came the freshmen girls to unload their cars and move into their new home away from home.

"Since numerous trips were required to unload all they had brought, Gene and I got multiple views of what the new Tiger ladies looked like," Kenny offered.

Kenny was quick to point out the reason the two of them didn't offer to help the new arrivals with their belongings was because of a Georgetown College rule involving boys in girls dorms. "In 1968 there was a rule that male students could not go past the lobby area," he said.

That Sunday afternoon Kenny's life was about to change forever.

Rita Sue Renfro, from Paint Lick, Kentucky, was one of those new Tiger ladies to arrive, and as she stepped from her family's car, there to meet her was none other than Kenneth Bryan Davis, who by now was a "big-man-on-campus."

"I was the first person she laid eyes on at Georgetown," Kenny likes to say years later. He quickly admits, however, for the record, that it was probably Gene she saw first. And she has reminded me over the years that she was more impressed with him that day.

For Kenny and Rita Sue, the courtship began almost immediately, and one year later they became engaged.

"I had always gone to a little country Baptist Church," says Rita. "So I think my parents wanted me to go to Georgetown College to marry a preacher. But I came home with a Church of Christ basketball player."

The following year on May 16, 1970, the two were married in Paint Lick.

"The plan was for an outdoor wedding on her parent's farm, however a persistent rain throughout the day forced us inside." Kenny's best man was Jim Porter, a fraternity brother from Danville, and Rita Sue's maid of honor was her roommate, Yvonne Robinson, from Covington.

The newly married Davis's honeymooned for four days at Cumberland Falls State Park near Corbin, before heading back to Georgetown.

"Rita had summer school, and I was in training for the tryouts to see if I could make the USA team in the World University Games," Kenny said. "We both had one more year before graduating."

Rita's mother, Virginia, was a basketball fan, rarely missing a college game Kenny played. Dallas, her dad, on the other hand, might get to a game every now and then.

"I was a cheerleader at Garrard County High and my brother Bo had played there," Rita added. "Mom was such a fan that she would go to some of the games at Berea College and Centre in Danville."

For Kenny and Rita, their education was important. After all, Kenny had gone to Georgetown to get an education and play basketball, and he found Rita. And Rita had gone to Georgetown to get an education, and found Kenny. Rita completed her required studies in three years and was able to join her husband as a member of Georgetown College's Class of '71.

Kenny and Rita moved into a three-room apartment at 702 B Warrendale Court, a designated housing area for married students.

"We affectionately called it "Cardboard Acres," Kenny laughed. "It was built from surplus Army buildings that the college acquired after WWII. When the wind blew our curtains would stand straight out. But no one complained as it was the first home for all of us, and we developed friendships from sharing meals, shoveling snow and playing games together."

It surprised no one, especially Kenny, that on nights before a basketball game that Coach Davis would drop in to make sure his star player was complying with the curfew.

"It took Rita awhile to get used to that," Kenny added.

One day Rita took matters into her own hands. Things had been tough for her and Kenny. Money was tight and she needed a job.

"I went to see Coach Davis. He could tell I was upset, so right off he says, 'Don't say anything you'll regret later.' He got me a student labor job in his office, and then he let Kenny and I eat some meals with the other players. I also had a class under Coach Davis, and like everyone else, I was scared of him."

The World University Games were held every two years, and by some considered a "dry run" in preparing United States sports teams for the grueling competition of the Olympics. All totaled there were 4,700 from 68 countries that would be participating in tennis, water polo, track & field, swimming & diving, volleyball, gymnastics, fencing, and, of course, basketball.

Prior to the World Games the team would practice at the U.S. Naval Academy in Annapolis before beginning a European tour to include Warsaw, Bucharest, and Belgrade. From there it was straight to Turin, Italy, where from August 22 through September 7, the U.S. would battle for the championship.

Kenny had made the team along with Jim McDaniels from Western Kentucky; Cliff Meely, Colorado; Dave Robisch, Kansas; George McGinnis, Indiana; Bob Ford, Purdue; Tom Parker, Kentucky; John Mengelt, Auburn; and Jim Cleamons, Ohio State.

During the tour, heading into the title game the American team had lost only one game. The Polish Nationals inflicted a five-point loss on the U.S. team, which turned around the following night and defeated the same team by 20.

And how did Kenny adjust to the European food? "I'll tell you what," he later said, "It made the cafeteria at Georgetown look like a five-star restaurant. I lived on bread and jelly for several days."

Coach Davis' American team was favored to beat the Russians in the finals. It was a game described by the Associated Press as "a series of body clashes between the players with a lot of pushing and elbowing."

The U.S. came into the game averaging just over 90-points a game, but the Soviets, playing a tight body-checking defense took a 78-71 victory.

Cleamons and a Soviet player were ejected from the game with one minute remaining in the game for fighting. Jim McDaniels led the U.S. team in scoring with 23.

"My players went back to the dressing room and cried like crazy after the game," Coach Davis said. "We stood there and watched them raise the communist flag. It was embarrassing. It was heartbreaking."

Coach Davis became the first man to coach a losing U.S. team in the World University Games.

"The Russians were in our dressing room within five minutes after they beat us, wanting to trade jerseys, sneakers and things," the coach said. "To me it proves that we can disagree and still have something in common."

But he added:

"When it came to the Russians we were walking on eggshells. 'Don't upset the Russians, everybody was saying. We knew we weren't going to get any breaks.'"

Years later, Coach Davis looking back on the loss said he should probably have played George McGinnis more late in the game.

And McDaniels remembered this about Kenny: "He was a great teammate…brought it every day, and laid it on the line in practice and the games. He was a person I enjoyed being around."

Chapter Ten

Kenny Davis, still with one more year at Georgetown, had defied all odds in becoming one of the all-time greats at the school. He had withstood, so far, some of the toughest basketball practice sessions on the planet, even losing a couple of teeth during one of them.

A disappointing junior year by the team, however, didn't dampen the prospects for the 1970-71 season.

Kenny was also coming off of a summer that would have made a lesser player want to take a year off. The Olympic Development Trials at the Air Force Academy, the World University Games practice at the Naval Academy, the multi-country tour behind the Iron Curtain, and then the Games themselves in Italy.

If Kenny never played another basketball game, it was Dr. Bob Davis who took a rawboned farm boy from Wayne County, Kentucky, with a desire like Coach Davis had never seen before, and turned him into a world class basketball player.

It didn't take any longer than the opening game of the season for Kenny Davis to let Tiger fans know his final season was going to be special. Hitting for 45 points in a 101-99 win over Lincoln Memorial, it was his highest single game point total since his sophomore year. And four nights later he bombed 44 in a win over Tennessee Wesleyan.

No longer was Jimmy Reid around, gone by graduation. The pair had formed one of the best guard combos in all of college basketball, and their play rivaled that of Dick Vories and Cecil Tuttle back in 1963-64. It was hoped that the play of Mike Calhoun, transfer John Owens, Steve Fritsch, Barry Zwick, Gary Moore, Tony Vance, Tom Stewart, and freshman Van Phillips would be enough to offset the point production of Reid and several others who left the program in what turned out to be a disappointing season.

Sure enough Calhoun began to show promise in an 86-75 win over Campbellsville when he and Kenny combined for 47 points, with Calhoun getting 22.

Phillips soon made his presence known, too. The kid was from Wayne County like Kenny, but he had played at cross-town Monticello High. Still, the Phillips and Davis families' back home were friends and at least for one year of college, they would be rooting for the same team.

The Monticello connection was strong. Phillips looked to Davis to show him the ropes and Kenny was willing to do his part. When Coach Davis was preparing to make room assignments for the team's first road trip, Kenny asked to room with Phillips.

"He knew I wouldn't get him in any trouble," Phillips laughed.

Kenny never lost his south-central Kentucky roots and solid values of life and work ethic that he had been exposed to from family, friends, and coaches. He still had one remaining basketball season at Georgetown, but already had achieved a success on the basketball court that only a very, very few would ever experience.

He would think back to the days not so long ago of boarding a yellow school bus with 'WAYNE COUNTY" painted on the side. But what were the odds three years later he would be boarding jet planes and traveling all over the world to play basketball?

With two families from Monticello now headed to Tiger games on a regular basis, the two fathers, Bruce Phillips and Clyde Davis, would often sit together. Kenny was already an all-time Tiger great, while Van Phillips was still trying to earn his stripes. It was a rare situation when Coach Davis substituted for his star. There was, however, one occasion that Phillips likes to talk about.

"My dad and Kenny's dad were together," recalls Van Phillips, "And Clyde would holler toward Coach Davis 'put Phillips in, put Phillips in!" Finally with about five minutes left in the game, Coach called for me to go in. I entered the game and replaced Kenny. Clyde leaned over to my dad and said, 'I didn't quite have that in mind.'"

There was another reason, Phillips jokingly talked about, as to why Kenny liked for him to be in the game. "It took me awhile, but I finally figured it out," he recalled. "I rarely shot and would always pass the ball to him."

Phillips may not have shot much that first year at Georgetown, but before he was through he had scored some 1,400 points, averaging 20 a game as a junior and 16 his senior year.

One game in particular the freshman from Monticello stepped up big time to pull a victory out over Lincoln Memorial. The Tigers had squandered a 17-point lead, and though Davis and Calhoun had scored 25 and 20 for the game, it came down to free throws. With a minute and half to go and LMU charging, every time they would score they would foul Phillips. He hit six in a row to pull out the win 91-89. "Kenny came over to me and said, 'Don't they know they're fouling the wrong guy?'"

Phillips continued:

"I was prone to foul out after being assigned the other team's best point guard. After a few games I noticed that Kenny never fouled out, so one night I asked him about it. He looked at me, smiled and said, 'You can't score from the bench.'"

Today Phillips is an attorney in Monticello.

John Owens was another transfer who came into the program and became eligible during Kenny's senior year. Coach Davis made a good living with transfers over his twenty-year career at Georgetown, and many of his great players had attended larger schools before finding their way to the little Baptist college in Scott County.

Owen's history came from nearby Lexington, where he was a 6'4" forward on the Henry Clay basketball team before he tore an ACL. Nevertheless, he made the U.K. freshman team as a walk-on playing with Tom Parker, Mark Soderberg, Randy Noll, Stan Key and Kent Hollenbeck.

"Coach (Joe B) Hall offered me a scholarship, but I dropped basketball when I decided to go into the ministry," Owens said.

But basketball wasn't out of Owen's blood. He had practiced some with Coach Lee Rose's team at nearby Transylvania College. And if that wasn't enough, he played numerous pick-up games that included Cliff Hagen, the former U.K. All-American who had recently retired after an NBA career with the St. Louis Hawks and ABA Dallas Chaparells.

"Hagan prepared me for playing physical," says Owens. "He was rough and knew all the tricks." (Hagan, a gentleman off the court, was considered one of the toughest players in pro ball and as a player-coach for Dallas in the old American Basketball Association he was involved in several fist-a-cuffs).

When Owens decided he still had some basketball left in his tank, he was well prepared for the practice sessions conducted by Coach Davis.

"My dad was a minister," says Owens. "So Coach Davis called me "Preacher Boy." When I came out for the team some of them didn't think I could make it. "But I knew how to fight and I made the team."

Anyone who ever played for Davis has their memories of a special practice drill, and Owens was no exception.

"It was the "loose towel" drill, "he laughed. "We (the players) would get in a circle…Coach would throw a towel in and whoever came out with the towel and made it to the stands got to sit down."

Looking back, Owens says after leaving U.K. he didn't have any preconceived ideas about the talent at Georgetown. "I knew about their history and I remember Coach Rupp talking about Cecil Tuttle and how good he was."

Owens was confident that his Georgetown team had always practiced more than their opponents, and he also felt good about the success the year he played with Kenny. We won 25 games his senior year."

John Owens, when graduated from the Southern Baptist Theology Seminary in 1973 with a doctorate, is quick to describe Kenny Davis as a mild mannered, small town, farm boy with a wonderful sense of humor, who was in the truest sense of the word, a student athlete. But then he went a step further in his observation.

"With all of the rough and tumble practices and fights," he said. "No one messed with Kenny. He had an air about him."

A number of years ago Owens recalled running into Joe B. Hall in Lexington, and the former Kentucky coach telling him a story about Coach Davis.

"I credit Bob Davis with helping me win the NCAA in 1978," Hall told Owens. "We played Auburn when they had John Mengelt and they out physicalled us. I knew then I had to get some tough guys. Because of the beating Coach Davis and Auburn gave us, I went out and got Rick Roby, Mike Phillips and James Lee."

At Georgetown, Owens scored 1,463 points, made Little All-American and played for the Kentucky College All-Stars against Ohio and Tennessee. He is now a minister in Winchester, Kentucky.

There might have been rumblings every now and then from the "big men" about the number of shots Georgetown guards took, but remember Coach Bob Davis was all about an offense built around guard play and their ability to score. Remember, three years back when Kenny arrived with intentions to take a few college credits and then transfer to the Air Force Academy? That is, until he soon realized he was in paradise and was smart enough to know it.

"There'd be some bickering every now and then about the ball not going inside enough," Kenny said. "But Coach Davis told them to 'knock it off, Davis and Calhoun will miss enough shots for you to get your share.'" Years later, friend Sherman York asked Kenny how he always ended up with the ball on a fast break. "You've got to know when to give it up so you can get it back to score."

All anyone had to do is look at the box score to see Kenny had a shooters mentality. More times than not it was shoot and think later. Never was it more evident than in a game against Belmont. Mike Calhoun picks up the story.

"We're undefeated and up by one with seven seconds to go and Kenny's at the line. When he was shooting free throws you could usually relax because he hit them. But, this time he missed and the ball came straight back to him. Instead of throwing the ball back out, he shot it again and missed. We were all hollering for him to throw it back out, but his instinct took over and he shot it."

Georgetown, for the record, won 82-81 and Kenny finished with 41.

In early January, the Tigers made their annual trip to Louisville, and the outcome was not pretty as the Cardinals won 115-76.

After the game U of L's star player Jim Price created a bit of a stir when after the game he said, "Davis is a good ball player, but he would be just average in the Missouri Valley Conference" (the conference Louisville was in at the time).

A college coach who saw the game and Price's comments offered that "Kenny wouldn't be average anywhere, and if I had my pick I'd take Davis without hesitation."

Years later Kenny was asked if he had responded to Price's comment. He answered:

"I did not. I was one who respected and congratulated my opponents, realizing that I had a full time job developing my game, which left me zero minutes to critique how others played.

"However, if one is looking for a commentary as to who played the best in that game, the box score which listed me as scoring 34, and Price scoring 19, is a stronger comment than any words that I could have said."

As good as Kenny Davis was, there would be times for some unexplainable reason he would go off the charts…the other way.

In a loss to Valdosta State in the West Florida Invitational, Kenny scored 37 points. But it was what he didn't do that became the news. He was 13 of 35 from the field and, get this, 11 for 20 at the free throw line. Stop the presses; Kenny Davis missed nine free throws in one game. Van Phillips, the other Monticello kid in the lineup, scored 14.

If Kenny's shooting percentages had gone in the tank the night before, he pulled them out in the consolation game with a 105-88 win over host West Florida. Forty-seven points he scored on 15 field goals and 17 of 18 free tosses. Shooting slump over.

Nevertheless, there were still games where defenses would be determined to put the clamps on Kenny, and when they did it usually meant that a teammate would be in position to pick up the slack. But more often than not, if Kenny was zeroing in, the Tigers won.

Pikeville was usually a formidable opponent. They had a reputation of recruiting good players from the mountains. One of Kenny's lowest point totals came in an 81-75 loss. He scored 18, but John Owens served notice that now that he was eligible after transferring in he was ready, as he scored 19.

The conversation about the style of "aggressive basketball" never went away when it came to Bob Davis coached teams. It seemed that someone, mainly opposing coaches or fans, had something to say. Several teams had even gone as far as to drop the Tigers from their schedules. Transylvania, Berea, Centre and Bellarmine, all within about an hour's drive, refused to play, thus causing Coach Davis to become more creative in his scheduling.

As the end to Kenny's career at Georgetown appeared on the horizon, he was focused on getting his team to the nationals.

Though Georgetown fell 91-87 to Union College, he banged in 44 points. Then it was 36 in an 89-88 win at Rio Grande.

As the season wound down, there was Pikeville one more time… never easy. This time the Tigers won 96-93 behind the play of Tom Stewart and John Owens who scored 27 and 21 points. But Kenny, like in the earlier loss to Pikeville, scored only 18 after getting in foul trouble, a rarity.

Only 18! Are you kidding? But that's the standard of play Kenny had established in his four-year career. When he didn't score at least 30 something was wrong. Forget it that some teams were hell bent on stopping him, double or triple teaming him, denying him the ball or roughing him up. Sometimes, he was a decoy that could free up teammates to pick up the slack. With Joe Ogletree, Gary Moore, Tom Stewart, George Lockwood, Van Phillips, Tony Vance, Mike Calhoun or John Owens, they were all capable.

Kenny quickly followed the 18-pointer with 44 in a 105-80 win over Northwood, Indiana, and then, against all odds, the kid from Wayne County dribbled and shot his way into Kentucky college basketball history. His 33 points in a 101-94 loss to Franklin, Indiana made him the highest scoring player in a state where basketball has often been called a religion.

The 2,974 points now scored broke the previous mark held by Dickie Vories.

With a 21-6 record, all that remained were one last home game, and then the NAIA playoffs in hopes of getting back to the nationals in Kansas City.

The bleachers were full to watch Kenny conclude, perhaps the greatest career in Georgetown basketball history. Averaging over 32 points, he held virtually every scoring record, and they were there to watch him.

With 30-seconds left and the score all even, Kenny nailed a basket for a 77-75 win over Thomas More. The basket gave him 25 for the game.

The NAIA Regionals were to be played in McKenzie, Tennessee, and the Tigers would be facing a tough Bethel team. Coach Davis knew if he was to get his team to Kansas City, they would have to go through not only Bethel, but defending national champion Kentucky State and their two All-Americans Travis Grant and Elmore Smith.

Davis had hoped that Thorobred Coach Lucias Mitchell would forego the NAIA tournament to either play in the NCAA small college regional or the NIT with other major college powers. Kentucky State, however, decided to stay put, and Georgetown, who during the season had been nationally ranked as high as fourth, would have to take their number ten ranking and deal with the task at hand—Bethel College.

Bethel, coached by Science Hill, Kentucky native Doug Hines, employed an aggressive style of their own, upsetting Georgetown 82-78. Kenny, playing his last game ever in a Georgetown uniform, scored a game high 29 points with help from Stewart's 18 points and 17 boards and Owen's 15 points and 11 rebounds.

Bethel players and Coach Hines knew all about Kenny's game, and they also knew they'd have to pull out all stops to win. And they did.

For sure it was not the way Kenny wanted to bow out. Before the game, Coach Davis had predicted to *Courier-Journal* sports writer John Flynn, "If Kenny's hitting, it won't make any difference what Bethel does because we're going to blow them out."

Kenny was hitting from the field with 10 baskets, but free throws, well, that was another matter.

Flynn continued in his reporting: "Davis, obviously worn out from the rigors of a 28-game season, missed nine of 18 free throws."

"Can you imagine us losing because I couldn't make free throws?" Davis told Flynn. "Goodness, I hit 85 percent during the season, but tonight I couldn't get anything in the basket. How do you explain it? You make free throws all your life and suddenly you can't buy one."

"I'm just glad it's over," Kenny Davis said. "It's been this way all year, the defense handling me. I complain and the officials act as if I'm a crybaby. The only thing that made the game (this year) fun was the winning, and tonight we didn't win. It wasn't any worse than usual, but they sure had their hands all over me."

One of Bethel's defenders was J.C. Popplewell, from Russell Springs, and he knew Kenny well.

"I had to use my hands on Kenny," he said. "You can't let him get the ball. I'm from the next town over from Kenny's and I found that out when we were in high school."

Bethel would go on to lose to Kentucky State the next night, and the Thorobreds would go on to win their second national NAIA title in Kansas City.

One thing was for sure, Kenny Davis, with 3,003 career points, was the first Kentucky collegian to ever score more than 3,000 points.

Perhaps now Kenny could put his Physical Education degree to good use and go into coaching, as many who knew him thought he would. Or would he?

Chapter Eleven

In order to score over 3,000 points, a player has to have a lot going for him. It isn't done that often, so the odds of almost anyone doing it are not good.

But for Kenny Davis, those odds increased when several key factors are taken into consideration. First, he had a coach who believed in his ability to make shots. Second, he had teammates who bought into it as well. And then, just as important, Kenny was able to avoid serious injuries or illness. In order to score you've got to be in the game, and save for several bruises and missing teeth, his career at Georgetown was injury free.

Over forty years later when anyone speaks of guards at Georgetown College, they may start with Cecil Tuttle and Dick Vories, but they end with Kenny Davis.

Kenny, in four years had averaged 12, 27.5, 29.5 and 32 points per game. He was a 3-time NAIA All-American, broke the all-time Kentucky collegiate scoring record (later broken by Travis Grant) and played basketball on five continents (North America, South America, Asia, Africa and Europe).

It was against all odds that the kid from Wayne County, who used to dribble a basketball while peddling his bike would ever in his wildest dreams accomplish so much.

And he wasn't done!

For a number of years Dr. Bob Davis had been involved as vice-chairman of the U.S. Olympic Basketball Committee, and the fact that he had been the head coach of the USA team that played in the World University Games meant that his clout could open a few doors. But just because a door was open didn't mean any more than just that. Could he get a player an invitation to try out for one of their touring American teams? Probably. But then it was up to those individual players to walk through that door on their own merits. And absolutely Kenny Davis could walk on his own.

Described in college as a supercharged sharpshooter, at 6'0", 175-pounds, the kid, who was now a man, some thought, was at the end of the line when it comes to playing basketball.

"I just assumed he'd always go into coaching," said his brother Ralph years later. "I'd think a lot of us around here (Monticello) did."

Can you imagine the high schools and even some colleges that would line up to hire him? The former high school and college honor student conducted his life the same way...with honor. He played the game on high octane, and just completing an incredible college career, playing for a legendary coach, it appeared that if coaching was his choice, he would be a superstar there, too.

His good buddy and teammate at Georgetown, Jim Reid, after all, had joined Coach Davis' staff, and prepared to position himself to become a good coach. Dr. Bob Davis couldn't coach forever, and who knows, maybe Reid could take over.

But wait. Kenny still had some ideas of his own, and for the time being they didn't include coaching.

Western Union telegrams began to arrive from the professional basketball teams who had drafted Kenny. The American Basketball Association held their draft in mid-March 1971, with hopes of beating the much more established NBA to the best players. Though there had been talk of a merger for several years, it appeared that the two sides were light years of reaching a compromise on what teams from the newer league would make the cut.

Kenny's ABA telegram came from the Carolina Cougars and its president Carl Scheer informing him that this was official notification that Carolina had selected him in their 1971 draft. "After your college season is concluded, I would like you to contact me to arrange an appointment to discuss your professional basketball career with the Carolina Cougars. Please call me collect."

Kenny had already received a letter in late November 1970 from Athletes Advisory Group, Inc., a New York City based company that represented professional basketball players. Although the letter was signed by Charles Kaufman, president of the company, the name that jumped off the letterhead was that of Norman Blass, Executive Vice President and General Counsel.

Blass was the ring leader in making the connection with Western Kentucky's Jim McDaniels and Carolina also in November 1970.

McDaniels recounted the story in the book, "Kentucky Colonels of the American Basketball Association…The Real Story of a Team Left Behind." The Hilltopper All-American told of how he met with Blass at a Bowling Green residence in late September 1970, and then two months later when Blass showed up at his one bedroom shanty-style home near the south part of the campus, in what was known as Vet Village. Not only did the New York sports agent have Cougar, President Carl Scheer and team owner Ted Munchak with him, but he also had a suitcase full of money and 15 signed ABA contracts of current college players. "I saw their names, everybody knew them," said McDaniels. "He said it plain and simple if I didn't sign with him I'd be left out (of the merger between the ABA and NBA) and all of the money would be gone."

For an instant McDaniels started to leave the room where Blass stood. Perhaps the merger wouldn't happen. But that's when Blass played the trump card, and it was a winner.

"He pulled out a nice black leather brief case and put it on the table with a contract," recalled McDaniels. "He opened it and it was stuffed full of money. It was $5's, $10's and $20's. He said there was $25,000. I tried to count it, but it was so overwhelming I had to stop."

Kenny Davis was only 6-foot tall and Jim McDaniels was 7-foot. The urgency back then for the ABA to sign the best big men in college league pulled out all stoops to nail down the likes of McDaniels and 7'2" Artis Gilmore.

The letter Kenny received, not only mentioned some of the big name players, but also emphasized they represent "those who play real well, but get less publicity." The letter went on to mention some players from small schools. It closed by saying, "We pride ourselves on our integrity."

Another Western Union telegram came Kenny's way on April 8, 1971. This one was from the New York Knickerbockers of the NBA informing they had selected him in their draft and to "please call me collect," signed William Holdman.

Even though Kenny hadn't played against the big-time marquee schools in scoring his more than 3,000 points at Georgetown, his game was still good enough to garner lots of attention. He had performed well in all-star games and international play, and it didn't take long for word to get around that Kenny Davis had a work ethic that equated to success—and to top it off he was coachable.

More letters were coming his way. One was Bill Fitch, Director of Player Personnel for the Cleveland Cavaliers. Another came from the Seattle SuperSonics, signed by Henry Akin, Head Scout. Akin had played at Morehead State a few years earlier. And then there was one from Marty Blake, who sent his letter to Coach Bob Davis telling him how he would like to represent Kenny in any negotiations with the NBA or ABA.

Just when you thought Kenny could not possibly play anymore basketball for a while, he agreed to play in several post season all-star games.

The first of those was the prestigious Portsmouth (Virginia) Invitational Tournament in late March. Originated in 1953 by the local recreation department, it had attracted some of the biggest names in the game such as Rick Barry, Earl "The Pearl" Monroe, Dave Cowens, Doug Moe and Larry Brown. There were players with Kentucky connections who played there, too. Dick Cunningham, from Murray; Tom Hagan, a Louisville native who played at Vanderbilt; Tom Boerwinkle, MMI High School, who starred at Tennessee: Garfield Smith, from Campbellsville, and played at Eastern; Wayne Chapman, from Owensboro, who played at Western; and Harley "Skeeter" Swift, a star at East Tennessee State who still holds the Diddle Arena single game scoring record by an opponent against Western with 42 points.

All of these players were either in the NBA or ABA.

"It was a venue where players had the opportunity to showcase their talent in front of professional scouts," says Kenny. "I played on Yale Dolsey's team. He was one of the founders of the PIT, and we won the tournament.

"We had on our team Jim O'Brien from Boston College, who later became the head coach at Ohio State (he also played for the Kentucky Colonels in the ABA), Jim Larrinaga from Providence, who now coaches at Miami (Florida), and Walt Szczerbiak. His son Wally plays in the NBA."

Kenny was named to the five-man all-star team at the tourney's conclusion.

"I remember Szczerbiak was named the MVP and his prize was a color T.V.," Kenny offered. "Back then that was considered a big deal.

"I didn't have to miss much school since the tournament was a Friday thru Monday, and I was already taking graduate classes the last semester, and most were in the evening."

Three days later on March 27th, Kenny was checking into what was then the Colonel Sanders Inn on Newburg Road at Watterson Expressway in Louisville. He would be a part of a Kentucky All-Star team that would take on a group from Tennessee in a preliminary game before a game involving the Kentucky Colonels. It was one of those in-and-out games: check in on Saturday, practice Sunday morning, play the game Sunday night, and go home. For Kenny it was one more visit to Freedom Hall, and the opportunity for family and friends to see him in an all-star game.

The roster was jammed with U.K. and Western players as could be expected. Jim McDaniels, Clarence Glover and Jim Rose from the Hilltoppers; Larry Steele, Mike Casey and Jim Dinwiddie from the Wildcats; Morehead's Jim Day, Eastern's Carl Greenfield, Bellarmine John Linneman, and Kenny Davis was there, too. Adolph Rupp would be in charge of the Kentucky team, and Vanderbilt's Roy Skinner, Tennessee.

"The last game I participated in that historic building will be forever etched in my memory. It was a "home and home" series…Tennessee game played in Vanderbilt's Memorial gymnasium, and Kentucky's game in Louisville's Freedom Hall.

"My first contact with Coach Rupp was in 1966 when I was invited as his guest (they were recruiting me at the time) to attend the Tennessee-Kentucky game played in Memorial Coliseum. Don't remember much about the game other than Adolph constantly throwing "barbs" toward referee Lou Bello. At the all-star game I had received positive comments from him about my play during my Georgetown career. I was in Lexington often playing in pick-up games with Mike Pratt, Dan Issel, and Mike Casey, so I was excited to get the opportunity to play for him.

"The established rules for this all-star game were that all players on the squad play equal amount of time in the first half and the coach could choose who he wished to play the second half.

"First half ended with me and several other Kentucky players never entering the game. Second half began and the same players who played most of the minutes the first-half were back out on the floor for the center circle jump. (Yes, still did that in 1971).

"I am sure Coach Rupp could have thought of a thousand places he would rather have been than coaching this game, as it was evident he was not too observant as to what was happening out on the court. On different occasions he would look over at Claude Vaughan, his assistant, and ask, "Who in the hell took that shot?" Sensing that, I decided to take matters into my own hands to ensure I would at least make an appearance into the game.

"A timeout was called about the seventeen minute mark and as our players were coming to the bench I jumped up and patted Jim Dinwiddie (one of Rupp's players from U.K.) on the back and said, 'I'm in for you,' ran to the scorer's table and checked myself into the game. I ended up playing extended minutes and scored several points that helped our team to victory.

"I certainly meant no disrespect to Coach Rupp for what I did, as I held him in high esteem and still do, but by becoming the all-time leading scorer in Kentucky college basketball history, I felt I had earned the opportunity to play some minutes in that game. Also I had family and friends there, and I did not want to disappoint them by never leaving the bench.

"I took that chance, as I felt if Coach Rupp detected what I had done, he would not make me leave the arena, rather he would simply make me sit back down…and I was doing that anyway!"

McDaniels scored 25 to lead Kentucky to a 108-94 win. Day had 18 points and 10 boards while Kenny Davis made the best use of his playing time by scoring 12 points. Rose also scored 12, and Casey 11. Ted "Hound Dog" McClain, the former Tennessee State great, had 23 for the losers.

A return game was played the following Sunday night in Nashville with Western's John Oldham, coaching the Kentucky team, while Tennessee State's Ed Martin handled Tennessee.

But there was more.

In between the pair of "local" all-star games was the annual East-West College game sponsored by the National Association of Basketball Coaches and played in Dayton, Ohio on April 3, 1971. The game was big, and an invitation to play meant that the recipient was considered to be among the nation's best. Coaches Adolph Rupp and Henry Iba were the brainchild in establishing the all-star game and you bet when Kenny Davis was named to the East team, he would definitely be there.

He joined East teammates Jim McDaniels, Artis Gilmore, Rich Yunkus, John Roche, Austin Carr, Jim Cleamons, and Charlie Davis. The West squad included Marv Roberts, Willie Humes, Dave Robisch, Willie Sojourner, Cliff Meely and Mike Newlin.

In an overtime shootout the East, coached by Northwestern's Dutch Louborg, won 106-104 with McDaniels earning the game's MVP honors by scoring 29 points. Kenny scored six.

Still the post season all-star games kept calling, and still Kenny kept playing.

"I participated in all of the games that sent me an invitation," he said. "I was honored that they felt I had the talent to participate. It also gave me the opportunity to measure my game against the best seniors in the country."

But for Kenny Davis it was more than just his game in the present. There was still something deep inside that drove him.

"The label that was attached to me and others who played for NAIA schools was we were "small college" players," said Davis. "I resented that and it was one of the reasons I played as well as I could in those games. I felt I was not only playing for myself, but for those other players who were not getting the opportunity to showcase their talents. I carried that "chip" into the Olympic Trials realizing I would probably have to do more than players from NCAA schools, because of the "label" I was carrying."

If Kenny was worn out he didn't show it, and when the North-South game promoter's called, he was ready.

It was a two game series with the first being played in the Carolina Coliseum on the campus of the University of South Carolina. Kenny, playing on the South team with Gilmore, John Mengelt (Auburn), and Rich Yunkus (Georgia Tech), lost 106-98 to a Randy Denton (Duke) led North team. Kenny scored 10.

A few days later in Dorton Arena in Raleigh, North Carolina, Kenny had 16 points as his South squad won 114-99.

"By this time I was off of scholarship at Georgetown and money was tight," Kenny offered. "The North-South promoters gave each player

$500 for playing. I needed the money as it would pay our rent for the remainder of the year. But in order to maintain my "amateur" status I had the game organizer to make out the check to a neighbor of ours who lived in married housing at Georgetown. I'm glad those archaic rules no longer exist for today's athletes."

Chapter Twelve

Bill Summers, Chairman of the U.S. Olympic Basketball Committee, was saddled with the responsibility of keeping basketball teams that competed internationally at a winning level.

There had been growing concerns that other countries were closing the gap on U.S. basketball, even to the point of actually winning championships. For years the United States had been able to send what was considered second and third tier teams and still win. Those days were over, and there were several reasons why.

The rest of the world had to put an emphasis on basketball, thus attracting better athletes who would have played other sports. Then, our best college and professional coaches had been hired to conduct clinics on foreign soil in an effort to "educate" their coaches. U.S. colleges then began to recruit internationally, bringing players here to receive better coaching, better competition, and train in our facilities. And what seemed like overnight, teams from throughout Europe and South America were appearing on college schedules throughout the country. Although most of their games were labeled "exhibition", it soon became evident that their teams were competitive. But the bottom line, however, was that some of our country's best collegians were not willing to play. Several of the top players just plain didn't want to go through the "tryout" process.

As the 1971 Pan-American Games in Cali, Columbia neared, it became very important to select a team that could win. And not to be lost in it all was this team could be a precursor to the 1972 Olympics in Munich, Germany. The Pan Am Games were regarded as a master tune-up for the Olympics, and the U.S. needed to get it right.

On June 12, 1971, Kenny received a letter from Bill Summers with congratulations on being selected to participate in the "Pan American & Olympic Development and Selection Camp" at the Air Force Academy in Colorado.

What the letter meant was that Kenny would be competing with 54 others in hopes of making the 12-man squad. There were no guarantees, but he just might have a leg-up in at least getting strong consideration as Coach Jim Gudger, of East Texas State had been named to coach the team. Gudger had become familiar with Kenny two years earlier when he coached a group of collegians in a 20-game tour in Africa.

The 55 players were split into six teams with individual coaches, and from July 5 thru July 26, the squads played against each other as well as games with nearby local teams.

Kenny was not the only Kentuckian trying out. Bird Averitt from Hopkinsville, who had played at Pepperdine, was there. Over the years several players with Kentucky connections had played in the Pan-Am Games, some even going on to make the Olympic team. The 1959 team included Jack Adams, Eastern Kentucky; Bill Evans, U.K.; Don Goldstein, U of L; Adrian Smith, U.K.; and Dan Swartz, Morehead. In 1963, Ed Smallwood, a Louisville Central High School grad who played at Evansville, made the team. And in 1967, Darel Carrier, Western Kentucky; Mike Silliman, Louisville St. X High School, and U.S. Military Academy; and Wes Unseld, U of L were on the squad.

When Kenny Davis was named to the team he kept the streak alive. Joining him on the team were Henry Wilmore, Michigan; Bob McAdoo (Vincennes Junior College), North Carolina; Paul Westphal, Southern Cal; Jim Chones, Marquette; Dwight Jones, Houston; Luke Witte, Ohio State; Chuck Terry, Long Beach State; Bob Ford, Purdue; Jim Forbes, Texas-El Paso; Don Buse, Evansville; and Brian Taylor, Princeton.

Legendary Coach Henry Iba had been heavily involved in the selection of the Pan-Am team, having already been chosen to coach the team the following year in the '72 Olympics in Munich. The hopes, of course, were for the Pan-Am team to demonstrate ability to adapt to international rules with a premium on teamwork, defense, and rebounding, all trademarks of Iba teams.

Immediately upon arriving in Cali, Columbia, U.S. officials knew there were problems. It started with the housing setup. The basketball team was assigned 12 to a room with six double-decker beds in the four-story dorms. It was crowded to say the least. And the coaches were not happy either. Toilets didn't work…only one faucet in the bathroom, and it was cold water only. "It took two days to get a plumber," said assistant coach John Bach. "We operated out of suitcases with no place to store or hang our clothes. And needless to say the players have not reacted favorable, which is another example of how our prime athletes have been spoiled."

All of this, and the games hadn't even started. But once they did the U.S. Basketball Olympics Committee's worse fears were realized.

In what was called the biggest upset in the history of the Pan-American Games, Cuba stunned the U.S. basketball team 73-69. It was the second loss in the history of the Games for the Americans, beaten in 1959 by Argentina.

"There are not many teams in the United States who can handle this Cuban team," said U.S. Coach Jim Gudger.

"We weren't cohesive," offered Bach, "but still had a chance in the last three minutes."

Looking for anything, just anything, officials pointed to all of the away-from-the-court activities that go along with such a ceremonial-driven event as the Pan Am Games.

The 4,000 plus athletes marched into the 60,000 seat soccer stadium amid flying doves, numerous speeches and a torch runner, and often it is these opening and closing happenings that long after the game is a blurred memory. Still it was hot and tiring…took hours, first lining up at the Village, then bussing in, waiting in the basketball arena…and then marching.

Apparently there was only one wooden basketball floor in South America, as the floor was moved from one gym to another for games. Most of the floors team's practiced on were concrete, tile, or terrazzo.

Before the games got underway, all of the 380 U.S. athletes were told there would be no complaints. "Our athletes were told not to make derogatory comments to the press," said Clifford H. Buck, president of the U.S. Olympic Committee. "We try to make them realize that they are ambassadors for the United States of America."

U.S. officials were cautious about being too quick to jump on the city of Cali, when the truth was that few others wanted the Games. Not many cities expressed an interest in absorbing the financial and physical obligations. Cali, a tropical city of 700,000 located 90 miles from the Pacific coast, made the best offer.

"It hurts morale to be jammed into double decker bunk beds in overcrowded rooms," added Buck. "But we will live with it."

If the U.S. athletes were supposed to be ambassadors for America, what was the host Colombians supposed to be? With shouts of "Yanqui go home" from the host nation's fans, whistles and jeers became commonplace when Americans competed.

"They don't like us here," complained Russ Hodge, a decathlon performer. "Even in Russia they gave us better applause than they do here for a good performance."

Against a weak Surinam team the U.S. won 128-48. By comparison Brazil defeated the same team 135-56. So when the two teams met, it was expected to be a close game. And it was.

The U.S. team trailed at the half 33-28, and then trailed by six with three minutes left in the game. Failing to convert several chances to win in regulation, the American's pulled it out in overtime 81-79.

Brian Taylor led the U.S. with 19, while Chones added 17, Jones 12, and McAdoo 10. Kenny scored three.

The end result for the U.S. basketball team was far beyond disappointment. In a complicated scoring formula to rate teams, the Americans failed to move beyond the preliminary round on "goal point average" after compiling the same 3-1 record as Brazil and Cuba.

Brazil won the gold medal, Puerto Rico the silver, and Cuba the bronze.

CHAPTER THIRTEEN

After the Pan American games Kenny had some decisions to make. No longer was he the kid from rural Wayne County who played for a little NAIA Baptist college in Georgetown, Kentucky. He was now Kenny Davis, worldwide traveler and world class basketball player. He had done much more than fill out rosters. More often than not, if not the top player, he was certainly among them.

Through it all he was able to raise his game to the level of competition.

Looking back on it, what would the odds have been in 1966 that Clyde and Zula Davis' son, Kenny, would someday play basketball in the Olympics? A million to one? Maybe higher?

When he finally returned to Georgetown after the Pan-Am Games where he and Rita now called home, it was thought that he would go into coaching. After all, there supposedly would be a job teaching and coaching at nearby Scott County High School. But suddenly things changed.

He had been drafted by the Carolina Cougars in the ABA and the New York Knickerbockers in the NBA, but without a "no-cut" contract job security would be questionable at best.

"After making the World Games and Pan-American Games, I felt I had a decent shot at making the '72 Olympic Team," he said. "But it meant I had a year to wait. But since I had graduated, I needed to find a way to make some money while in training for the trials."

Georgetown College had permitted Kenny and Rita to continue paying a modest rent to remain in their house at 702B Warrendale. And that would prove to be invaluable in allowing Kenny Davis, one of their own, to pursue a dream, against all odds.

"The ideal position for me was to find a spot at Scott County High School to teach and coach. Coach Everett "Mutt" Varney was a friend, and a man I had great respect for, but he didn't have a position available to hire me," Kenny said. "Rita got a position there teaching business education, so I had to look elsewhere."

It became big news, at least around Georgetown and Frankfort, when Kenny landed a job in state government as an employee with the Department of Economic Security as a computer programmer.

"David Lee had been a former Tiger basketball great, and was the head coach at Franklin County High School," recalled Kenny. "He grew up in Frankfort and had lots of contacts, and suggested to Jim Thompson that I was looking for a job. He gave me a position. Soon I settled into making the short drive to Frankfort and back each day."

Though Rita and Kenny were now gainfully employed and relatively comfortable with their lives, basketball was still Kenny's priority, especially his hopes of making the 1972 Olympic basketball team.

But, still there was a major hill to climb. No longer a student-athlete at Georgetown College, he realized that in order to fulfill a dream, in order to make the team, he would have to do it as an AAU representative and not NAIA.

And the road he would have to travel would be with Marathon Oil, the AAU team based out of Lexington

Kenny's job in Frankfort permitted him to play a full schedule with Lexington-based Marathon Oil, an AAU affiliate. Even though the odds were against Kenny, it was the AAU route that he hoped would lead to a spot on the Olympic roster. Over the last several years there had been a tug-of-war power struggle between the AAU and NCAA when it came to the selection of international basketball teams, but still the AAU was assured of at least one spot on the team.

This is where Kenny was focused, first getting an invitation to the Olympic Trials, and when he did, he would prove to any doubters that might still be out there, he could and would do it.

The progression of Kenny's foray into competitive international basketball had been almost text book. First there had been a collegiate all-star team, then a bump up to the World Games, followed by a roster spot on the Pan-American team. In fact the Pan-Am Games were under the auspice of the Olympic Committee, and it was hoped by those in charge that those earning their way onto this team would have a leg up toward the Olympics.

Kenny's initial contact for the Pan Am team had been with a letter from the Olympic Basketball Committee, informing him he had been nominated by the NAIA to try out for the team. Cutting through the chase, making the Pan-Am team had been for years a stepping stone to the Olympics. So when Kenny was selected for the Pan-Am team in 1971, the odds for him to at least have a chance to make the Olympics had greatly increased.

When Kenny let it be known that he had hopes of being on the '72 Olympic basketball team, there might have been a few who believed him. Being an Olympian was a far cry from playing in the World University Games or even the prestigious Pan-American Games. What were the odds that he would even be invited to the tryouts?

In the meantime there was a young man in Lexington, Kentucky named Henry Scott Baesler, who went by the name of Scotty, who had become active in organizing a team of former college players around the Lexington area. Most of them had been stars, but for an assortment of reasons, not selected to play at the professional level. They did, however, feel there was still some basketball left in their lives and Baesler was doing his part to fill the void.

Scotty Baesler was the perfect person to do it. A local boy who had played at Bryan Station High School, he went on to fight and claw his way into Adolph Rupp's starting lineup at the University of Kentucky, averaging double figures his final two years while captaining the team.

Though never a mega star in the Wildcat tradition of teammate Cotton Nash, he was quite popular with the sold out crowds in Memorial Coliseum, and when he graduated in 1963, he, like so many others, still wanted to play. Keep in mind, this was a time before European teams were luring American players to foreign countries with lucrative paydays.

Baesler had entered law school, but still found time to put together a team sponsored by Jerry's Restaurants in 1964. "We had plenty of guys who still wanted to play," says Baesler.

As a player-coach his Jerry's team played all over the area and with Baesler's contacts his team was now playing exhibition games against college teams. It didn't surprise those who knew Baesler, when several years later, he became Lexington's mayor and then a U.S. Congressman.

Soon the teams evolved into Marathon Oil and meshed into the National AAU Basketball League, a group of teams each sponsored by private business and industrial firms which provide financial support for the operation of the teams and the league.

By now another U.K. player, Pat Doyle, had joined Baesler as a coach. Doyle brought a pretty fair resume' of his own to the team. A 1959 Mr. Basketball in Kentucky, he led his North Marshall high school team to the state title, and now working in state government in Frankfort, he was more interested in coaching than playing.

With this said, Kenny Davis' timing was everything. There was now a place for him to maintain his amateur status, be gainfully employed and still be able to chase a longshot dream—making the Olympic basketball team.

The AAU had long been the driving force for assembling Olympic basketball teams, and by 1968 the NCAA had emerged in the eyes of the so-called basketball authorities as the major influence in keeping the U.S. competitive in international basketball.

Baesler had become political in regard to serving as a member of the Executive Committee for the AAU as well as a member of the Olympic Basketball Committee. While there was now a movement for the NCAA to be more of a determining factor who made the team, it was people like Baesler who battled to keep at least one roster spot available for an AAU player. After all, the AAU had a proven record of international success and an unblemished record when it came to the Olympics, having never lost a single game. And believe it or not, there was a day when playing for the Phillips Oilers or Akron Goodyear was more lucrative than an NBA contract.

Kenny had a brief fling in AAU ball soon after graduating from Georgetown, when he played in a 5-day national tournament in London – London, Kentucky. He played on a team called the Southeastern All-Stars, a team of just-graduated seniors and all from Kentucky colleges. Also competing in the tournament was Marathon Oil. But it was the powerful Armed Forces team that won the tourney, defeating first Southeastern 86-81 in the semis and then Marathon Oil in the finals, 90-77.

So now that Kenny had a taste of AAU ball locally, he was confident he could play at Marathon Oil's level of play. And so was Scotty Baesler.

"We handpicked our players," Baesler said, "And we knew all about Kenny. We already had Cecil Tuttle who was really, really good for us, so if we could get Kenny he'd add to our offense."

Marathon Oil in the beginning played a 10 to 15 game schedule from early til late November.

"We were one of the first amateur teams that played colleges, like the AAC (Atlantic Coast Conference)," Baesler says. "They paid us about $2,000 a game for travel expenses."

As Kenny had hoped, on April 21, the letter inviting him to the Colorado Springs Air Force Academy complex finally arrived. Not long after, his airline ticket and details on what clothing to bring arrived by mail. The instructions were to the point: "We suggest that you bring practice trunks, strap, and basketball shoes. Since your entire stay will be on the Air Force Academy rounds, you need only bring slacks, sports shirts with collars, sufficient underwear and street shoes. Evenings will be cold and a jacket is advisable. Under no circumstances will you be permitted in the dining room in a T-shirt or any shirt without a collar. This is an Academy regulation. Above all, travel "light"—one suitcase only, please."

The letter was signed by M.K. "Bill" Summers, Chairman, Men's Olympic Basketball Committee. And then Summers handwrote a personal note: "This is the year Kenny."

On June 10, 1972, Kenny Davis, with 65 other young men, all hoping for a chance at basketball glory, arrived in Colorado.

Chapter Fourteen

Originally the Olympic Committee had planned on bringing sixty-six candidates to Colorado Springs beginning June 12 through June 24, but only 59 were on hand when eight teams were announced with each having seven or eight players, a coach, manager, and even two officials with international rules experience.

Coach Henry Iba was the man in charge and his assistant coaches were Penn States John Bach, and Don Haskins, who had defeated Adolph Rupp and his heavily favored Kentucky team in 1966 for an NCAA championship, at what then was Texas Western. Haskins knew Iba well, having played for him at Oklahoma State.

Along with Summers, from Brownstown, Indiana, Herb Mols from Buffalo, New York, the Olympic team's assistant manager, was on hand to scrutinize the assembling of the team. These two, away from the basketball court were the face of basketball in the United States as their team prepared for Munich.

Only five players from the 1971 Pan-Am team for various reasons were present when the trials began. Kenny, Jim Forbes, Dwight Jones, Chuck Terry, and Luke Witte were the only ones invited. These were, however, several big names not there. Among them Bill Walton, Julius Erving, Jim Chones, and David Thompson were noticeably absent.

But it wasn't just the missing players that were discussed.

Some said Iba should have never been the coach. Others said the game at that point in his life had already passed him by. As fantastic as his coaching records were, there were those who could easily point to the 68-year-old legendary coach's numbers over the last few years as proof.

Though he had coached teams to two Olympic golds in '64 and '68, his defense at all cost had fallen out of favor with many of the so-called experts. Before Iba's retirement at Oklahoma State in 1970, his record in the previous five years was an unimpressive 47-80, and the last Iba team to play in a Final Four was back in 1951. Numbers don't lie and by all indications Coach Iba was not a coach on the upswing, despite winning 767 college games that included back-to-back NCAA titles in 1945 and 1946. His style really never changed. With a strict control offense and physical man-to-man defense, Iba felt that "keeping possession of the ball was the strength of his defense."

His offense was unmistakable; set play...no freelancing...run the set...back it out...reset...run it again. This is the way he had always done it, and when it wasn't, his raspy voice that sounded like a man who had screamed way too much, would demand it be done again... and again.

Bobby Knight was about to begin his second year of coaching at Indiana when he was tapped to be one of the coaches at the 1972 Olympic Trials. Even at 31-years-old he wasn't much for keeping his opinions to himself. He told anyone within earshot, including referees, what he thought.

He had become upset over the number of whistles. "Damn it, let 'em play," he said. "Stick that whistle up your butt." Of course he got a technical foul. But the next day Knight wore his own referee shirt with a whistle around his neck just to make a point. The following morning he saw Iba while walking past him. Iba, eating breakfast, never looking up, said loud enough for Knight to hear, "I don't want to see that damn referee shirt today."

It was the Iba way or no way. Head strong, demanding and assertive because he had earned the right to be, there is no better example of "do-it-my-way" than in a college game against Kansas. His team finished with only four players on the court even though he had players on the bench. He simply did it because he didn't want to play them.

But before being too critical consider some facts: Henry Iba did not politic for the Olympic job. More than less, he was a compromise choice.

UCLA's John Wooden was a logical choice. His Bruins were on top of the collegiate basketball world at the time, and his selection would surely have meant his star Bill Walton, too, would have been a part of the team. It was strongly felt that a team with Walton and anybody else was sure-fire gold medal winners.

Insiders said Wooden resented having to fill out an application for the "job". They said he had earned the right to be appointed, not having to compete. There was even another thought. Not only should Wooden be the coach, but he should also bring the core of his UCLA team with him. After all, it had been done before when Adolph Rupp, as an assistant coach in 1948 brought his 1948 NCAA championship Kentucky team with him.

"That damn Wooden was upset about not getting the job", said Bobby Knight. And if he cared about basketball like he said he did, he'd have made Walton play. Hell, Walton was given a pass all the way to Munich. He said he was hurt or something, but hell he was okay by the time the Olympics came around."

And speaking of Rupp, there were supporters pushing for him to be the coach. However, at 65-years-old, not in the best of health, and with his collegiate coaching career coming to a close, he was ruled out. So, too was a rising star, Dean Smith at the University of North Carolina. It was felt he lacked the experience to oversee an Olympic team on the world's biggest hoops stage. And with the vast improvement of international competition, mainly the Russians, almost through the process of elimination, the Olympic Committee turned to their proven "old-salt", Henry Iba.

Worrying about who was and who wasn't the coach, or anything else for that matter, was the furthest thing from Kenny Davis' mind. He would leave the gossip and rumors to others. He was in Colorado to play basketball.

He knew there were some really good basketball players there. He also knew he had played more international games than anyone else. And there was a huge difference in the rules that most were used to in the college game. That's why Iba and Summers were insistent in assigning game experienced referees to each of the eight teams.

Summers' letter of congratulations to Kenny made it clear that the "Selection Committee" would watch the games and select the final twelve players. And because each team was few in numbers, individual playing time would be equal. The letter went on to say players would be judged on "individual ability on the floor, dedication to team work, all around attitude, coachability, and willingness to corporate."

Scotty Baesler picks it up here:

"I was there as a member of the overall selection committee, but wasn't one of those that made the final selection," he said. "The AAU guys were really outnumbered by the NCAA members."

There was one person, however, that Baesler says carried the AAU torch and pushed Kenny Davis in particular, for making the team.

"Carl Slavosky was an insurance businessman in Cincinnati who was very active in AAU basketball (remember AAU ball back then was totally different than what it is today)," said Baesler. "He was in on all the discussions, so every day I'd ask him what the hell is going on. He carried the water for Kenny and the AAU. He was impressed with Kenny and felt Kenny was deserving, because of what he had done at the trials. If Carl had anything to say about it, Kenny was not going to be left off of the team. Carl was Kenny's biggest fan at the Trials and he kept telling me everything would be okay. I wasn't in the room when Kenny was selected, but Carl was.

"Playing at Georgetown really had nothing to do with Kenny making the team," Baesler continued. "It was what he did in Colorado Springs. He earned it, and Carl Slavosky never let up in pushing for him."

Now, more than forty years later, this is the first time Kenny is aware of Carl Slavosky.

"I never met nor knew who he was," Kenny says. "This is a new name that I was not aware of." It's amazing as we go through life how many people are watching us that we aren't even aware of. Apparently Mr. Slavosky was watching me and I didn't even know it."

The 1972 Olympics were the last year the AAU was involved with picking a basketball team, and even though Scotty Baesler says the NCAA outnumbered the AAU members on the final selection committee, the official listing of members showed the AAU with 24, the NCAA with 12, Armed Forces four, NAIA six, Junior College one, National High Schools, two, and YMCA one.

For sure the AAU representatives were feeling the pinch of being, not necessarily left out, but their influence being diminished over the last decade.

Officially at the Trials Kenny and Gene Kirk were representing Marathon Oil, but in a strange sort of way former Kentucky star Mike Casey was there and also listed from Marathon Oil. Casey had an outstanding two weeks, but narrowly missed making the team. But then when the Shelby County native was named as an alternate, his affiliation was tagged with Southeastern All-Stars AAU. Though Casey had played a game here and there for Marathon Oil over the years, it was his association with Southeastern that led to an invitation to the Olympic Trials.

Kirk had played in college at Delta State in Mississippi.

"He could defend and rebound," recalled Kenny, who played with Kirk at Marathon. "He was unselfish and his most difficult task each game was deciding whether to pass the ball to Phil Argento, George Bryant or me, as we all three always thought we were "wide open." Gene claimed he always had spending money as bribes came his way from all three of us before every game."

There was no way of knowing it back then, but several people involved as either a coach or a player at the Trials went on to have celebrated careers. In fact at the Pan-Am Trials in 1971, Kenny was on the same team as a kid from Army named Mike Krzyzewski. Also trying to make the team was James Brown, from Dartmouth, who went on to be one of the top television sportscasters in the country. At the Olympic Trials players in contention for a spot on the '72 team were Gregg Popovich, Air Force Academy; George Karl, North Carolina; Mike D'Antoni, Marshall University, and Bobby Crimins, South Carolina.

There was, however, one person, neither a player nor a coach, but a referee who became infamous among Western Kentucky University fans for a call he made against the Hilltoppers in an NCAA tournament game in Iowa City against Michigan in 1966. With Western leading 79-78 and only seconds remaining, Western's Greg Smith and Michigan's Cazzie Russell were involved in a jump ball. Referee Steve Honzo whistled Smith for a foul on the jump against Russell, who to his credit sank both free throws for an 80-79 win. To Hilltopper crazies Honzo is one of the all-time villains. But in the picture with all of the Olympic Trial participants, there was Honzo in his stripped shirt standing behind Bobby Knight.

Chapter Fifteen

As Kenny Davis was poised to possibly achieve one of the highest honors any athlete can receive…representing his country in the Olympics, he couldn't help but think back to when his trek began, at least mentally.

"The seed for me even thinking about playing in the Olympics began in the rec room of Anderson Hall on Georgetown's campus," recalls Kenny. "There was a black and white TV located in the dorm where our team lived, and every moment between classes and fall practice we were glued to the set watching the '68 games in Mexico City. I can still recall the announcer's excitement at the spectacular play of Spencer Haywood and his teammates at those games."

Now with the first few days of practices out of the way in Colorado Springs, Kenny felt good about his chances to make the team.

"My dream began to emerge in my mind after successfully making both the World Games and Pan-Am squads," says Kenny. "I was a starter for some games on both of those teams, and knew that the majority of the '72 team would probably be selected from those units due to the international experience I had gained playing in those world tournaments."

It was one thing to have the experience of 26 international games under his belt, but it was another to play well at the Trials and exhibit a focus of being a team player that would impress the coaches…especially Coach Henry Iba.

"I had 26 additional state department games under my belt," continued Kenny. "So I was feeling confident about my chances."

The knowledge of international rules gave him a jumpstart.

"I performed a move that took the other guys a little time to pick up," he said. "The referees don't have to touch the ball after a turnover. As soon as he would blow the whistle and made his call,

I would immediately strip the ball from the offender's hand and inbounds to a teammate before the defense was set for an easy fast break basket. Time after time I got away with that until they finally caught on to it."

But there was another element…one that doesn't show up in a box score, a team photo or even in a conversation. It's called desire.

From those days of riding his bicycle all over Monticello as a youngster, Kenny's motivation to play basketball more often came from within himself. Even at an early age he had figured it out. If he wanted to be good, it was up to him. Not a family member or even a coach.

That same desire continued into and through his days at Georgetown and into those post-season all-star games where he competed with and against the "big-name" guys. He fared very well. And now with the competition reaching another level he was more than ready for the challenge.

"I respected the players who were here from the NCAA who had made a name for themselves," Kenny said. "But since I had competed against them for the past three summers, I was not fearful they would out play me."

Deep down he still had a "rub." It wasn't personal against any one team, player, or even a coach. But still it was an underlying issue that kept him going in his pursuit of excellence to become a basketball player. It stayed in the back of his mind, not something he dwelled on, but something he never really let go of.

Labeled as a little guy from a little school in Wayne County, he was overlooked for many of the high profile post season all-star games even though he was the top scorer in Kentucky. And then he was passed over by the "big blue" in Lexington, only getting a courteous invite to a game and a country ham dinner. And though he did wind up with a scholarship to Western, things just didn't work out.

And there he was again at a little school, this time Georgetown College. It's what kept him motivated.

But there was still another ace Kenny had up his sleeve.

"I also knew that for many of those players it would be their first experience playing in the thin air of the Colorado altitude. If you have never competed in those conditions, it can be a shock as I found out on my first training camp there in 1970," he offered. "If you were not in top shape, a week could go by before you felt comfortable in those conditions, and since the duration of the trials was only two weeks, you would have no chance to make the squad."

Kenny knew absolutely that he needed to be in the best physical condition of his life. And even before he was selected for the Trials, he set out to accomplish that. He followed a rigid training schedule, pushing himself while using the facilities on Georgetown's campus. He was primed and ready when he was notified of his inclusion in the group to make the Olympic basketball team.

"The night before I left for Colorado, I ran the fastest mile that I had ever run with a 5:15 time," he said. "It might not have been something an Olympian miler would be proud of, but it wasn't bad for a basketball player. I also knew that once the season was over and the lack of a coach pressing you to stay in shape, many players did not have the discipline to keep them in top form."

Just to get to this point as a basketball player from a small town in Kentucky might seem to be against all odds. But the way Kenny looked at it, the odds had now increased in his favor. Now, betting against him to make the team would be like betting against the house in Vegas.

"To go there and not make the squad because someone had greater talent than me was something I could live with. But I knew if I did not make the team because I was not in peak physical shape would haunt me for the rest of my life."

Kenny was confident that whatever they threw at him in practice would not compare to what he had gone through for five years (counting red shirt period) of playing in college for Bob Davis.

And speaking of Coach Davis, he had for a number of years been involved as a member of the Olympic basketball committee, and had been selected to be a part of the coaching staff in Colorado Springs.

When Kenny discovered that his college coach would also be his "unit" coach at the trials, he wasn't particularly thrilled about it.

"You've got to remember he was a coach and I was a player," he says. "Even at Georgetown he didn't get close to his players, so in Colorado I was only around him at practice and games. We never interacted away from the court.

"He remained distant so as not to show any favoritism toward me. No doubt he was pulling for me, but I was going to have to make the team on my own merits, not from any help from him. The majority of the players at that camp had no idea he was my college coach."

Kenny further points to a statistic that in his opinion is proof no favoritism was shown. "Twelve players, including three on my team, played more minutes in the exhibition games that I did."

Most of the coaches for the eight teams at the Trials had their successful ways of doing things with their college teams, but their roles here would be entirely different. They would not be implementing any particular styles or strategies here. Instead they had been selected for this prestigious assignment to only carry out Coach Iba's plan for winning another gold medal in Munich.

Iba instructed the coaches as to what he wanted to see offensively and defensively from the teams. And it was up to the coaches to make sure they did. Their roles were somewhat limited.

Kenny picks it up again:

"This gave Iba an idea how each player could fit into their role using his motion offense and hard-nosed defense. Coach Iba was criticized for his slow down play, but his strategy was that the foreign teams had not progressed as well on defense as they had offensively. He felt that if we passed the ball enough times their defense would break down and a good shot would result."

While the practices and games were high spirited, the stakes for each of the participants were equally high. Making the Olympic team would be life altering. But with it all, a business-like approach came from most of the players, realizing that making this team was different from anything they had ever experienced before. After all, this was the Olympics.

"We were cautioned to keep our emotions under control as we were reminded that foreign teams at times would use subs to provoke the other team's best player as a strategy to get him ejected from the game," Kenny said.

Today, decades later, Kenny is reminded of a practice incident.

"Each time I look in the mirror, I see it," he says. "As I was going for a loose ball I sustained an injury to my lip. And without any numbing medicine and on the sidelines while my teammates continued to practice, they used five stitches to put it back together. Five minutes later I was back out on the court. Don't know if it was a doctor or a trainer that did the stitching, but whoever, it was wasn't very professional as I still have the scar."

Later Kenny learned that Coach Iba was there and had seen it all. "I think he admired my ability to withstand the pain."

All of the practices and games were conducted using international rules, and soon it was easy for the coaches to spot those who had only competed using American rules.

"There were certain things I could do to exploit this weakness and those of us who had played against foreign teams had a skill set that gave us an advantage once the scrimmage games began."

(Kenny felt like the lack of international experience may have prevented Kentucky's Mike Casey from making the Olympic team, as he had an excellent Trial).

At the conclusion of the first week of the Trials, none of the players were privy to any information that might be out there as to how anyone measured up to each other as competitors. But soon after the second week was underway with full-court games being played, the players begin to see where they stood, as statistics from each of the eight teams were posted on a regular basis.

Coaches Iba, Haskins and Bach confirmed their roles as "observers" only during the practices and games.

"I don't recall a single time during the two weeks that they provided any coaching input whatsoever while we were on the court," Kenny recalled. "They gave no signals as how they felt about one player versus another."

Kenny found out later that after the day's practices were concluded, the three Olympic coaches would meet, review what they had seen and decide what they wanted implemented the following day.

Practice, eating and sleeping comprised the majority of each player's 24-hour days, leaving little time to just "hang out".

"Our sleeping quarters were some distance from where we ate and occasionally I would cross paths with Gene (Kirk) and Mike (Casey)," said Kenny. "However, each team, and we were on different teams, had a different schedule. I was limited with my time spent with them. And there definitely was no time with Coach Davis. Most of my time was spent with our "green" team (squads were named according to the color of our uniforms.)

Kenny had been a big scorer at Wayne County High, and after four years at Georgetown College he had scored 3,000-plus points, but now all of that was out the window. Now the game was defense.

"It began to change when I was playing on those international teams," he says. "I soon realized that everyone on those teams could score, and I knew if I was to get significant playing time I must also play defense like I had never played before."

It wasn't that Kenny Davis couldn't play defense. Before, it hadn't been his role as a team player. Defense wasn't difficult. All he had to do was revert back to his freshman year in high school at Wayne County.

"Coach Ray Mills demonstrated those fundamentals to me as a freshman," he said. "The key to successful defense is whether you wish to apply the effort and take ownership in keeping your opponent from scoring."

And Kenny didn't have to look far for an example.

"I played one year with Van Phillips at Georgetown. He was a Monticello boy who had played for Joe Harper there, and he was one of the best at guarding me. In practice that year he drew the assignment in practice. He was relentless, and I credit him for making me a better player because in most games I did not face a better defender than Van was.

"While I didn't play a lot of defense at Georgetown, Jim Reid and Mike Calhoun both claimed they had to guard their man and mine, it didn't mean that I couldn't. Also there was a greater chance I could foul out playing defense, and Coach Davis would not be pleased if that occurred."

With Kenny on the brink of making the team, he still found time to think about the folks back home, especially wife, Rita.

But now Kenny wasn't the only Davis that was tough. So was Rita Davis.

"By the time I went to Colorado Springs, Rita was conditioned to my absence while playing basketball," he says. "We had been married six weeks, and then I was gone for nine straight, playing in the World Games in Italy. During our courtship she quickly bought into my dream of making the Olympic team, and she became very supportive in my efforts to realize that dream. She kept busy with her college classes, graduating in three years with a degree in business."

Rita, though, was not the only one who had bought into Kenny's dream.

"Both of our parents helped financially, which made it possible for me to compete. And because of this support, possibly I had a greater incentive to make the team than some of the other players at the Trials. The least I could do to show my appreciation was to compete as hard as possible," Kenny said.

"I just thought Kenny would play basketball in college, and it would be over," Rita laughed. "I never dreamed basketball would be his life. I knew he couldn't play forever."

Chapter Sixteen

As the final days turned into the final hours at Colorado Springs, a slight edginess appeared among the players and coaches. It had been a tough two weeks and everybody was tired. Everybody was ready to find out who was in and who was out. And besides that, they were ready to go home.

"In my mind going into the final two games, based on stats, twenty of us still felt we had a shot of making the team," Kenny said. "The other 39 probably knew that whatever they did would not be sufficient to garner a spot.

"I don't recall, however, those final two games being any more spirited than the first six exhibition games we had played. But I did not see every game, because as soon as we finished ours we were bused back to the academy due to some of the scrimmages being off site."

After the last game all 59 players were called together, and informed that the selection committee would meet later that night to finalize the '72 Munich Olympic basketball team. The 12 names would be posted the following morning at 9 a.m. outside their meeting room.

Looking back, Kenny suspected the committee had been meeting every night since the scrimmage games began the second week, and he felt they probably had at least four spots nailed down as to who they wanted on the team.

"Swen Nater, Dwight Jones, Doug Collins, and Ed Ratleff were some of the guys who had been dominant in the scrimmages," said Kenny. "So I really doubt that the final night's selection was a lengthy process.

"We played a scrimmage our last night and didn't get back to the academy until late. We were excited that it was over so we kind of celebrated back at our room (the "green" team). None of us slept well, I can assure you."

As they had done the previous two weeks, the players were up and out to breakfast early the next morning.

"After that we all moseyed over to the meeting room where they were going to post the names of who made it," Kenny said. "It was more of a relief than anything when I realized my name was on the list. There were some really disappointed faces, but for our "green" team there was some shouts of happiness. Ed Ratleff and I had made it. (James Forbes would later be added to the team), and Gene Kirk also shared in my happiness."

Mister Iba wasn't one to scratch and claw for a certain player. The other members of the selection committee could do that, but for the most part they knew how he felt from the previous nightly meetings. He did, say however, he wanted the right to pick the twelfth player on the team.

The "chosen twelve" created a bit of a stir. There were some who made the team that were considered shoo-ins, while there were others who were left off who had also been considered shoo-ins.

Collins had had a great Trial. So, too, had Nater, Ed Ratleff, and Tom McMillen. They were expected to make it. So were Marvin Barnes, Larry Kenon, Allan Hornyak, Barry Parkhill, Jim Forbes, and Kermit Washington.

The nation hadn't heard of Collins until the Olympics. Growing up in Benton, Illinois, a town of 6,000, his dad was the County Sheriff.

"I lived in a jail for four years," laughs Collins. "I was Benton's Opie. As a junior I was 6-foot and about 130-pounds. I didn't start on the varsity until my senior year when I began to grow."

Collins had a good year, and several schools began to show interest, one of which was Western Kentucky University, the same school Kenny had signed with in 1966. At the time Jim Richards was Western's assistant coach and he remembers the recruitment of Collins.

"We already had a youngster from Benton (Danny Johnson) so we knew the program. Doug had really developed as a senior, but his coach, Rich Herrin, said he wasn't sure Collins could play at our level, so we backed off. Man, did we miss out."

Instead Collins went to Illinois State, where he averaged over 32 points his senior year and played for Will Robinson, who had coached Spencer Haywood at Detroit Pershing High School at Illinois State. Robinson became the first black Division I head coach in the nation.

"Coach Robinson became a father to me," says Collins. "He didn't teach me basketball, he taught me about life. He wasn't an X and O guy, he was an all about life guy."

But along with Kenny Davis (Marathon Oil), the Olympic team was Mike Bantom (St. Joseph), Jim Brewer (Minnesota), Tom Burleson (North Carolina State), Doug Collins (Illinois State), Tom Henderson (San Jacinto Junior College), Bobby Jones (North Carolina), Dwight Jones (Houston), Kevin Joyce (South Carolina), Ed Ratleff (Long Beach State), John Brown (Missiouri) and Swen Nater (UCLA).

And who was Iba's personal pick? Tom Henderson, the junior college kid. Kenny was the only AAU player named.

While Kenny's dream lived on, for the others, theirs was over, at least for making the Olympics. Those who didn't make the team went back to their dorms to retrieve their clothing and prepare for their trip home. The new Olympic basketball team was held over for an extra day to go over the upcoming schedule and to begin the "Iba indoctrination" in getting ready for the remainder of the summer leading up to Munich.

"Coach Davis was one of the first to congratulate me after the team's announcement," Kenny said. "His personality did not allow him to show a lot of emotion, but I could sense that he was proud for me. And it was also an achievement in his coaching career as he understood that I had now become the most decorated player he had ever coached."

Kenny is quick to point out that many had felt Cecil Tuttle should have been Georgetown College's first Olympian based on his play at the '64 Trials.

"Knowing how talented he was from our years playing together for Marathon Oil, if I had been the second player from Georgetown, I would still have been just as thrilled as I definitely would have been following in great footsteps. Cecil was one Hazel Green (high school) Bullfrog that could play."

Kenny continues:

"My first call was to Rita sharing the news that I had made the team and that I would be delayed an additional day coming home. I recall her mother, who was a big sports fan, telling her that she knew all along I would make the squad. It would have been nice and I would have slept better if she had shared that confidence with me.

"Rita immediately called mom and dad, who were informed of the good news and I am sure it did not take long to hit the local radio station, as calls began to pour in from my Monticello hometown friends."

It might have seemed like a lifetime effort had gone into his becoming an Olympian and maybe it was. He couldn't remember when he didn't play basketball. And now here he was, still in Colorado Springs. While most were saying their good-byes, and wishing each other well, the chosen-twelve's journey was far from over.

Kenny's departure from Colorado would be at least one more day before he could return to Kentucky and Rita.

"The next day Kenny was on his way back home, where Rita met him at Bluegrass Field in Lexington.

"Although it was the end of a journey that I had been on for three years, it didn't totally sink in until I arrived back home, and was immediately greeted with well-wishers from everyone that it seemed I had ever known. It also felt like everyone wanted a moment of my time to either do a TV, radio, or newspaper interview."

Kenny only had ten days before he would have to report to San Francisco, and then fly to Hawaii where he and his teammates would be, for the next 26 days preparing for Munich.

"Rita and I needed to get away, but with limited money it had to be a short trip," he said. "A friend got us a room at the Weston Hotel downtown Cincinnati. It was a short drive from Georgetown, so we went up to Kings Island and then to watch the Reds play baseball."

Although the twelve players weren't given any specific instructions from Coach Iba or Committee Chairman Summers when they left Colorado Springs, Kenny sensed what was in store for him in Hawaii. He had heard the Iba stories and he had seen the veteran coach watching, watching, and more watching at the Trials.

"I just knew what we would be facing, so I continued to work out as hard as I did before the Trials," he said.

It was a good thing he did.

The first week of July 1972, Kenny's airline ticket arrived in the mail to his home in Georgetown. Bill Summers, in a letter, reminded Kenny about several things to bring with them: birth certificate; passport application completely filled out; and his AAU card. "Please make application at once, enclosing $1.50 with your application," he was instructed. He was also told "heavy clothing is not essential in Hawaii as temperatures will be around 78-80 degrees, so travel light with only summer clothing."

Rita drove Kenny to Lexington the morning of July 10, where they kissed each other and said goodbye as he boarded his flight to San Francisco. The strain and stress had subsided a bit, as there were no more worries of making the team. It now had become more of a business…a business about winning games. One game in particular…beating the Russians. In all of the international games Kenny had played in, in four tries he had never played on a team that beat the Russians.

What would the odds have been of that happening?

When Kenny arrived in San Francisco, he went to a private phone near the baggage area. He picked it up and rang directly in to the Airport Marina Hotel. In minutes a limo was on its way to pick up the kid from Monticello, Kentucky. This is the way Olympians were supposed to be treated.

For the next three days the team would be living in luxury in one of the great cities of the world. What a start. Kenny could only imagine what Hawaii would be like if San Francisco was like this.

Mister Iba (he was called "Mister" more than Coach, Henry or Hank) had requested that all of the players and coaching staff gather for a late lunch before heading over to Stanford University for their first practice session. The following two days were spent at nearby Travis Air Force Base practicing.

This was the first sign of things to come. It wasn't a vacation; they weren't here to see the sights. If they could see anything from their hotel window, that would be as good as it got. They were on a mission… one they hoped would end with an Olympic gold medal.

"It seemed like Coach Iba always liked to do things at a military base," Kenny said. "And if he was near one, that's where he went."

During the three days in the Bay area, Sears (official outfitters) clothing people came in and took measurements for each member of the team. For Kenny, his Olympic street and parade clothing wouldn't be out of the ordinary size-wise, but for several others like 7'4" Tom Burleson, 6'11" Tom McMillen, and 6'9" Jim Brewer it was a little more involved. The plan was to present the team with their new wardrobe just before departing for Munich in September.

"The weather in San Francisco was spectacular and it would have been my wish to have stayed there instead of Hawaii," says Kenny.

Kenny probably wasn't alone in his feelings about San Francisco, but still there was the allure of Hawaii. Who wouldn't want to go to this vacation paradise, especially to play basketball?

"When I first heard about going to Hawaii, I thought it would be the highlight of the summer," Kenny said. "But that was in the beginning."

While the Olympic basketball was leaving their hearts in San Francisco, the coaches, Iba, Haskins, and Bach, had set their sights on the Naval Submarine Base at Pearl Harbor, Hawaii, and on July 14, that's where they arrived.

Chapter Seventeen

Most the 12 players were a seasoned group, though not nearly to the degree of the Russians who they expected to be playing in Munich. Their seasoning had come from playing on various teams while growing up, grade school, junior high, high school, and college. The Russians were not only seasoned, but cured, like a good country ham. They had played together for years…on the same team.

The U.S. team actually was the youngest in Olympic history, averaging just over 20 years, with Kenny being the oldest, just turning 24 in Munich.

And now here was Iba, with just 21 days, challenged to whip his unit into a well-oiled basketball machine. It was pretty much the same process he had used in coaching his American teams to two Olympic gold's in 1964, and 1968. It would surely mean success in 1972.

Upon arriving in Hawaii, the brief taste of luxury accommodations was quickly forgotten. Iba's military-style philosophy meant that his team would live like soldiers…or, in this case, sailors.

Housed in barracks and sleeping on cots, the players were not prepared for those Spartan conditions. And besides that the heat and humidity was much worse than the 80 degrees Bill Summers had told them to expect. The heat, beds, mosquitoes, and lack of air conditioning began to quickly become issues with the team. Was this the way Olympians were to be treated? But the truth was, even though they were Olympian's, as of yet, they hadn't won anything.

But as tough as the living conditions were, the practices were just as bad. For Kenny, it did cross his mind that Coach Bob Davis had done a good job in preparing him for days like this.

"At Colorado Springs Coach Iba just watched," Kenny offered. "But in Hawaii we were now down to one team, and it was like he had a microscope zeroed in on us."

From day one their schedule was set. Could boot camp or even prison been much different? A 6:30 a.m. wake-up, followed by breakfast, the team took the court by 7 a.m. Two or three hours of practices, depending what needed to be worked on, was followed by an early lunch. The team would return to the barracks for a short rest and another practice. Dinner was usually served around 5:30 p.m., and then another practice.

"This was Coach Iba's way of getting us ready to beat the Russians," says Kenny. "It was really the only way he knew how and he was the coach."

The practice facility was something the players would never forget either. In the book "Stolen Glory" by Mike Brewster and Taps Gallagher, it was described as "an open-air gym sunk several steps into the ground and protected from the sun and heat by a mere canopy."

There was something else about the facility, however, they not only heard about, but saw with their own eyes. On December 7, 1941, in the aftermath of the Japanese attack on Pearl Harbor, some 400 bodies were laid out on the gym floor. The day before the attack the new gym had been dedicated by a band from the U.S.S. *Arizona*. Many of those sailors, who had been involved in the ceremony, had now returned, this time with their blood spilling into the gym's floor. Those blood stains were still there for the Americans to see every day for 21 days.

Some of the players weren't up to the rigors of three-a-days, others were unaccustomed to the frequent berating dished out on broken or missed assignments. However, there was one among the group who never missed a beat. He had done it all and heard it all in practice. It was Kenny Davis, from a little Baptist college in Georgetown, Kentucky. Coach Davis had prepared him well.

Even in Hawaii there was underlying signs that the power struggle between the AAU and NCAA had not been completely put to rest. Throughout most of the Olympic basketball history, the AAU had the power position when it came to the coaches and players. But, in 1972, though the best players were from NCAA schools, the AAU still maintained control over the selection process, so there was no way a basketball team would be going to Munich without at least one AAU player.

"My stats were strong enough for me to make the team," Kenny said. "I'm sure it riled some NCAA people who wanted to once and for all wrestle the power from the AAU.

"Their next move was to try to run me off when we got to Pearl Harbor. Coach Haskins was the main person involved. He had me do personal things in my street clothes and then make me run laps for being late to practice…didn't happen, but he did it enough times that I knew it had to be planned."

Compared to how hard Kenny had worked to become a basketball player, this was nothing.

"After ten days it finally stopped as he realized it was not going to be effective," Kenny said. "In fact I believe I earned his respect before we left Pearl Harbor. It gave me a great deal of satisfaction.

Kenny wasn't through.

"He (Haskins) had no idea of my background playing for Coach Davis or he would have realized that his efforts were a waste of time. Another incentive for Coach Haskins running me off was the opportunity to replace me with one of his own players from UTEP, Jim Forbes. That was borne out when Forbes was added to the squad later when John Brown got hurt."

It was Iba's way of doing things. He thrived on the tension that had been created and relished the hand-to-hand combat being displayed around the basket.

Although the last thing Iba, Haskins and Bach would ever let on to their team was a concern of beating the Russians. But all one had to do was look no further than Iba's style. More than forty years later there was a strong sense that Iba got it all wrong with his style of play. Mister Iba didn't get this far without knowing the game. And he also had the pulse of the Russians.

He had seen them coming on for years. He also had seen who wasn't on his '72 team. Deep down Iba probably thought the Russians could move up and down the floor with his team. Yes, he would do it the only way he knew how to win—just like he had done all those times before: tough man-to-man defense, on offense pass it, pass it, pass it again, and look for a shot.

Kenny recalled a meeting in the locker room at Pearl Harbor. There was a chalkboard nearby and Coach Iba found a piece of chalk and in a herky-jerky style wrote "50" on the board.

"He said keep the Russians from scoring 50 points and we would win in Munich."

Now remember, this was still while the team was practicing—long before they had played their first game in Munich. If this had been a pre-game talk before his team took the floor for the gold medal game in Munich it would possibly have been easier for the Olympians to understand. But here it was, "50", halfway through the wretched practice sessions in Hawaii.

That's how far ahead of the game Iba was. That's how brilliant of a coach he was.

It was even talked about that there was a chance Bill Walton might join the team, not necessarily in Pearl Harbor, but just before the team left for Munich.

Kenny had his take on that happening:

"The rest of us would have resented that happening with what we all had gone through at Colorado Springs and especially Pearl Harbor," he said years later.

But as talk continued about Walton's "will he or won't he" be there, it was the other UCLA guy, Swen Nater, who was also in the conversation.

Nater, even though Walton's back-up at UCLA, had been a star at the Olympic Trials. With the highest point average among the 59 players at 21 per game, the 7'2" center showed some offensive skills that Iba felt would make up for Walton's absence. But Nater let it be known that he was having a problem with food. As a big man he had always had trouble eating soon after practice. It was his routine of pouring in liquids and eating later. Here in Pearl Harbor however, he had to eat on a regular schedule. In fact the Olympians had to eat when the pilots and sailors ate on the base. Nater claimed to have lost close to 30 pounds in the short time he had been there, so he had decided he had had enough. He quit the team and headed back to the mainland.

The loss was big, but in typical Iba-style he didn't show it or say it. Later, however, others did.

"We didn't have a real go-to player," says Kenny. "When the chips were down, Nater could have been one of those who could have made a difference because of his offense."

No sooner than Nater was on the plane back to California, Iba quickly named Tom McMillen as his replacement. And soon after the

Maryland player's arrival the team was moved out of their bug-infested barracks and into some apartments at the naval base.

Doug Collins recalled that upon his arrival, the 6'10" Maryland player was getting worked over pretty good by some of the others who had discovered new blood. Coach Iba told him to fill a pillowcase with soap bars and take care of 'em.

Finally, Iba and his staff allowed for a few tours of the island, particularly the surrounding area that included Pearl Harbor and its history. In an attempt to show that Iba and his coaches did indeed have a humane side to them, the players had access to bowling and movies on the base, and even an out-of-character luau was planned for an evening.

But it was Kenny Davis who had the "away-from-basketball" experience of the trip.

Assistant Coach Bach invited Kenny to accompany him on a little excursion. Bach, a former Navy pilot, had rented a small two-seater aircraft and wanted Kenny to join him in the air as he re-traced the Japanese sneak attack on Pearl Harbor.

"We were up there on a beautiful day when Coach Bach said we might be running low on fuel," said Kenny. "He said just to be safe we were going back."

In the meantime Bach's plane had lost radio communication with the ground tower, and the Penn State coach had a few anxious moments before safely landing.

"I didn't know there was a real problem until after we were on the ground," Kenny said. "Coach Bach was calm in the air, but once we landed I could see he was shaking."

One of the reasons Iba had been keen on practicing in Hawaii was, of course the isolation, but so too the fact that he could scrimmage against some of the nearby military teams. They wouldn't be as talented as his team, but by being older they perhaps would offer up some very competitive maturity and toughness. Something on the order of what the Russians would bring to the hardwood in Munich.

"They were older guys," said Kenny who was 23 and the oldest member of the U.S. team. "We played four games and won them all, but there weren't any crowds watching us because they were all closed to the public."

An August 4 date had been established to finish the practices and fly from Hawaii back to each player's home, where they would re-charge for a few days before reuniting again in order to play several exhibition games against some better competition before heading to Munich.

But on the day before the team departed Pearl Harbor, one of Kenny's teammates, John Brown from Missouri, had sprained an ankle while cutting for the basket. An X-ray determined no fracture, so perhaps the few days off would allow it to heal. But it didn't, and when a second X-ray revealed a stress fracture, Iba had to make a tough decision, a business decision that dropped Brown from the team. It was devastating to Brown. The Trials and 21-day grind at Pearl Harbor were all for naught. In Iba's system he needed twelve players playing, not eleven with one watching. No one on the team particularly liked it, but that's the way it was. Mister Iba, the coach, had spoken. "When John left the team, I think it caught all of us by surprise when we found out he wouldn't be going to Munich with us," Kenny recalled. "We didn't protest. Back then you just didn't do that…especially with Coach Iba. We didn't question him."

For Kenny, when he returned to Kentucky, there had not been enough time for him to share his stories with everyone who wanted to hear them. But he was not alone. There were eleven others just like him experiencing the same thing back at their homes.

The Olympians once again came together on August 10 in Dayton, Ohio, to take on a team made up of Oscar Robertson, Spencer Haywood, Bill Bradley, Charlie Scott, Terry Dischinger, Bill Hosket, and Adrian "Odie" Smith, the ex-U.K. star still playing at the age of 37. It was the first time the team had been tested against top flight competition, and Iba's system of controlling the game at both ends of the floor led to a 65-52 win. Holding this group of all-stars to 52 points was impressive.

Even though it was Iba's system, the coach was not actually there for the game, and neither were the national television cameras, which had planned on airing the team's first "official" game other than practice. Iba had remained at his home in Stillwater, Oklahoma to take care of personal business before leaving for Germany, and the Hughes Television Network was unable to generate enough sponsorship to make it a go.

Still, assistants Haskins and Bach were not out of their element when it came to head coaching.

With Dayton being the first gathering spot after the team had traveled back to their homes, Doug Collins never made it home to Illinois.

He told a Dayton sportswriter that instead, "I spent the last four days at my girl's house in Iowa."

The second exhibition game was played in Louisville with a watered down team of pro all-stars. But it didn't start out that way. Initially several of the ABA Kentucky Colonels, including Dan Issel and Claude Virden were going to play until the team's president Mike Storen stepped in.

"No one is a bigger advocate of the United Fund, the Martin Luther King game, the muscular dystrophy fund, the U.S. Olympics, any of them, than the Colonels. But if a player is signed to a multiple-year contract and is injured in August and unable to play in October, who is going to pick up his contract? Are the promoters going to pay him? Nine out of 10 times the answer is no," Storen said.

The pro all-stars were composed of Clem Haskins, Butch Beard, Mike Grosso, Jim "Goose" Ligon, Howard Wright, George Tinsley, Jim Rose, and the Olympians won 84-71 but, Beard and Haskins were not overly impressed.

Beard said the team was going to have trouble with the Russians, and Haskins felt the team was too deliberate on offense and needed to run.

With John Brown now gone, Iba quickly turned to his pool of alternates again, but there were still a few voices out there that wanted Walton. Iba nixed that and the logical choice was Jim Forbes. He had played for Coach Don Haskins at UTEP, and remember Haskins had played for Iba at Oklahoma State. The system stayed the same, so when Forbes arrived he hit the court knowing what to do.

To further point out the precisioned detail in which Iba demanded from his team, the proper way to stand at attention with the playing of the national anthem was even practiced. There would be no slouching, rocking back and forth or leaning. In a rigid position, with right hand over heart, all eyes on the American flag. After all, that's the way they would be standing on the podium for the gold medal ceremony in Munich.

The Olympians won next in Los Angeles by two points, 65-63, against the likes of Henry Bibby, Paul Westphal, Ron Taylor, Curtis Rowe, Sidney Wicks, Jim Chones and Bill Hewitt.

It was then a cross-country flight to Greensboro, North Carolina for an 82-76 win over a team led by Dr. J. (Julius Erving), Jim Cardwell, Mike Grosso, and Ted McClain. And in winding up their five game exhibition tour, the Olympians defeated an all-star group in Buffalo, New York 76-65. That team featured Randy Denton, Randy Smith, Wendell Ladner, Jerry Crocker and Johnny Green.

Finally on August 16, the team arrived in Washington, D.C. for a ceremonial sendoff at the White House. Here it wasn't just the basketball team, it was all of the United States Olympians, all 528 of them. This gathering was followed by a luncheon hosted by First Lady Pat Nixon. It was here in Washington D.C. the team received the clothing they would wear during the march into Olympic Stadium.

President Nixon sent a form letter to all of the U.S. Olympians before the games began. The letter was about patriotism and being an American, yet he quoted Roger Bannister, an Englishman just after he broke the four minute mile barrier. And then Nixon wrote, "A wise Roman remarked that in great attempts, it is glorious even to fail."

Chapter Eighteen

The Olympic teams flew charter flights out of Washington, D.C. for a seven-hour trip to Munich, arriving on September 19. Also making the trip, but on commercial flights, were Kevin Joyce's mother, Tom McMillen's dad, along with his college coach at Maryland, Lefty Driesell, the fiancées of Tom Burleson and Doug Collins, and Lucias Mitchell, the Kentucky State coach.

"We never really talked about me going to Munich," says Rita. "We didn't have the money, and I really didn't have the desire. If I went Kenny would be worried about me, and I'd become a distraction for him."

The entire U.S. Olympic team, shortly after their arrival, toured the infamous German concentration camp at Dachau. For Kenny and his teammates it was a break from basketball and a lesson on how cruel the world can often be to innocent victims.

Soon, however, it was back to basketball.

Housed in the Olympic Village, the American basketball team, like all of the others, was expected to conduct their practices in Basketballhalle less than five miles away, but Coach Iba would have none of that. Instead he had made arrangements with the United States government before arriving in Germany to utilize a CIA base some 50-miles outside of Munich.

"Coach Iba wanted to make sure none of the other teams saw what we had been working on all of the time in Hawaii," Kenny said. "And it was really secure. We had to drive our bus through several checkpoints so for sure no one else was going to see our practices."

The opening ceremonies were scheduled for August 26, and if any of the basketball players even had an inkling of skipping them, Iba quickly put that notion to rest. His players would be a part of the 122 countries and more than 7,000 athletes who would march into the stadium.

It was Coach Iba's third Olympics and he knew the importance of this day for all the athletes," Kenny said, "So when he declared the opening ceremonies mandatory all of us began to look forward to it. Other than the moment an athlete wins a medal, the most memorable event in an Olympian's life is being a part of the opening."

It also afforded the U.S. contingency the opportunity to show off their new clothing—Sears finest. Sporting white blazers, red slacks, blue ties and white shoes, the team, along with all of the other Americans, were required to gather four hours before in a designated area to ensure their entrance into the stadium would be well organized and everyone on time.

Unbeknownst to most of the U.S. athletes, controversy brewed concerning the American flag-bearer. In past Olympics' the USOC had made the selection, but this time the athletes had voted on it. By a two-vote margin discus thrower Olga Connolly won. She had won a gold medal in 1956 representing Czechoslovakia, but was now married to American thrower Hal Connolly, and was now competing in her fourth Olympic for the U.S.

Olga Connolly was considered by the USOC to be somewhat a rebel who got behind liberal causes, even to the point of circulating a petition demanding that during the Olympics the U.S. stop their efforts in the Vietnam War.

The immediate concerns for the USOC, however, was that Connolly might ignore a 64-year-old tradition and dip the American flag as she paraded in front of Germany's president. There was good reason for worry, as husband Hal at the '68 Mexico Games was replaced as the flag bearer when he let it be known he would dip the flag. Because she had been elected by the other athletes she could not be replaced. Olga Connolly, however, did not dip the flag as she strolled past the reviewing stand, but instead she lowered it later during the reciting of the Olympic oath.

It had rained that morning and when the sun broke through, Kenny offered that it was one of the nicest days of all in Munich.

"To a TV spectator, you probably think that getting to the stadium and preparing to walk in is a simple task," Kenny said. "But it's not. While the four hours seems like a long time, it passed quickly, and it was the first time we got to seek out those U.S. athletes who had become famous prior to the Olympics. We were all trying to get a glimpse of Mark Spitz and (diver) Micki King.

Marathon Oil Team 1973 AAU National Champions. Front Row: Jim LeMaster, Cecil Tuttle, Scotty Baesler, George Bryant, Kenny Davis, Gene Kirk, Ketchel Strauss, John Adams, Darryl Dunagan, Jim Day. Coach Pat Doyle.

Kenny's "official" picture for the annual Converse yearbook, 1973.

Kenny and Rita with their dog, Pierre, 1973.

Kenny and Rita at King's Island outside of Cincinnati, Ohio, 1973.

Kenny shakes hands with Larry Bird.

Jim Reid (left) with Kenny, 1976.

Marathon's AAU Champions Begin World Cup Defense

By Tom Easterling
Executive Sports Editor

SAO PAULO, Brazil — While Russia's Olympic champion basketball team is touring the United States, the team the Soviets will meet in Lexington on May 11 will be getting in its final preps in the annual World Cup Competition here.

Lexington Marathon Oil, national Amateur Athletic Union champion, will be defending the title it won here last year in this round-robin tournament that also included the Russian Olympic team.

Although Brazil, Russia and Marathon posted identical 2-1 records here last year, Marathon was declared the winner as a result of beating Brazil by 22 points. The Brazilians had beaten Russia by one point, and the Russians, in turn, had defeated Marathon by 10 points.

Marathon will be seeking to beome only the second team to put together back-to-back victories in this tourney. The old Akron Goodyear team won consecutive tournaments. However, no winner of the national AAU tournament has gone on to win the World Cup competition.

The Marathon team, which arrived here Friday, will meet host Brazil in the first game Wednesday night. Puerto Rico will be the foe on Thursday followed by Italy on Friday and Yugoslavia on Saturday night.

The Marathon team is composed mostly of former Kentucky college players. The only exceptions are Ketchel Strauss, who played his high school ball at Jessamine County and college ball at Tennessee Tech, and Larry Bauer, former Illinois player who is joining the team especially for the tournament.

Paul Andrews, who is now completing his Army service, played his college basketball at Union. Kenny Davis, a member of the U.S. Olympic team that lost that disputed decision to the Russians, is a Georgetown graduate.

Eastern will furnish three players on the team. They are George Bryant, Daryl Dunagan and Dan Argabright.

From the University of Kentucky will come Jim Andrews, John Adams, Phil Argento and Jim LeMaster. Two other former UK players are also members of the team. Scotty Baesler is general manager and Pat Doyle is the coach.

When Marathon returns for the Russian game, two undergraduates from last year's UK team will join Andrews from last year's Wildcats. They are juniors-to-be Jimmy Dan Conner and Kevin Grevey.

Tickets for the May 11 game against the Russians are currently on sale at all nine offices of the First Security National Bank and Trust Company.

TO DEFEND TITLE — Lexington Marathon Oil, which left Thursday for the World Cup Competition in Sao Paulo, Brazil, will play Brazil Wednesday night. Seated left to right are Jim Day, Jim Andrews, Dan Argabright, John Adams and Ketchel Strauss. Standing are Scotty Baesler, Kenny Davis, Jim LeMaster Darryl Dunagan, George Bryant, Phil Argento and Pat Doyle. Paul Anderson was not present. (Staff Photo).

Chris Evert (left) with Kenny, 1976.

Kenny with football great, Tony Dorsett. Photo courtesy of Bill Smith Photography.

Davis wins Monticello tennis tourn

Kenny Davis overcame cold weather and strong winds Sunday afternoon to defeat Gary Dick for the 1976 Monticello Open Tennis title 6-2, 6-2.

Dick had combined earlier with Mike Murrell to capture the doubles title over Alan Rankin and John Ricketts by a 6-1, 6-2 score.

Judy Dabney won the woman's division rather easily taking both of her opponents in straight sets, and whipping Ms. Gerald Pratt 6-0, 6-0 Sunday in the finals of the Women's Singles division.

Davis had advanced to the finals by marching through the lower bracket of the pairings rather easily except for a his semi-final match against Murrell, who took the champion to three sets before succumbing.

The former Wayne County Hihg, Georgetwon College, and United States Olympic star in basketball who has given up the sport that had made him such a familiar figure to so many Wayne Countians and now sells tennis and basketball shoes for Converse in both Kentucky and Tennessee.

He has been playing tennis competively for only three years now, but true to the tradition of exceptionally athletes, he has used his athletic ability to overcome other faults in his tennis game to become the 1976 Monticello Open Tennis Singles champion.

Davis defeated John Ricketss, the No. 1 player for Monticello High School in an opening round match 6-1, 6-1, and defeated Jerry Lair by a 6-1, 6-3 total in his Saturday morning quarterfinal match.

In the semifinals Davis ran into a little trouble however, with his opponent Mike Murrell taking the first set rather handily 6-3, but Davis came right back and took the second set at 6-1 to even the match.

After Murrell had taken a 4-3 edge in the final set, the eventual champion reeled off several winners to take the match and gain the finals.

Dick also had little trouble reaching the finals, and failed to even lose a set before the final match on Sunday, taking the measure of Jim Bridgeman 6-1, 6-3, beating Gary Dabney 6-2, 6-4, defeating Alan Rankin 6-2, 6-1, and finally outscoring Doug Roy of Somerest 6-2, 7-5 to gain the finals.

Dick proved to be no match for Davis however, with the winner breaking away from 2-2 scores in both sets to take the last four games and compile his final 6-2, 6-2 margin.

Dick and Murrell also captured the doubles title with little trouble, defeating the team of Doug Roy and Tim Bourne 6-1, 7-5 in he opening round, coming back later that afternoon to take the of the Jerry Lair-Jerry team 6-1, 6-3.

The doubles champ cidentally competing in competition as a team virtue of a forfeit in the s over the Somerset team Haymie.

The finals were played conditions and the winer to be able the weather, a away the doubles crow

With only three cont the women's division it little time for Dabney her superiority over opponents and win the

The tournament was despite weather proble first day and the poor for the finals, with to director Blane Guffey admirable job, and goo truning out for the several occasions.

#140

Sports

KENNY DAVIS, the former Wayne County High School, Georgetown College, and United States Olympic Team basketball star, returned home to Wayne County to excell in another sport these past two weekends. Davis won the Men's Singles title in the Open Tennis Tournament, losing only one set in the entire tournament and defeating Gary Dick 6-2, 6-2 for the title Sunday afternoon. +

GARY DICK

MIKE MURREL

Kenny standing between two Russian players at the 1976 Montreal Olympics.

Kenny presents Converse shoes to members of the Russian basketball team, 1976, Montreal.

Kenny, Mike Calhoun, and Jim Reid, at a coach's clinic in Lexington, 1978.

Kenny and son, Bryan, in 1983.

Pictured l-r: Jill, Kenny and Bryan, 1983.

Kenny receiving his induction into the NAIA Hall of Fame, 1984.

Kenny and Rita at a Converse meeting in Miami, Florida, 1984.

Dr. Bob Davis and wife Joyce with Gov. Martha Layne Collins and husband, Bill.

Pictured l-r: Kenny Davis, Ralph Beard, Gov. Collins, Mike Silliman, and Kenny Rollins, all past basketball Olympians from Kentucky hosted by the governor, 1984.

Kenny at the Banana Open tennis tournament, Hilton Head, SC, 1991.

Jim Reid, Kenny Davis, Mickey Bell (President of Converse), and Mike Calhoun at a coach's clinic in Louisville, 1992.

Pictured l-r: Mike Calhoun, Coach Bob Davis, Rita Davis, Kenny Davis, and Coach Jim Reid, Georgetown College Outstanding Alumni Awards, 1993.

DAVIS: Final game relived

Continued from Page 10

awards ceremony, letting emptiness represent them on the awards platform.

"We felt that the American people wanted us to stand up for what we believed in," Davis said.

Feeling bewildered and cheated, Davis and his teammates returned home with no medal. His basketball career was over.

PART IV

The silver medals are in a bank vault in Switzerland. The Olympic Committee calls every four years to offer the medals to the American team members.

"The U.S. Basketball Hall of Fame wants a medal, just one for their museum, but in order for them to receive one, one of the team members would have to accept the medal, and we won't do that," Davis said.

"I don't feel any bitterness," Davis said. "The judges made a ruling, and we abided by that ruling. You have that in any sport."

Davis credits the many years he played in team sports with his ability to accept things that are not always pleasant. He also says that sports have helped him build a career and get on with his life.

"Life goes on," Davis said. "People move on. That team has gone beyond that game."

The 12 members of the team have not been together since they left Munich, although 10 of them were reunited a few years ago for an interview.

A few years ago a promoter tried to reunite the team for an exhibition game, Davis said. It never materialized.

"Basketball is something that has to played regularly to keep the ability to play," Davis said."When you go into that gym and can't make the shots that were once so natural, you know you are ready to give it up."

"I play a lot of tennis now," he added.

Davis does not plan to go to Atlanta this year. He notes, "You can see it better on TV."

Although his hairline has receded, Davis has maintained the leanness of an athlete. He wore a Converse polo shirt and casual slacks as he told his story to one more reporter last week.

He noted that the 1996 torch bearers are allowed to keep the torch they carried in the run through America. He put it in his trophy case at home and said that is his "medal."

"Losing that gold medal was put into perspective when I saw those Israeli kids carried out in caskets," he remembered with tears in his eyes.

"They didn't get to go home. I did. I came home to my family. I came home alive."

Kenny shakes hands with University of Louisville Athletic Director Bill Olsen, while the Cardinal mascot looks on, 1998.

Kenny and Rita, 1998.

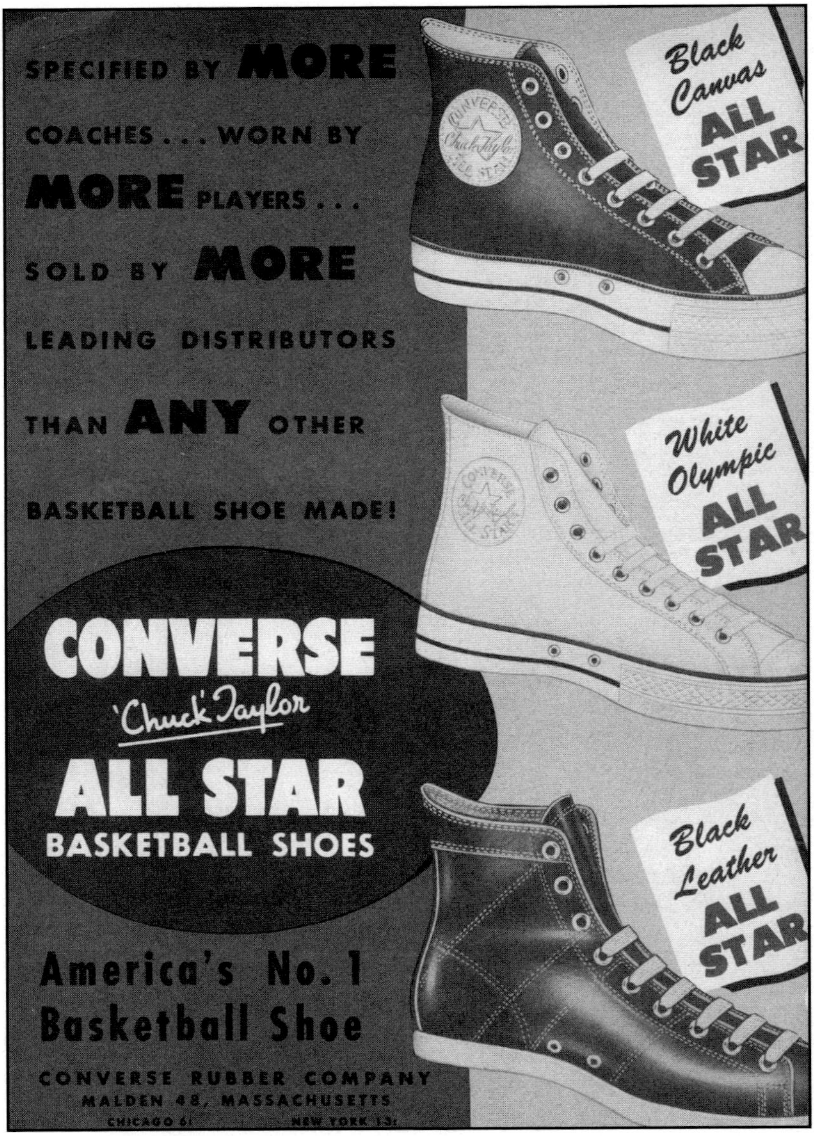
SPECIFIED BY MORE
COACHES . . . WORN BY
MORE PLAYERS . . .
SOLD BY MORE
LEADING DISTRIBUTORS
THAN ANY OTHER
BASKETBALL SHOE MADE!
CONVERSE
'Chuck' Taylor
ALL STAR
BASKETBALL SHOES
America's No. 1
Basketball Shoe
CONVERSE RUBBER COMPANY
MALDEN 48, MASSACHUSETTS
CHICAGO 6 NEW YORK 13
Black Canvas ALL STAR
White Olympic ALL STAR
Black Leather ALL STAR

Dr. Leroy Walker, President Emeritus United States Olympic Committee.

Coach Denny Crum (U. of Louisville) and J.B. Hall (U. of Kentucky) with Kenny Davis in a Converse ad.

Clyde Davis, Kenny's father, on his back porch, September 13, 2013.

Downtown Monticello, Kentucky.

Wayne Theatre, downtown Monticello.

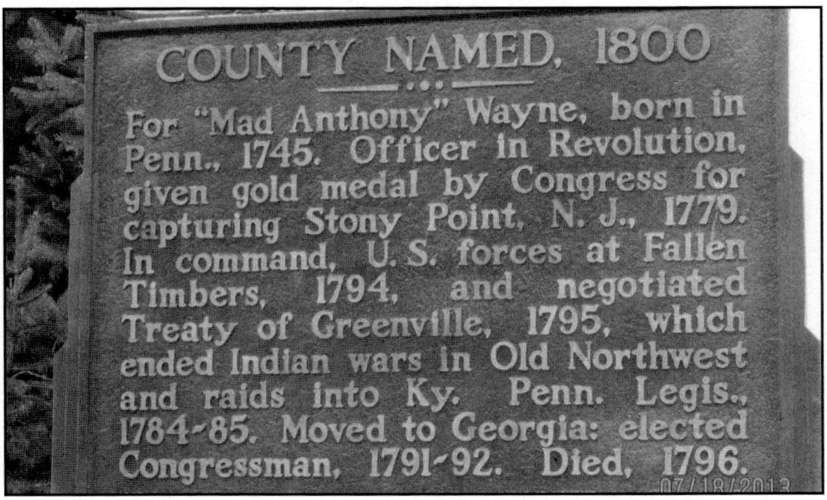

Wayne County historic sign. Note that at least one person from Wayne County received a gold medal!

Kenny in front of the Monticello War Memorial.

Kenny and Juanita Coffey at the history museum.

Kenny with his brother, Ralph, and grandson, Dalton Carter, at The Pool Room.

Wayne County High School

U.S.A. Olympic Men's Basketball Team. Front Row Sitting: Jim Forbes, Ed Ratleff, Tom Burleson, Kenny Davis. Standing: Dwight Jones, Kevin Joyce, Bobby Jones, Tom Henderson, Tom McMillen, Doug Collins. Taken in Washington DC, 1992.

CARRYING THE TORCH

Paint Lick resident and former Olympian Ken Davis talks about Munich, terrorists, medals and keeping life in perspective. *Page 10.*

SPORTS

Torch Song

Ex-Olympian relives memories of Munich 24 years later

By Danetta Barker
Editor

The flame was lit in Greece by sun passing through a piece of cabolic glass. A torch with 22 aluminum reeds, representing the 22 countries that have hosted the Olympic games since 1896, is then lit and begins the journey to Atlanta. Six other torches traveled with the first one to insure that the original flame lit in Greece will light the torch in the Olympic Stadium.

PART I THE ANSWER IS STILL NO

As Ken Davis reached over to ignite his torch from the flame of the previous runner, the light rain that had been falling in North Carrollton, Ky., stopped. He hoisted his torch, and as he began to run the kilometer that marked his second Olympic performance — this time as 1996 Torchbearer, the sun broke through.

"The factories let people come out to watch. Little kids waved American flags. It really made you feel great pride in our country and the Olympic games," Davis said.

"They told me the time passes quickly and that I should run slowly and savor the moment."

Davis knows how quickly time passes. It has been 24 years since he wore a USA uniform as an Olympic basketball player.

That June day in North Carrollton reminded him of the pre-game ceremonies before the 1972 Olympics in Munich, two decades and a continent away.

"It had rained every day since we arrived," Davis remembered. "Everybody thought the rain would spoil the ceremonies, but just before it all started the sun came out and we had a beautiful day."

Davis, now a sales representative for Converse who lives on a farm in nearby Paint Lick, was captain of the men's Olympic basketball team in 1972.

His wife, Rita, is associate vice president for academic affairs and research at Eastern. Daughter Jill is a senior and son Bryan, a sophomore, at Eastern.

Davis and his family live on a farm far removed from the events of the 1972 Olympics — marred in basketball history by the most controversial basketball game ever played; marred in human history by a tragic terrorist action.

But the memories are still vivid, and every four years the world comes calling. Inquiries from "Sports Illustrated," Tom Brokaw of NBC News, and even letters from Switzerland.

Every four years the same questions are asked: "Can you give an interview? Will you accept the medal?"

And the answers are the same.

"I will be happy to be interviewed."

"No, thank you. I will not accept the medal."

With the grace and maturity that only true Olympians can possess, Davis and the 11 other young men on the 1972 USA basketball team made a decision that shocked the sports world.

They refused to accept second best when they had earned the right to wear the gold. They refused to sell their dignity for 12 pieces of silver.

PART II MUNICH 1972

Other players on the team knew that after the Olympics, they had a shot at the pros.

Not 6-foot 1-inch Davis, who coming from a small NAIA school, knew that the Olympic games would be the zenith of his basketball career.

As an All-American player from Georgetown College, Davis averaged 30 points a game, he could easily sink a shot from thirty feet. Because of these skills he was chosen to train for the Olympic team in 1969.

Players were selected differently then. The Olympic coaches tried to put together a team that represented all of America.

Davis and the team arrived in Munich eight days before the opening ceremonies.

On Sept. 5, 1972 at 5 a.m., Arab terrorists broke into the Israeli dorm, shooting two athletes and the coach who was trying to protect them.

The terrorists held eight more athletes hostage and demanded passage out of the country. A helicopter was provided at the airport. The terrorists forced the hostages into the helicopter, but when security fired shots at the Arabs, one of the terrorists threw a hand grenade into the helicopter, killing the hostages.

Davis and his teammates watched from their room.

"You could look through our window into the window of the room the terrorists were using to hold the hostages," Davis said. "We could see the black ski masks the terrorists were wearing."

When the horror was over, 11 Israelis were dead. And the games were postponed for a day.

PART III THE GAME

"We had three games left," Davis said. "You'd like to think that had something to do with our performance, but it probably didn't. Once the game started you blocked everything else out."

The American team had won all 63 games they had played in the history of the Olympics.

But the '72 team went into the game as the underdogs. The press had doubted their ability to beat any team, especially the Russians.

"We had only been together as a team for four weeks. The Russians had played together as a unit for 10 years," Davis said.

The Russians played hard. The Americans played a slower game, not ready to increase the pace until the last half of the game. Realizing they had to get to the basket, to run as hard as the Russians, they closed the 10-point lead in the last seconds of the game.

With six seconds left, guard Doug Collins, from the University of Illinois, intercepted a pass and was fouled. The Americans took the lead for the first time on his two foul shots: 50-49.

With three seconds left, the Russians inbounded the ball. The Russian coach tried to call a timeout to set up a play, running on to the court with members of the team. But he had not followed international rules which allow timeouts only in dead ball situations. The referee stopped play with one second left to clear the court. The Russians inbounded again, but the pass was deflected. The buzzer sounds. The Americans celebrate wildly.

Then the outrage. An international basketball official comes down out of the stands. He overrules the officials and demands that the Russians be given a timeout, the ball and three seconds back on the clock.

"We were out on the floor celebrating, and the next thing we know the game is not over. We have to play three more seconds." Davis said.

The Russian inbounded a pass the length of the floor to a 6-foot 7-inch player, who grabs the pass and makes the winning basket.

In a frenzy of horns, whistles, shouts, cries, arms and legs, the USA team lost 51-50.

"We didn't think they could score in three seconds. They did. We couldn't believe it," Davis said.

Some players wept openly while others had to physically restrain U.S. Coach Hank Iba from attacking the officials. Iba refused to sign the scoresheets and promptly issued a formal complaint. While the international appeals jury reviewed the game to determine the gold medal winner, the U.S. team was holding a meeting of its own.

"We decided unanimously that we would not accept the silver medal," Davis said. "We had to take a stand. We felt that if they were allowed to get away with this that they would try this with every USA team. We felt in our hearts that we had won the gold medal and we would not accept anything less."

Davis, as captain and the oldest member of the team at 23, gave the unanimous decision to the Olympic committee the next morning.

In the midst of an Olympiad that had already gone as mad as anyone could possibly imagine, the Americans boycotted the

SEE DAVIS PAGE 11

Photo submitted

In June Davis took his turn carrying the Olympic torch through the rain-soaked streets of North Carrollton. His one kilometer run was part of the 84-day relay to Atlanta.

Photo submitted

The team which refused its medal included Davis, second from left in row two, Tom Burleson, back row center, and Doug Collins, No. 5. Coach Hank Iba is third from left front

Kenny carrying the torch across Kentucky for the 1996 Atlanta Olympic games.

Kenny displays the Olympic torch he carried on part of his run through Kentucky on the way to the 1966 Atlanta games.

Kenny's son, Bryan, Madison Southern High School prom, 1994.

Kenny's daughter Jill and Eastern Kentucky University athletic trainer, Bobby Barton.

Sandy, Bruce, Kenny, Ralph and Gene at the 60th wedding anniversary celebration for Kenny's parents, July 2000.

Kenny's dad at his 60th wedding anniversary.

Wayne County High School Hall of Fame ceremony, 2002. Courtesy of Wade Upchurch Photography

Kenny and Rita's home near Paint Lick, a house they originally built in 1977.

Kentucky Athletic Hall of Fame induction in Louisville, 2004.

Kenny and Rita in 2004 at the Hall of Fame induction.

Kenny in front of Walker Elementary School.

Kenny at the Olympic team 40th Reunion party, 2012.

Coach Bob Davis stands in his home in front of a painting depicting his years at Auburn University, 2013.

Author Gary P. West with Coach Bob Davis and Kenny in Georgetown, 2013.

Oil Valley Elementary School as it looks in 2014, remodeled into a home.

Bill Moss (right) holds up a 1972 Munich travel bag he had as he ate with Ed Ratleff.

Kenny and Rita at their home.

Kenny and son, Bryan, on their farm.

Kenny's 1998 Harley softtail classic.

Biking across Clay's Ferry with Dennis and Darlene Grant.

Kenny now rides his bike 5,000 miles per year.

Kenny and the scooter he rides today.

1979 Ford pick-up owned by Clyde Davis, Kenny's father. Said Kenny, "It was the only new vehicle he bought his entire life."

Phillips & Phillips law firm in Monticello. Bruce Phillips often traveled with the Davis family to Georgetown to see their son, Van, who was a teammate of Kenny.

Tom Burleson with an over-size putter he used at the reunion golf outing.

Crowd at Georgetown College during a reunion of the 1972 Olympic team.

Ladies at the reunion, sitting l-r: Mrs. John Bach, Stephanie Hassel, Mrs. Jim C. Brewer, Mrs. Kenny Davis, Mrs. Bobby Jones. Standing: Mrs. Jim Forbes and Mrs. Kevin Joyce.

C.M. Newton and Micki King (1972 gold medal diving champion) with Kenny at the reunion.

Neely Thomas, the all-time women's leading basketball scorer at Georgetown College, and Kenny Davis, the all-time men's leading scoring.

Kenny and Billy Reed (right) with Jessica Casebolt (former Georgetown student), Miss Kentucky 2012, who sang the national anthem at the reunion.

A Special Olympics group leads Kenny into the reunion banquet in Lexington.

The entire Kenny Davis family at the Reunion with other Olympians.

Picture of rings given to each team member at the reunion.

Kenny talking to attendees at Georgetown College.

Kenny talking to the banquet crowd at the reunion.

40th Anniversary reunion photo, 2012. Front row, l-r: Asst. Coach John Bach, Tom Burleson, Dwight Jones, Doug Collins, Tom McMillen, Bobby Jones. Back row: John Brown, Jim Forbes, Ed Ratleff, Dwight Jones, Tom Henderson, Bill Moss, Kevin Joyce, and Kenny Davis.

Georgetown College put the welcome sign out for the 1972 Reunion.

Author Gary West with Coach Ray Mills at the reunion.

Converse employees who came to support Kenny at the '72 Olympic reunion, from left: Joe Rogers, Ross Harms, Kenny, David Allen, and Ken Moody.

Kenny and Coach John Bach at the Reunion.

Kenny waiting for the Courage in Munich session to begin, sitting with Joe Rogers, Ross Harms, Ken Moody, and Miranda Harvey.

Kenny with Coach Joe B. Hall.

Kenny with Dwight Jones. Dwight was the USA leading scorer for the '72 Olympic team.

Jessica Casebolt singing the National Anthem at the Courage in Munich banquet.

Kenny's family at the Courage in Munich banquet. Kneeling, l-r: Kellie Carter, Emm Carter, Caroline McCracken, and Davis McCracken. Standing: Junior Worley, Sandy Worley, Shannon Carter, Dalton Carter, Rita Davis, Kenny Davis, Ralph Davis, Carolyn Davis, Shannon McCracken, R.G. Davis, and Tony McCracken.

The original Chuck Taylor shoe in 1948.

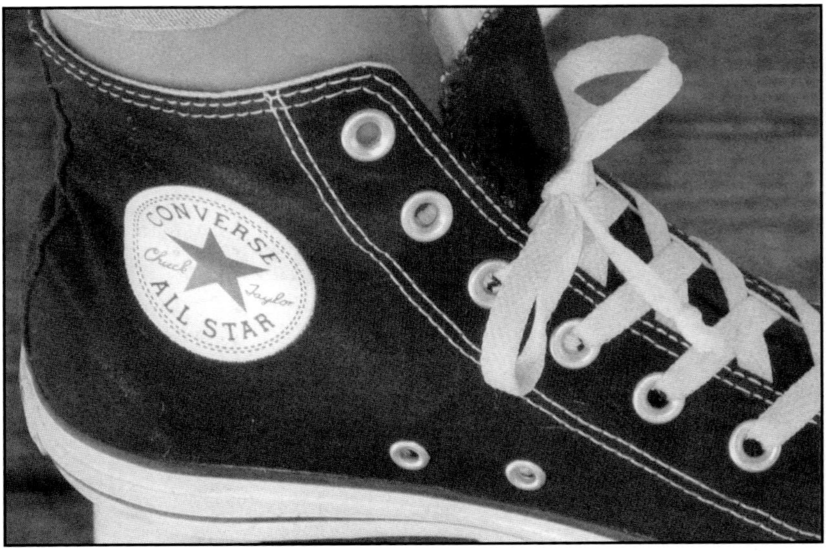

Coverse All-Stars lifestyle shoe, 2014. Still a classic after 66 years!

"We kept hearing about this swimming phenomen who was the world's best. So we really wanted to see him. Based on the rumors, I pictured someone 6'4", 240-pounds. When someone finally pointed him out to me, I was amazed to see that I had been riding up and down the elevator for the past week with him, and did not know who he was. Being 5'11" and 160-pounds caused him to blend in and did not fit his superstar image."

Organizers wanted the Americans to line-up according to height as they marched into the stadium with shortest first, and naturally the basketball team would be the last to enter. Being 6'1", Kenny was positioned about ten rows in front of his teammates.

"As we began to march, I realized I was not with my teammates and felt out of place," he said. "So I fell back and joined them. We had shared so much together and I did not want to miss being with them at this special moment in our lives."

After the U.S. group had paraded in front of the huge crowd to a rendition of "When the Saints Go Marching In," they gathered in the large infield to listen to speeches and for the lighting of the Olympic torch. It was, however, when the thousands of white doves were released, that the unsuspecting Americans realized for the first time they were in a vulnerable spot.

"Some of our fellow Munich Olympians had participated in Mexico City in '68," laughed Kenny. "And we noticed they were carrying rolled-up newspapers. When those doves flew over we realized the wisdom they exhibited in remembering what had happened to them as rookies four years prior. Needless to say most of us first-timers had a major cleaning task when we arrived back to the village."

Coach Iba's micro-control was somewhat compromised with his team being quartered in Olympic Village. They were in fact, for the first time in a long time, able to relax and have a little fun. For those who had family there, they were able to get together and enjoy the various foods from different countries, trade pins and head to the game room.

Athletes were free to roam just about anywhere they wanted in their warm-ups and with proof of identification. Although the some 20,000 blue uniformed German security guards were a presence, they for the most part were unarmed, and certainly not intrusive.

The two-a-day workouts were now behind the Americans, and it was time to play basketball for real.

The 16 basketball teams that had internationally qualified to compete in the Olympics had been divided into two groups, with the United States and Russia seeded number one in each. The Americans had played and lost to one of the teams in their division in the Pan American Games—Cuba, by a 73-69 score. Brazil was also there. And they were good, even a threat to win gold.

Gene Bartow, who had coached at Memphis State, UCLA and UAB, and later was a front runner for the Kentucky job when Joe B. Hall retired, was the coach of the Puerto Rican team that figured to be the stiffest competition for the Russians. (Kentucky hired Eddie Sutton).

One of the stars for Bartow's team was Hector Blondet, who played at Murray State for Coach Cal Luther. Luther was in Munich with a friend, Gene Landolt, who had played basketball at the University of Missouri two decades before, and the two of them had a few event tickets, but not many.

"We bluffed our way in to see Sugar Ray Leonard in the last night of boxing," Luther said. "Each door had German security, but I had picked up a little dialect and told the guard Gene was one of the trainers. We had warm-up suits on and made up a story that we had to deliver something and would be right back out. We didn't have I.D. one, and we were able to get right next to the ring and could even hear Howard Cosell (announcer) talking."

Luther said he got to see Mark Spitz swim as well as the basketball games. The former Murray State coach later coached the Egyptian National team in 1989, and later was involved in the 1990 World Games in Argentina.

An easy 66-35 win for the Americans over Czechoslovakia in the opening game gave the U.S. team a sense of confidence, even though in their minds and that of their coaches, they knew this game really didn't prove they were gold medal worthy—at least not yet.

Then came the Australian's and, as expected, the United States easily won 81-55.

The third encounter would be against the Cubans. Of course they were confident. After all, they had that win the previous year over the U.S. and in their minds they would win again. This American team, however, had only three players from that squad, Kenny, Dwight Jones and Jim Forbes.

For the first time in Munich, Iba and his team were emotionally ready to play. It had been common knowledge that several of the U.S. players had tried to be friendly with some of the Cubans in the Olympic Village, but were turned away. Suddenly this game had become more than just a game. The players felt it and Iba, as only he could, in a five word sentence told his team before they left the locker room: "Let the damn blood run."

And they did, kicking the Cuban team 67-48. Fidel Castro, Cuba's dictator, had been deprived of coming to Munich and personally congratulating his team if they defeated the Americans.

The next team was Brazil. And as expected, the competition had suddenly risen to another level. Tied 26-all at the half, and down by seven with under 12 to go, the U.S. squad rallied to win 61-54.

Iba's team was 4-0 and the most points they had given up was 55. That's what his team had always been about—tough defense.

In the book "Stolen Glory" it was written that to this point in time the American team still seemed uncomfortable with international rules, not throwing the ball inbounds quick enough, not challenging shots near the rim for fear of goal tending, and not being decisive or when to shoot free throws or take the ball out of bounds after being fouled.

With Iba's Olympic experience this would be difficult to understand. After all, he was all about repetition, doing it until you get it right. But still it was hard to argue against his success.

The Americans picked up Olympic win number 60 with a cakewalk 96-31 win over Egypt. Kenny scored six points in this one, logging almost a half of playing time. "I needed some playing time," he said. "It gave me the opportunity to run our offense and it helped my confidence."

Regardless of the score, Iba never let up in his intensity to play defense. With the U.S. leading Egypt 90-20 late in the game, the Egyptians scored two straight baskets. Iba had seen enough…called time out, and sent in five substitutes. "If you don't want to guard someone, these guys will," he told the replaced subs.

Spain, a rapidly improving team on the international scene was next. Even though the U.S. convincingly won 72-56, the game gave a hint of things to come.

Mike Bantom scored on a put-back to supposedly give his team a 43-36 lead. Even though one of the referees had held up his two fingers indicating a made basket, the scoreboard failed to post the score. A timeout and a meeting at the scorer's table with all of the coaches failed to rectify an obvious error. It was never corrected and it seemed that the referee, who by most accounts should be in charge, really wasn't.

Japan was the next to fall, losing 99-56. Now with a 6-0 division record, everyone was naturally keeping a close eye on the Russians. And they were lighting up the scoreboard. While the U.S. was holding their opposition for an average of well under 50 points a game, the Russians were posting wins of 94-52, 94-64, 87-63, 79-66, and 100-87.

While Kenny Davis was focused only on basketball and winning Olympic gold with his teammates, all hell seemed to be breaking loose for the Americans in other events. It could have been described as a comedy of errors, because that's exactly what it was.

Jim Ryan, a kid from Kansas with high hopes of medaling for the U.S. in the 1,500 meters fell, and lost out. Then Frank Shorter entered the Olympic Stadium leading the marathon or at least he thought he was. Suddenly another runner appeared ahead of him. But wait! It was an imposter, a runner who had slipped by security and ran onto the track ahead of Shorter. The shock on Shorter's face told it all, until he realized he was the winner. Initially Shorter couldn't understand why all of the booing, instead of cheering. It was the imposter being booed, however, not Shorter.

The U.S. track team continued to grab the headlines when the team's coach, Stan Wright, gave two of his 100-meter gold medal favorites the wrong starting time. Ray Robinson and Eddie Hart missed the start for a qualifying heat and were disqualified. Wright, the coach, blamed some of the problem with not being able to read German. While America's top two sprinters watched from the sidelines, Russia's Valery Borzov won the 100-meter finals.

And the swimmers were not without their issues.

Sixteen-year-old Rick DeMont, though he had made known a medication he was taking for asthma, was disqualified and forced to return his gold medal after setting a world record in the 1,500-meter freestyle. His coaches knew all about it, but failed to realize the medication was banned.

Even though the Russians were leading the medal count, still there were wondrous Olympic moments for the Americans.

One of those was the swimmer, Mark Spitz, which Kenny and a host of others just wanted a glimpse of. Spitz's quest for seven gold medals was almost derailed when he either purposely or by accident waved to the cheering crowd with a shoe in hand that clearly displayed the Adidas logo. Believe it or not, there was discussion among Olympic officials as to whether or not to let him continue swimming. Ultimately he did, and won seven gold's.

Any event that relied on judges and referees to determine a winner created controversy. But what happened next was something the world had never seen before or even could imagine.

Chapter Nineteen

For three straight Olympiads the city of Detroit had lost out in the final balloting to host the Summer Games. And in 1966 when the I.O.C. came together to select the host city of the '72 Games, Detroit once again had been the United States first choice, but once again the Motor City lost, this time to Munich, Germany, a city chomping at the bit for a chance to show the world a softer, far less confrontational side of their country than Hitler's Nazis had displayed in 1936 in Berlin.

Visitors to Munich saw the beauty of a country immersed in the arts. They heard beautiful music, saw thousands of young people smiling, and the architecture of their centuries old buildings were post cards waiting to be sent back to the States. The country had put its Nazi past behind it and was now marching forward bringing their beautiful city with them while showing the world.

"The streets were full of activity, both day and night, making the pageantry surrounding the games even more colorful," Kenny recalled. "Stores, churches, and gift stand operators went out of their way to make us feel at home. And even at our quarters in the village we had views of the village and lots of flowers. Our building was modern German architecture, built in a stair-step design so that each floor had a balcony. The underground roads left the ground level free of traffic congestion except for pedestrians."

For Munich in 1972, it was the best of times.

However, in the early morning hours of September 5, eight Arab terrorists entered the Olympic Village and headed straight to Building 31. It was here that the Israeli athletes were housed, and it was here that the Olympics changed forever.

There are many variations of how the eight terrorists that called themselves Black September, slipped into the Olympic Village and into Building 31 where the Israelis' were.

Everyone agrees that the Black September group killed two Israelis, a wrestling coach and weightlifter, soon after entering because they resisted. Nine other athletes and coaches were taken hostage, with a demand to cancel the Games, release 200 Palestinian terrorists held in prisons in Israel, and provide them safe passage out of Germany.

Instead, the West German government offered the Black September group unlimited dollars to release the hostages and leave. But they refused.

With the world watching, Olympic head Avery Brundage did in fact bring the Games to a halt, but only temporarily.

In the meantime, ABC television's Jim McKay, a newsman in his earlier years, but now a sportscaster, stayed on the air for 15 straight hours. What the viewers didn't know was under his clothing McKay was wearing the yellow swimsuit he had on when he received the call to go on the air. Quickly he had put his television clothing over the swimsuit.

Former Kentucky Governor John Y. Brown was only a few feet away from McKay's live broadcast.

"I was a guest of Roone Arledge, the head of ABC sports," Brown said. "I was sitting with Roone near Jim McKay when he went on the air. Many, me included, consider McKay's performance, which by the way was without script, to be one of the greatest on-air reporting jobs in television history."

An Arabic-speaking German policewoman, wearing glasses, a skirt and white blouse, was the lead negotiator. The only thing she held in her hand was a walkie-talkie that she used to relay information to German officials. Standing on a balcony of Building 31, she could be seen talking face-to-face with one of the terrorists who appeared to be dressed in a leisure suit and wearing a white brimmed hat. All the while German policemen armed with submachine guns, and dressed as athletes, maneuvered into position just waiting. Waiting for the terrorists to let down their guard. They never did.

Finally after hours of uneasy negotiations, the Germans allowed the terrorists and their hostages to helicopter to a nearby military base, where they would then be flown to Egypt. But the German plan was to never let the terrorist leave their country. Sharpshooters had been positioned to eliminate the terrorist at the airport. However, it was discovered upon leaving Building 31 and boarding a bus to the helicopters, there weren't three or four terrorists as first believed, but eight. So when they reached the airport the sharpshooters were outnumbered when they began their attempt to pick off the terrorists. Five of them were killed and three were captured, but not before they machine-gunned one helicopter and tossed a grenade through the door of the other.

In a bit of irony, the three captured terrorists were sentenced to long prison terms, but two months later the West Germans exchanged them for passengers and a crew of a German Lufthansa airplane that had been skyjacked by Palestinians. Two of the three terrorists were later tracked down by Israeli operatives and killed.

At one time various news reports surfaced indicating all of the hostages were saved. But then when a tired-looking Jim McKay was handed a piece of paper, trying to hold his composure despite a quiver in his voice, he told the world: "Our worst fears have been realized…two athletes were killed yesterday in their rooms…nine were killed at the airport…they're all gone." McKay didn't report at the time that a West German policeman also died.

Munich had been the perfect place for Olympic politics at its worst. By murdering the Israelis, Black September had taken its message of the ways of the world to the Olympic Games. At the time, this is where the world's power was concentrated for all to see.

An El Al jetliner carried 10 coffins back to Israel, where they were placed in 10 brown army vehicles, each flanked by six Israeli soldiers. Soon the coffins vanished under heaps of flowers and wreaths.

The eleventh murdered Israeli, weightlifter David Berger, was flown back to his home in Cleveland, Ohio. Eighteen months before, he immigrated to Jerusalem to be a part of their weightlifting team.

It received only a footnote, but four years earlier, at the '68 Games in Mexico City, more than 200 students who had decided the Olympics would be the best venue to protest Mexico's social conditions, were shot by their government.

For Iba's '68 Olympic basketball team selecting the team also had its issues. A boycott campaign led by black sociology professor Harry Edwards fell pretty much on deaf ears. At the moment of truth, the August 1972 issue of "Sport Magazine" wrote that only one U.S. athlete actually boycotted the Games—an All-American player at UCLA who played under the name of Lew Alcindor. (Kareem Abdul Jabbar)

With total chaos and confusion now in Munich, it was not easy letting family and friends know back in the States each athletes situation.

The only way the U.S. had of knowing was what they saw on ABC television.

Basketball players weren't the only ones staying in the building with the basketball team. So, too, were the boxers and swimmers. "Duane Bobick was the highest profile boxer, and, of course, Spitz the swimmer," Kenny said. "I remember Bobick was beaten almost to a pulp by Teofilio Stevenson (Cuba) in his gold medal bout.

"We had a phone in our building out in the foyer that we all used to call back home. Most of the time it wasn't being used, but after the attack we had to stand in line, it was so busy, all of us calling back home to let them know we were okay. Our Olympic people gave us a pre-paid calling card to use. I guess I talked to Rita four or five times during the 20 days I was there. Then she'd call the rest of the family and give them any news from here."

Back in Kentucky, the Davis and Renfroe families were glued to their TV's.

"That's all we did," says Rita. "We watched it all night. Someone literally watched it all the time…we were so afraid we'd miss something. That's the only way we had of knowing what was happening. None of us could believe what we were seeing and hearing."

While many versions have the terrorists climbing the 7-foot fence that surrounded the village while dressed in warm-up outfits to look like athletes, there was another account that Olympic historian Tom Ecker developed in his book "Olympic Facts and Fables."

Brewster and Gallagher's book, "Stolen Glory," wrote that it was not uncommon for some of the American athletes, including several of the basketball players to scale the fence around the Village rather than walk all the way around to the front gate. They had even been linked to innocently helping the three or four terrorists over the fence. Then some slightly drunk Canadians, returning from watching a hockey game, reported they might have been the ones who assisted the Black September group over the fence.

But here's what Ecker's book reported: Authorities first assumed the intruders had changed clothes once inside since they were not wearing warm-up suits the rest of the time. Ecker says at least six books and three motion pictures have been produced describing the events of that day and none of them agree.

One of those books, "The Blood of Israel," by French journalist Serge Groussard, may have conducted the most in-depth look into what really happened, Ecker wrote.

The writer tells of four athletes from Arab nations in warm-ups seen climbing the fence. This was reported by two passers-by who later refused to give their names. Groussard says the obvious question is why the terrorists would be wearing Arab-nation warm-ups that might attract attention. He also questioned the timeline. German officials reported the terrorists entering the village at 4 a.m., and then walked 50 meters to the building where the shooting began at 4:25 a.m. Why did it take 25 minutes to get from the fence to Building 31? Why did they bother to change from warm-ups into clothing they wore throughout the ordeal? And what happened to the warm-ups? They were never found.

Three Swedish athletes came forward some 20 years after Munich with another version: Most of the Swedish team had been out for dinner on September 4, and returned to the village well after midnight. They were all wearing their blue and yellow Swedish warm-ups. Some of the women in the group invited three of the men to join them in the women's area of the village for coffee. Men were strictly forbidden there, so after playing cards until 4 a.m., they left to return to the men's area which required climbing the fence again. A guard in the area heard them and began yelling at the three, who ran to the nearest building on the men's side of the fence—Building 31—and hid in the garage area beneath the building. Soon they made their way back to their quarters, one street over.

The following morning, when the Swedes' learned of the attack and that the terrorists had not yet been identified as Arabs, but had climbed over the fence at 4 a.m., they were fearful their fingerprints might be found on the fence because they were the ones climbing that fence at 4 a.m. That was the reason everyone believed there were only three or four terrorists, and not eight.

So how did the terrorists get into the Village? Groussard says they did it with a key to the padlock on Gate 25A, a service gate locked every night at midnight and unguarded until the following morning. This was different from the main entrance that remained open all night, but required identification to enter.

The theory was that the terrorists got the key to the gate and the key to the Israeli quarters from a locksmith, who was part of Black September's operation. Groussard's research established two of their

Both the American and Russian teams had to sit around all day and half the night before playing the most important basketball game of their lives in order that television could be served. For sure, money talks at the Olympics, while at the same time the operative word was amateurism.

"Actually we had all adjusted to the time changes by then, and I don't really remember it being that much of an issue," Kenny said. "In our building there was a large foyer, and the coaches got us together there and we did a walk-through of some of the plays we were going to run. It was a long day so we just hung out in the village. The food area was open 20 out of 24 hours so we spent some time there."

As the 6,500 spectators crowded into the arena, and despite an apparent flippant attitude by basketball fans back in the U.S. who had little reason to believe their American team would not win their 64th consecutive Olympic game, getting into Basketballhalle that night was a tough ticket.

As was customary in international play, before each game the teams exchanged pleasantries in the form of token gifts. However, the two game captains, Kenny Davis of the U.S. and Modestas Paulouskas for the Russians, exchanged their national Olympic banners.

"We gave the opposing teams little pins," Kenny offered. The Russians, I remember, gave us little dolls that opened up with another doll inside and then another. Most the times the gifts we received were more valuable that what we gave."

With everything else going on in the world of sports, "Sports Illustrated" magazine named Billie Jean King and John Wooden its 1972 Sportsman and Sportswomen of The Year.

Tennis player King used the magazine as a mouthpiece to declare that amateurism in the Olympics is a farce. "I have trouble interpreting college basketball players as amateurs," she said. "No matter how small it is, if they are given financial aid for excelling at sports, calling them amateurs is incorrect. As an amateur tennis player, whether they gave me $10 or $4,000 under the table, I still consider myself a professional and I don't like being called an amateur. The amateur idea is ridiculous."

Johnny Wooden, for a coach who always seemed to have the best big men in the nation at UCLA, had some rather surprising opinions about the game. He said he was in favor of the 30-second clock (not yet implemented in 1972) to cut down on inactivity and stall games;

and also thought jump balls and offensive rebound baskets should be eliminated. "A rebound should be passed off before another shot went up," he said. "This would take away the advantage of the unusually big player, cut down on fouls, and make for some pretty play around the basket." Didn't he coach Lew Alcindor and Bill Walton?

Billie Jean King was not through with her take on the Olympics.

"We must lift ourselves out of the glass jar. We can't divorce ourselves from politics, either. I haven't met one human being who agrees with Avery Brundage that sport is above politics. The nationalistic flavor of the Olympics breeds political problems. Athletes should represent themselves, not their countries. Using one's position in sports to influence a political situation is a personal, individual matter.

Wooden brought up that Walton, in the spring of 1971, had been arrested in an anti-Vietnam War protest. The Hall of Fame coach pointed out that "he was representing himself and not his UCLA team," but the team had been criticized.

King admitted she had become less nationalistic over the years. "In most European countries they don't play their anthem," she said. "But I kind of like ours because it seems to settle things. And I don't like the Olympic victory celebration ceremonies. They're political."

It was interesting that King spent a great deal of talking about the Olympics, while Wooden never mentioned the Games—not one time.

The starting lineup Iba put on the floor that night was Tom Henderson, Bobby Jones, Dwight Jones, Jim Brewer and Ed Ratleff.

Henderson had been the surprise of the Olympics, and the fact that he had been Iba's personal pick to the team made the "old coach" feel good in that he could still recognize talent when others couldn't. That Henderson had been a junior college player made it all the better.

Bobby Jones was an up and coming star for Dean Smith at North Carolina; Jim Brewer had been sensational at the trials, in the exhibition games and in Munich. Iba knew he would be a physical force inside that the Russians would not be able to push around; Dwight Jones, out of Houston, to this point was the team's leading scorer at 9.6 points per game in an offense that had every player on the team scoring; Ed Ratleff had been an All-American at Long Beach State and coached by Jerry Tarkanian. Ratleff's game in college had been all-about offense, but now with a four-pass-before-you-shoot-system, he was relegated to being a very good team player.

Collins, Joyce, McMillen, Forbes, Davis, and Bantom would get their chances later. But there was one player that night that wouldn't be playing, and it wasn't because of an injury.

Tom Burleson, who at North Carolina State had been listed at 7'4", but at the Olympic Trials was officially measured at 7'2 ½", had been benched for having his fiancée in his room. Had this happened anytime other than the night before, Burleson would probably have been sent home.

There had been skeptics from the beginning about the capability of Iba's team winning gold, but now it was time to play basketball, and surely an American win would shut the mouths of all the naysayers. Some thought the fact that Russia's average age of 23 years, compared to the Americans 20 years, would make a difference.

The Russians controlled the opening tip and before the Americans knew what had happened they trailed 15-7. Sergei Belov had quickly put to rest the perception that the Russians weren't fast. He was quick, too. (Remember it was a Russian who had just won the Olympic 100 meters). Billed as the Jerry West of Europe, he was using his 300-game experience in international play, and maturity as a 28-year-old, to school the younger U.S. guards.

Trailing 21-11, the U.S. scored four quick points to make it 21-15, and then pretty trading points, they went into halftime down 26-21. Iba's system looked like it was working. The 26 points by the previously high scoring Russians gave every indication that if the Americans could cut down on their sloppy play, they would win this game and the gold.

The second half was back and forth with neither team able to display much offense. In Iba's controlling style, when his team had the ball, if a wide open layup wasn't available it was pass it back out again. On the other hand the defense thrown up by the Russians was effective, too.

With 12 minutes remaining in the game, the Russians led 34-28. But it was here that something Iba had warned his team about weeks before happened. Dwight Jones and a Russian substitute were tossed out of the game. Iba had cautioned that international teams will often send in a player to rough-up a star player in order to create retaliation. And in the gold medal game of the Olympics it worked, as one of the U.S.'s top scorers had been baited into losing his cool.

With slow tempo by both teams, Russia's 44-36 point lead with a little over five minutes remaining was reason for concern, but Iba's proclamation to hold them to under 50 points, at this point appeared to be in jeopardy.

"We knew we were in trouble if something didn't change, "offered Kenny Davis, who had played on teams that had lost to the Russians in four previous international games. "It was crazy in our huddle during timeouts. (Kevin) Joyce and (Doug) Collins told the coaches we needed to pick up the tempo."

Not in the lineup for the Americans now were two of their best players. Dwight Jones had been booted for fighting, and Brewer had suffered a blow to the head earlier that rendered him almost senseless. "He wasn't really sure what was going on," Davis said. "But at the time we really didn't know how bad he had hit his head. And, then don't forget, Burleson had been benched for violating team rules."

Joyce, who had played at South Carolina for Coach Frank McGuire, took it upon himself to force the action. Most observers weren't aware that he had suffered a back injury during training in Hawaii, and Iba had considered sending him home and calling up an alternate. But now Joyce was rallying the team, and with only seconds remaining in the game, the Russians led 49-48.

It was here that Doug Collins made what has been called the greatest play in Olympic basketball history. Picking off a Russian pass, he sprinted for the other end with a wide open court. Going in for a game winning layup, he was fouled hard from behind, causing him to crash head first into the basket support. The fall left him dazed for a few seconds, and it appeared he would be unable to shoot the two free throws awarded to him.

Collins, from the very beginning in Colorado Springs, had emerged as a rising star. The previous year he had been the number three collegiate scorer in the nation at 29 a game, but still in a slow-down offense he had shown Iba enough of his all-around ability during the 21 days in Hawaii, that he was the star of the team. Iba looked at the clock, making sure he correctly saw the three seconds that remained and was all that separated his team from Olympic gold.

"If Doug can walk, he's going to shoot." Iba said loud and clear. And Doug could walk.

Collins was now doing what every kid who has ever bounced a basketball on a dirt court had thought about...standing at the line with the game's outcome determined by hitting or missing.

With the two most pressurized free throws in American basketball history, Collins sank the first, tying the score at 49 all. This is where things however began to go haywire. Just as he let go of his second shot, the horn sounded from the sideline. He made it anyway, and the U.S. led 50-49.

"The place went wild. It was our first lead of the game," Kenny said. "They threw the ball in but then the referee (Renato Righetto from Brazil) stopped the game with one second on the clock. The Russian coaches and players were all on the court."

The Russians claimed they had tried to get a timeout, and that was the reason for the horn sounding during Collin's second made free throw. It was total chaos. With no one speaking the same language, it was like someone yelling fire, with no exits.

Accordingly, the rule offered that no one could call a timeout once the ball was in the possession of the shooter. And what about the Russians inbounding the ball and the referee stopping the game with one second remaining? Righetto, the referee, tried to sort it out with bedlam all around him. His decision awarded the ball back to the Russians on the baseline and ordered the timekeeper to put three seconds back on the clock.

Righetto's decision was bolstered by the appearance on the court by R. William Jones, the president of the FIBA, which was the governing body of international basketball. Jones, in earlier times had been a British spy, but now he had built a kingdom in basketball circles, as many of the referees, scorekeepers, timekeepers, and even coaches owed their jobs to him. After all, he was the founding father of international basketball, dating back to 1932, and he was credited with bringing the sport to the Olympics in 1936. Jones had been seated near mid-court, behind the scorer's table, so he was able to quickly get to the floor.

Jones held up three fingers in front of the referees, signifying three seconds be put back on the game clock. Artenik Arabadjion, the other referee was from Bulgaria, and the timekeeper from Germany meant there was no common language in all of the confusion.

For the second time the Russians inbounded the ball with three seconds left. A half-court shot didn't come close, and the Americans erupted onto the court in celebration. They had won their gold and Iba was a genius. The Russians had not scored 50 points.

"We won the game," says Kenny. "Everyone knew we won, even the Russians." "Everything we'd gone through was worth it. The gold medal was ours."

But wait!

Confusion among the referees and scorer's table once again raised its ugly head. Jones, the basketball czar, had returned to the scorer's table.

"It was awful, horrible," Kenny Davis recalled. "We had gone from jubilation like you can't believe to being told the game wasn't over. They said when the Russians inbounded the ball the last time, the clock hadn't been reset properly."

R. William Jones ordered that three seconds be put on the clock one more time. Tom McMillen compared Jones' appearance to being like David Stern coming out of the stands during an NBA game.

Don Haskins, the assistant coach, wanted Iba to take the team to the locker room. As far as he was concerned the game was over. The U.S. had won it twice. Jones, however, told the American coaches if they left the court they would forfeit the gold and possibly be barred from future Olympic basketball games.

"We had to do it all over again," Kenny said. "But this time the Russians did it different than the time before when they threw the ball in and got off a half-court shot. Their guy (Ivan Edeshko) threw it the length of the floor to his big 6'10" teammate (Alexsandr Belov). We had Forbes and Joyce back there with him and Kevin missed the ball and fell down and Jim got shoved out of the way. Belov lays it in."

There had even been some confusion on McMillen's part. Told to guard and disrupt Edeshko pass as much as possible, the 6'11" McMillen, jumping and wildly swinging his arms, the Bulgarian referee pointed toward McMillen warning him not to reach over the inbound line in his efforts. Not wanting to get a technical foul, he backed off. And in doing so the Russian had a much easier pass to complete at the other end of the floor.

Russia wins 51-49. They had been given three chances to score, and third time was charm.

The normally calm Iba, who for the most part stayed in his seat except for timeouts, was going crazy, shouting at the referees and scorer's table. If the humiliation of losing the first U.S. basketball game in Olympic history was not enough, Iba was pick-pocketed for $350 dollars.

The locker room was a mess. Some were crushed. "We couldn't believe the score would stand," Kenny says. "We were screaming and crying, wondering how did this happen. When Coach Iba came in the locker room and told us we needed to get out there and accept our medals, I think it was Joyce who told the coaches to get out."

The Americans had been told a protest would be filed, but just in case it wasn't ruled in their favor, then and there as a team they decided they wouldn't accept the silver. In their minds they won gold… not silver.

"As the team captain, I went out and told the press what we had decided," Kenny said.

Iba filed the official protest and R. William Jones appointed a five-member committee to hear it. It was well past 1 a.m. by now, and both the Americans and Russian players were still in their uniforms.

Finally, after meeting for several hours the protest committee took a break at 6 a.m. Reconvening at 11 a.m., two hours later they voted 3-2 against the U.S. protest. As somewhat anticipated, the vote had been swayed by the three communist countries appointed by Jones.

At the hearing, sitting in the mob of newsmen, were two of the American players, Kevin Joyce and Tom Burleson.

When the final verdict was announced denying the U.S. protest, Joyce was asked for a comment.

"Why should we accept the silver medal?" He added. "We won the gold. What's a medal anyway? It's just something to show your buddies."

Bill Summers, U.S. Olympic Basketball Committee President, then addressed the FIBA group: "The Russian basketball team played an excellent game, but I regret we cannot accept this decision. Our team will not be present for the awarding of the silver medals. We do not wish this to be misconstrued. We respect your integrity. We regret that all this confusion has come about."

Iba said later, "It was the first time in 50 years I've been in athletics that they've played an overtime ball game when the game wasn't tied."

Jones offered that the reason for his presence at the scorer's table was the Russians were not given their timeout when they had asked for it. "The American's need to learn how to lose," he added.

"Americans are whiners," said Edeshko, who threw the pass for the final Russian basket. "They always want to be first…if they're not, they're always looking for a reason. That's their national problem."

With the U.S. refusal to accept the silver, it was briefly discussed by the I.O.C. about moving bronze medal winner Cuba up to silver, and Italy, who finished fourth into bronze. Now with the Americans out, the medal ceremony was moved from Olympic Stadium to an indoor facility. "None of us were there," says Kenny, "But some of us did watch it on T.V. in our building."

"We left Munich as quick as we could," Kenny said. "The I.O.C. didn't want the basketball medal ceremony in front of 80,000 people because it would just add to the controversy, so they got it out of sight."

"The only thing I fault is that Coach Iba didn't get his team to the locker room and stay there," offered Bobby Knight years later. "But Henry was too much of a gentleman to piss any of 'em off. What right did that son-of-a-bitch from England, or wherever he was from, to come on the floor? He had absolutely no right to be there. The loss was the greatest miscarriages of justice in the history of sports. In my opinion Henry won three Olympics."

Today Knight says, "Without any reservations, Henry Iba was the most innovative coach in the history of the game in terms of what he did defensively. It required smart players who could concentrate.

"All of those other coaches like Lefty Driesell can piss and moan all they want about whether he played too slow. But all he had done was win two Olympics and two NCAA's. What had most of them ever done but complain."

Knight, in 1984, coached the U.S. Olympic basketball team and asked Iba to be a part of his staff. Following a gold medal win over Spain, Iba was carried off the floor by the American players.

Former University of Kentucky coach Joe B. Hall was also a part of the Olympic Trials in Colorado Springs and knew Iba well.

"Mister Iba was such a respected man," Hall says. "He was ahead of his time when it came to defense. He was so appreciative to all of us who helped out with the Olympics. When I was coaching at Regis College, he brought his team to Denver to play my team. If you can believe it, we upset his team and my players were carrying me around the floors on their shoulders. Mister Iba kept following them around until he could shake my hand. That's how he was. It was his wife who made him get out of coaching. She thought the game was passing him by."

Memories and facts can often become distorted with the passage of time. But recorded video can more often than not set the record straight. Each frame of ABC film of the game, particularly the ending, has been run and rerun, slowed down, and backed up until there can be no distortion or misreading of the events that took place.

Chapter Twenty-One

What happened in Munich in September 1972 outraged the American public, even those who weren't basketball fans. But for the most part other countries weren't that concerned. For several it was almost like "it's about time the Americans got theirs."

Soon after returning from Munich, Clifford H. Buck, president of the United States Olympic Committee, said he was going to recommend that the United States suspend indefinitely any further participation in the Olympic basketball "as a protest to the unconscionable injustice done to the USA basketball team in Munich."

Buck went on to say that his proposed action would be directed to the FIBA and not the International Olympic Committee.

But don't be misled to think it was just basketball that failed to deliver gold. Buck also said there would be a full review of America's distressing performance in the Munich Games, the nation's most dismal in history.

"Medals aren't everything," he said back then. "But I must confess that I thought we would do better. I thought we would at least be even with the Russians in winning golds. When we get home we will have a meeting to evaluate our performance. We spent more money during the past four years than ever before to field world class teams. We must decide if we are spending it properly, putting the right emphasis in the right areas."

The gold medal count wasn't close, as the Russians garnered 50 while the U.S. had 33. Next was East Germany with 20, and West Germany and Japan with 13 each. Total medal count was a bit closer, with Russia's 99 to America's 94.

Bill Wall at the time worked for the U.S. Olympic Basketball Committee. He had succeeded Adolph Rupp as the president of the National Association of Basketball Coaches, an NCAA organization of which he had been a part of during his 18 years at MacMurray State in Jacksonville, Illinois.

"Henry Iba, Cliff Wells, and Adolph were part of my committee," said Wall. "But we had no say in the selection of the '72 Olympic team."

It was Wall who probably had more insight on R. William Jones of any in the American contingent. He was well aware of the bureaucracy involved in who controlled what when it came to the NCAA, AAU and FIBA. He was equally aware of the power Jones wielded in the Olympics.

"He started basketball in the Olympics," says Wall, "And he was literally a dictator among anyone involved in international basketball.

"Jones was chairman of the (IOC) technical committee, and I felt like he thought he was authorized to come on to the floor if he thought something was not right."

"The one official (Righetto) who refused to sign the scorebook never worked another FIBA game," Wall said. "And the other (Arabadiig) worked a few more and then moved to the United States from Bulgaria. That's how strong his influence was."

Jones, because of his position, according to Wall, received lots of gifts on his visits to other countries over the years. "I know once he went to Italy and came back with a Rolex (watch)."

Wall, however, is quick to give credit to R. William Jones as far as promoting basketball globally.

"He developed the Olympics for men and in 1976 he was the one who got it introduced into the Olympics for women. Ninety-five percent of what Jones did was good, but the other five percent was bad decisions he made."

Wall says two efforts were made to give the silver medals to the U.S. team members who wanted them, but Olympic rules stated it was all or none.

"I wasn't at that gold medal game," continued Wall. "But I agree with them not accepting the medals."

Wall, nevertheless, in a play on words, found a silver lining with the Olympic loss for the Americans.

"The Russians then became the "bad guys," and when they came over here (U.S.) to tour we sold out every game when we played them."

In retrospect, had the U.S. won as expected, there would have been little written about this team over the years. They would have been just another in the long line of gold medal U.S. basketball teams. The same can probably be said if the Americans had lost by five or ten points. They would have graciously, but disappointedly, stood on the podium, accepted their silver medals, listened to the Russian national anthem, and gone down as the first team to ever lose an Olympic basketball game. End of story.

Well, not yet.

In 1976, Dean Smith coached the U.S. back to a gold medal, but the Olympic spirit and politics remained deeply entwined. And in 1980 it was about to come to head. A boycott of the 1980 Summer Games in Moscow by the Americans had become a reality when President Jimmy Carter recommended the U.S. teams stay home. The reason: Russia in December 1979 had invaded Afghanistan.

Naturally, it brought out mixed emotions by former Olympians and those athletes who had trained a lifetime in hopes of becoming an Olympian, not just in name, but also in actual competition.

Keeping the Games from becoming politicized had been the Olympic theme from the very beginning. But some thought with Carter's talk of a boycott, as a break with the ideal of separating politics and sports.

When the U.S. decided to be a no-show in Moscow, it made the Soviet's decision not to be a part of the '84 Games in Los Angeles much easier.

John Thompson (Georgetown University) coached the 1988 U.S. team to third place, winning the bronze medal. With future NBA players David Robinson, Hersey Hawkins, Mitch Richmond, Dan Majerle, Danny Manning, J.R. Reid, and Stacey Augmon, the Americans lost its only game to the Russians 82-76. It was the first Olympic meeting between these two since the 1972 gold medal game.

It was this performance that led to future U.S. Olympic teams selecting NBA stars.

Finally, the Munich Games were over. But once again there was a degree of uneasiness even in the closing ceremonies.

A threat of more terror and violence occurred when an anonymous tip reported that an aircraft was in flight to bomb Olympic Stadium. Taking no chances, the West German government scrambled jets into the sky. Apparently a DC-8 charter had unintentionally drifted off course and was not a threat.

The mood of the capacity crowd of 80,000 seemed to exhibit more relief than joy. What had begun as Germany's dream to show the world a new face had ended in a series of nightmares that pointed out a vulnerability that threatened the future of the Olympics regardless of where they were conducted.

Surprisingly, of the 8,500 athletes from 124 nations that had marched in the opening ceremonies, only 2,000 were on hand when it ended. Death, politics, and blatant nationalism overshadowed the goal of brotherhood, goodwill, and the Olympic spirit.

Long after the memories of who won and lost have been forgotten, the '72 Munich Games will be remembered for chaos and tragedy.

Kenny was glad to be headed home. When his plane landed at the Cincinnati Airport in northern Kentucky, he was a different person than the young man from Wayne County was when he left a few months before heading to Colorado Springs and the Olympic Trials.

"His brother Gene and I met him when he returned," said wife Rita. "He was exhausted. He was so tired he couldn't talk. It was three or four days before he was acclimated to being home."

He had been a world traveler, and in spite of never traveling outside of Kentucky until he went to college, his young career had taken him to five continents, and he was only 24-years-old.

"I thought I had seen a lot, maybe not everything," he said. "But when I came back from Munich I was changed. All of us were. What we had seen and done affected all of us. Returning to the United States, and especially Kentucky, sure did look good.

"At no time in my life did going home feel better. Friendly, warm faces are always welcome, but this time they seemed even more pleasing after spending the majority of the summer traveling."

It didn't take long for Kenny's hometown to put together a day to honor him. Throughout the entire area, not just Monticello and Wayne County, everyone was proud of his against-all-odds accomplishments.

On Saturday afternoon on September 16, Kenny and Rita climbed into the back of a convertible on Kendrick Avenue in Monticello to kick-off a parade that would end at the Wayne County High School football stadium. It wasn't quite Olympic Stadium in Munich, but it meant just as much to him. There weren't any world leaders, Olympic presidents or 80,000 people who didn't have a clue who Kenny was. Instead, there was family, friends, and others who just wanted to pay their respects.

Wayne County Judge Wilson Shearer and Monticello Mayor Carl Shearer both spoke at the event. So did Wayne County School Superintendent Clarence Bates, and Principal George Horton. Even former principal A.J. Lloyd said a few words. All the while Kenny's wife Rita beamed as everyone shook their hands and told them how proud they were of them. But no one there that day was any prouder than Kenny's parents, Clyde and Zula, as they waited to hear the featured speaker, Dr. Bob Davis, Kenny's college coach. Perhaps, now seeing all of this, Zula Davis had a better understanding about those late night post-game practices Coach Davis implemented immediately following a tough loss at Georgetown a couple of years before.

In the meantime, Kenny and Rita knew that together they had sacrificed in order for Kenny to reach for a dream, and against all odds, he lived it. He had been playing basketball all of his life, but now the two of them were ready to settle down and somehow put their lives in order. It was something they really hadn't been able to do since they married.

It seemed almost too good to be true when Kenny was approached with an unbelievable job offer with Converse Rubber Company on their sales staff.

"When the Converse offer came along it was considered a premier job," Kenny said. "Coaches and sports celebrities were leaving their jobs to come to work with Converse. Hot Rod Hundley, Larry Conley, Phil Rollins, and free throw legend Bunny Leavette were just a few working with them."

Two weeks after returning from Munich, Joe Dean, Converse's national sales manager, hired Kenny.

"At the Olympic Trials, Joe told Coach Iba they needed someone and Coach Iba told me about it," said Kenny.

There was a bit of downside, initially, with the job, Kenny and Rita would have to move.

"There were a few places we could go, but we decided on Springfield, Ohio, because it seemed so much like where we lived in Georgetown. So we moved there in late December 1972.

All of the Olympians knew they would have a shot at the pros. But Kenny, being a realist at the age of 24, knew the Olympics would be the zenith of his basketball career.

It had been written that when Kenny returned home his basketball career was over. Far from it.

He had earned his Olympic spot by representing Marathon Oil the AAU team out of Lexington, so he picked up where he left off with them.

"The location actually worked out pretty good because I wanted to continue playing for Marathon Oil if I could, and since many of our games were in Cincinnati and Dayton, that made it much easier for me to get to the games," he said.

"I actually went on the payroll on October 1 with Converse," Kenny said. "Rita and I didn't have much money and I needed to go to work. Phil Rollins was training me then.

"Mike Pratt and I had been hired at the same time and he was assigned to Kentucky, so I went to Springfield, Ohio. (Pratt was a native of Ohio, but had made a name for himself as an All-American at U.K.).

"Springfield was a larger city than both of us were accustomed to, but it was a wonderful place we grew to love, and it was the birthplace of our daughter Jill," said Kenny. "I spent a lot of time at Wittenberg University watching athletic events. At the time they were one of the top division three basketball and football schools in the country. Ray Mears had coached their basketball team before becoming the University of Tennessee's head coach."

Kenny continued playing with Marathon Oil as much as he could on weekends. Basketball was still his life, professionally selling shoes, and now playing as a hobby. He thrived on the competition, but equally relished the camaraderie. "It was a great bunch of guys to be around," he said.

In April 1973, Marathon coached by Scotty Baesler and Pat Doyle won the National AAU tournament held in Ashland, Kentucky. The team as usual was comprised of players who had played their college ball in Kentucky. From U.K. was Jim LeMaster, Phil Argento, and John Adams; from Eastern, George Bryant, Don Argabright and Darryl Dunagan; Gene Kirk was then coaching at Woodford County and had played at Delta State; from Morehead, Jim Day; and Paul Andrews from Union College by way of the Armed Forces AAU team.

"We then headed for Sao Paulo, Brazil to defend a title we had won the year before," Kenny said. "We also added a few players to take with us. (Jim Andrews, U.K.; Ketchel Strauss, Tennessee Tech; and Larry Bauer, Illinois)."

The year before in Brazil is where Marathon Oil coach Pat Doyle saw one of the Russian players warming up wearing a Johnson Central High School sweatshirt. After asking around, Doyle found out the Russians acquired the shirt while playing an exhibition game in Paintsville.

Marathon Oil was once again successful in winning the International Cup Basketball Tournament.

Upon their return to Lexington, there was still one more high profile game for Marathon Oil, however, this time it would be on their home turf. But, and it was a big but, it would be against the Russians.

The Russians had been on an eight-game tour of the U.S., and just as Olympic committee member Bill Wall predicted, the American loss to the Russians in Munich would ensure a sellout wherever they played on the tour.

On May 11, 1973, over 4,000 fans squeezed into the gym at Henry Clay High School to watch the Russians pound Marathon Oil 109-87. George Bryant scored 23, Kevin Grevey (added to team) 22, and Jim Andrews 21.

Kenny, by now on a first name basis with several of the Russian players, scored four points.

"They had actually played us in Memorial Coliseum before the Olympics," Kenny said. "So I got to know a few of them. Out of eight games I played against the Russians, I was only on the winning team once."

Another twist to the game in Lexington was that Alexsandr Belov, the player who scored the final shot to beat the U.S. in Munich, did not play in the game although he was on the bench. He had injured his ankle a few days earlier in Baltimore.

And then…are you ready for this? One of the referees in the game was…Renato Righetto, the international referee from Brazil who was on tour with the Russian team in the U.S.

In 1975, Mike Pratt decided he wanted to try his hand at coaching, and when Lee Rose asked him to be a part of his coaching staff at the

University of North Carolina Charlotte, he jumped at the chance. "I loved Converse," he said. "But there was something inside of me that wanted to coach."

So when Pratt left it opened up the Kentucky territory, and Kenny and Rita moved to Louisville.

"In Ohio one of my responsibilities had been to service the account for the Cleveland Cavaliers, and then when I got to Louisville I had the Kentucky Colonels, and the Cincinnati Reds," Kenny said.

Soon after the move to Louisville in August 1976, son Bryan was born.

"Joe Dean wanted me to live in Louisville to be close to the Kentucky Colonels," says Kenny. "It was a major emphasis for Converse to place shoes on the pro athletes at that time."

But things were about to change for the ABA Colonels. In existence since 1967, owner John Y. and Ellie Brown, cashed in and folded the team in 1976.

"When that happened Joe gave me permission to live anywhere in the state we chose," Kenny said. "Rita had grown up in Paint Lick, and after spending some time there when we were dating, I fell in love with the area. We had talked that if the opportunity ever presented we would like to settle there and raise our family."

Kenny and Rita had similar backgrounds being from families that had raised tobacco and cattle, so when some land in Paint Lick went up for auction not far from Rita's childhood home, they bought it.

"In January 1977, we moved into our new home," Kenny said. "It's the same home we still live in today.

"To me the most appealing aspect of any job is to be able to work in an area that you enjoy living in. Converse allowed me to do that, and it is one of the reasons I made my career with them."

There were several times Kenny turned down promotions with Converse that would have taken him to much larger cities.

"They (Converse) could not understand why I didn't take them," he said. "It would have taken us to Denver, Chicago, Charlotte, Dallas, and Boston. But I had been to those cities and none offered me and my family the quality of life we were enjoying on our farm here in central Kentucky."

Calling on stores, schools, and teams over the years has piled up some tall tales from Kenny throughout the years. But there's one that he still repeats.

"I had just moved back to Kentucky to take over the territory and was making a sales call in Pikeville before heading over to Hatfield Sporting Goods in Williamson, West Virginia," he says. "It was late afternoon, but I thought since it was only 32 miles, I could drive it in no more than an hour. I got behind a bunch of coal trucks on this curving, winding road, and it took me over two hours. The store had closed by the time I got there, and plus there wasn't any motels. I knew I couldn't drive back to Pikeville, so I made some calls and was told there was this lady who rented out rooms to tourists for the night. I went there and got a room. A little later the lady and I were talking and she said her ex-husband would sometime drive by and see what cars were there. She said sometimes he'd just go crazy. Well, when I went to my room I scooted the chest-of-drawers over in front of the door. I figured I probably couldn't stop him from coming in, but if I was asleep, at least I would hear him. I was awake most of the night . . . might have slept an hour."

By this time Rita had established her own career at Eastern Kentucky University, where she served as Associate Vice President for Academic Affairs and Research. Paint Lick is where they wanted to be.

Paint Lick now lays claim to Kenny Davis, putting him in the same category of another one of their native sons, baseball Hall of Famer Earl Combs, who played in the same New York Yankee outfield with Babe Ruth.

Kenny is fortunate in that there are at least three Kentucky towns now that can legitimately call him their own. Monticello is where it all began, Georgetown is where he developed his game, and Paint Lick is where he has raised his family and capped off a career with Converse.

Over the years, however, the athletic shoe business began to change. With aggressive competition coming from other shoe brands, and millions of dollars being pumped into the pockets of coaches and athletes, Kenny Davis' role with Converse began to change, too.

"I went from calling on professional and college teams to calling on rock stars," he said.

Perhaps no product in history has taken a more dramatic turn in its function than the Converse Chuck Taylor All Star athletic shoe. From its introduction in the twenties to the mid-80's, it was the one and only shoe of choice for the serious basketball player.

"Almost everyone from my era can still quote the price and date when they got their first pair of "Chucks"," Kenny says. "Mine came from Riherd's Sports Shop in Glasgow in 1963, and cost $5.75."

But just as he has done throughout his life (remember he went from scorer to playmaker), Kenny was able to adjust as the focus of Converse began to change.

"For fifteen years my primary job was placing our shoe on pro athletes," he said. While many players required a special fit, Lenny Wilkens of the Cleveland Cavaliers for example wore the "low cuts" right off the shelf. But as the shoe began to lose its luster as a performance product, and serious players began to demand a leather upper, the shoe gained fame as a "cult" accessory for rock stars. Ellen Degeneres, Miley Cyrus, Renée Zellwegar, Reese Witherspoon and Drew Barrymore sport them on a daily basis.

"So for the last twenty-five years of my Converse career, I no longer was required to enter smelly locker rooms to promote our product. I was now getting the opportunity to go backstage and deliver free "Chucks" to silver screen stars. And I was getting paid to do that…not a bad gig for a guy from Wayne County."

Chapter Twenty-Two

The Converse story ranks among the top when it comes to athletics…especially basketball.

The Converse Rubber Company began in 1908, first making rubber working shoes in Malden, Massachusetts. Because these shoes were seasonal, the company began turning out athletic shoes only because they needed to keep their employees year-round.

As basketball began to catch on around the country, Converse, in 1917, after several years of research and development, produced their first "All Star" shoe line. Even though it was the first mass produced basketball shoe in North America, in the beginning sales were slow.

A young man playing basketball for the Akron Firestones saw the shoe and liked it so much he convinced Converse to hire him as a salesman. He became so successful that in 1932 Converse put Charles H. Taylor's name on their best basketball shoe.

"Chuck Taylor All-Stars" became the most popular basketball shoe in the world and is still today the best-selling shoe of all time.

Taylor would go to small towns, meet the coach, and put on clinics. He did this all over the country at high schools and YMCA's, and when WWII began, Taylor became fitness consultant for the U.S. military, and before long soldiers were doing calisthenics while wearing Chuck Taylor sneakers that had become the official sneaker of the U.S. Armed Services.

Taylor designed the white high tops worn by the U.S. Olympic teams in 1936, the first time basketball was played on a world stage. In 1949, the classic black and white high top was released, and before long Chuck Taylor All Stars were on the feet of professional, college, high school, and anyone playing basketball.

Taylor's name became synonymous with the game as he crisscrossed the United States putting on clinics. By 1949 he had even put his name on a high school All-American game in, of all places, Murray, Kentucky. Murray State College made its arena available and put together sponsors that enticed Converse and Chuck Taylor to be a part of their North-South Cage Classic. It predated the McDonald's games, and from 1949 through 1955 it was THE high school All-American game. The best prep players across the country played in Murray, among them Mason Cope, Gayle Rose, Togo Palazzi, Bob Pettit, Tom Gola, Jerry Bird, Robin Freeman, Howie Crittenden, Tom Heinsohn, Earl Adkins, Charlie Tyra, Archie Dees, Vernon Hatton, Bevo Francis, Phil Rollins, Doodle Floyd, Billy Ray Cassidy, and Tom Marshall.

Every player in these games wore the white Converse Chuck Taylor All Star (#9162) with special colored shoelaces that Converse had produced.

Taylor's influence was such that he was able to assemble over 180 radio, newspapers, and college coaches who selected the participating players each year. And at the conclusion of each All Star game, Taylor and two other Converse representatives, Grady Lewis and Johnny Norlander, would select five players to the Chuck Taylor All-American team.

Taylor was aptly described in most basketball publications as an "internationally known basketball expert." But it wasn't just high school teams he found time for. He and Converse were deeply immersed in the college and pro games as well. In 1921 Converse began publishing an annual Basketball Yearbook that soon became the "bible" of what was happening in hoops. The book chronicled every aspect of the game as its popularity began to spread nationally.

His sales approach never seemed to change and Taylor had a hand in selling 600 million pair of the shoes. It is interesting to note that he never received one penny in commissions as his income came from a salary. It was said, however, that he did know how to stretch the expense account.

Converse introduced the first all-white high tops in 1947 made especially for the 1948 Olympics team, and by 1966, Converse claimed an 80% share of the sneaker industry. Chuck Taylor, called the "Ambassador to Basketball," was the reason. In 1968 he was inducted into the Basketball Hall of Fame, and a year later he died.

In the fall of 1957, Frank Selvy (the Division I NCAA record holder for most points scored in a game, 100 in 1954 at Furman) had been released from the Army and re-joined his St. Louis Hawks team.

"Alex Hannum was the coach and he wouldn't play me," says Selvy. "The owner, Ben Kerner, however, wanted me to play instead of sitting on the bench. There was a rift of sorts so I was thinking about quitting basketball. In the meantime Converse offered me a job. It was a good salary with a car and expense account."

But here's where it got interesting for Selvy.

"Converse had printed my picture in one of their magazines that I was now with Converse, I think there were several hundred thousand that had been distributed. But then Kerner said I was still under contract with the Hawks and threatened to sue Converse. So I went back to the Hawks. My time with Converse lasted about a month. Back then everybody wore their shoes. When I was coaching later at Furman, Hot Rod Hundley was one of their sales reps in Greenville (S.C.), and he used to stay with me when he was in the area."

When Frank Selvy left Converse and returned to the NBA, it created an opening in the rapidly growing shoe company. So in 1958 Converse hired Joe Dean.

"I think Frank was with Converse six weeks," Dean said. "And I ended up with them for 28 years. It changed my life."

Dean, called Jo-Jo in his earlier days, had been a good basketball player at New Albany High School (Indiana) before going to LSU in 1949. "I also had offers from Wake Forrest and Purdue, but my high school coach, Gordon Raney, told me I would have a better chance of playing at LSU than at a school in the ACC or Big 10. He said basketball wasn't quite as good in the south at that time."

Dean had a Hall of Fame playing career at LSU, and although he was drafted in the NBA, like many at the time, he decided instead to play for the AAU Phillips 66 Oilers. "I played in an East-West All-Star game after my senior year, and Coach Iba was one of the coaches, he recommended me to the Phillips Oilers and I played with them for four years and was an alternate on the '56 Olympic team.

Dean's smooth approach in bringing in former big name college stars to promote Converse took the company to greater heights. Following the example of Chuck Taylor, he was everywhere. "Taylor knew every basketball coach in the country and that's what I wanted to do."

Back then I did most of the hiring at Converse," said Dean, who in 1981 along with 48 other executives bought the company. "We had an opening in the Kentucky-Ohio region and I knew Kenny Davis was our man. I actually met him when he was a senior at Georgetown College. I just really liked the guy. We even talked about making him a regional manager, but he would have to move, and he didn't want to do that."

All the while a start-up television group headed up by a young Eddie Einhorn was in the process of putting together a college basketball network he called TVS. In the beginning his contract was with the Southeastern Conference, and Einhorn needed someone who knew basketball and also the SEC.

Hello "string music"!

Joe Dean was his man and it didn't hurt Converse shoe sales that their national sales manager had his face and the most recognizable voice in sports, talking about basketball to hundreds of thousands of people every Saturday afternoon during basketball season.

"I started out with 'nothing but the bottom of the net,' and then 'tickling of the twine', laughed Dean, "But then at a game in Charlotte, N.C., I just said 'string music' and Eddie told me to keep using it."

Dean, with a mix of southern twang and midwestern drawl, became a fixture in college basketball for 18 years, and with his star power he enjoyed attending the Kentucky Derby for 45 straight years.

"Going to Louisville every year also gave me a chance to get over the river (Ohio River), and visit family and friends in New Albany."

At the Derby, Joe Dean was more recognizable than many of the movie stars, and anyone who saw him couldn't help calling to him, "string music" or another basketball word he coined, "stufferino". Dean would simply smile and wave, always appreciating the recognition.

Dean was a master at signing sports stars to shoe contracts, among them Magic Johnson, Larry Bird, and tennis star Chris Evert. But one star he wasn't able to close the deal on was with pop sensation Michael Jackson. Dean and Converse had designed a shoe to complement Jackson's famous white glove, but for various reasons it didn't work out.

In 1987, Dean returned to LSU as the director of athletics, until he retired in 2000.

(I interviewed Joe Dean for this book on September 17, 2013, and two months later to the day, he died of a heart attack).

Phil Rollins had been an outstanding basketball player for the University of Louisville in the late 50's and had gone into high school coaching when his opportunity with Converse came about.

"I was coaching at Flaget High School in Louisville when Grady Lewis (Converse) hired me," Rollins says. "I worked with him, and of course, Joe Dean."

Rollins was around when Kenny Davis was hired and some of his responsibilities were to show Kenny the ropes.

"We drove up to the northern part of Indiana in Kenny's VW," Rollins recalled. "We were gone for more than a week…had dinner with Digger Phelps at Notre Dame…toured the football area. But Kenny, for whatever reason, forgot to pack many clothes. We went out and he bought some underwear, but it was the wrong size. He thought he bought size 32, but it was a 42 instead."

Larry Conley had played for Adolph Rupp at U.K. and was a member of the 1966 Rupp's Runts that lost to Don Haskins' Texas Western team. He had planned on becoming a lawyer, but after one year of law school he decided that wasn't it, after all "I coached at George Washington University for a year and then played a short time with the Kentucky Colonels until I had to serve my military duty," Conley said. "And then I interviewed with Grady Lewis at Converse, and was hired by Joe Dean."

Conley was with Converse during exciting times for the company. "We were the only game in town for a while, and then the other shoe companies like Nike and Adidas started to pay coaches to use their shoes. Joe (Dean) and Gibb (Ford, President of Converse) were adamant they weren't going to do that. I remember Joe saying 'what about loyalty?'"

Conley left the company in 1979 after 10 years. "I absolutely loved it. I called on all the colleges. We didn't make football shoes or baseball shoes. It was strictly basketball."

Looking back on it, Conley says UCLA's John Wooden might have been the first college coach to ever be paid to have his team wear a certain brand.

Conley said the first time he had any knowledge of who Kenny Davis was, came from his brother. "My brother Joe went to Georgetown and played a little basketball with Kenny. 'You've got to see him play,' he told me."

Bailey Howell was exactly the big name star Converse was looking for when Joe Dean hired him in 1972. He had been an All-American at Mississippi State playing for Babe McCarthy, and then enjoyed a 12-year Hall of Fame career in the NBA that included four championship years with the Boston Celtics.

"When I quit playing professionally, suddenly the game I had been playing most of my life was gone," said Howell. "I was pretty low to tell you the truth, and then Converse came along. The quality of people that worked there was exceptional, and at the top of the list was Kenny Davis."

Howell's association with Converse gave him a new life that still revolved around basketball.

"The company couldn't produce the demand fast enough," says Howell. "The Chuck Taylor All Stars were put together by little old ladies here and there, and everyone wanted them. I went to NCAA tournaments, Junior College tournaments…if it was about basketball Converse was there. We were primarily order takers, not necessarily salesmen. Every now and then we might get them to take on another color. We had a special personal relationship with all of the coaches, and they wouldn't wear another shoe other than Converse. But then Nike bought their way in by paying the coaches and then went to the AD's and bought the whole program. Today Converse is selling more shoes than they ever have…after Nike bought them."

With all of the relatively young guns then coming to work for Converse, most of them still had the urge to compete in something even though for the most part their basketball playing days were over.

"Joe (Dean) liked people who were competitive," Howell continued. "And Kenny Davis was one of the most competitive guys walking around then. "I didn't play basketball after my playing days were over in the pros, but I did play some tennis with Kenny and Bill Justus. Kenny dedicated himself to the game and soon he became the best tennis player on the sales staff."

Bailey Howell retired from Converse in 1994 after 22 years.

Bill Justus had been a star football and basketball player at Fulton High School in Knoxville, Tennessee, before deciding to play only basketball at the University of Tennessee in the early 60's. Following graduation he had his choice of playing two professional sports, basketball or football.

"Tom Landry was the coach of the Dallas Cowboys, and they flew me down and offered me a contract even though I hadn't played since high school," said Justus.

That was a period when the Cowboys were looking for, not necessarily football players, but good athletes. They had signed one of Justus' basketball teammates at U.T. to an NFL contract. Ron Widby played for them several years and was one of the top punters in the league.

Justus was also drafted by Denver in the ABA and Philadelphia in the NBA.

Joe Dean thought Justus was a natural for Converse, and in 1969 hired him.

"The idea was to hire a group of basketball guys to put on clinics and work in group sales. We were a team," says Justus. "I became a regional manager and Kenny worked for me when he came on board. He was really, really smart. He could look at something and figure out how to do it better or easier. That's not a slam, it's a compliment."

The competitive fire still burned, too, when it came to playing pick-up games on the hardwood. Looking back on it Justus still remembers how good Kenny Davis was.

"The Kentucky Converse guys called him Kenny, "No D". But he'd guard me and I couldn't get a shot off. He may have been Kenny "No D" then, but he was Kenny "Plenty of D" when he guarded me."

And, how about those tennis games? "In the beginning I beat him easily, but all of a sudden he started concentrating on improving and I don't think I ever beat him again."

In Monticello there were no tennis courts, so the first ones he saw were at Western, but when he transferred to Georgetown he took a tennis P.E. class, and by chance he roomed with the Tiger's number one tennis player, Rick Denker. And then when he moved to Ohio he began to take the game a little more seriously so he could keep up with all of those Converse guys like Justus and Howell.

"I started to play a lot," he says. "When I was in the Murray area working, I'd try to schedule a game with Bennie Purcell. He was always one of the best players in the south in his age group, and his son Mel Purcell at one time had a world ranking."

Kenny's game advanced so much that in 1993 he received a USTA sanctioned number two ranking in Kentucky's 45 age group.

It was in Springfield that Kenny also decided to check off one more thing he had always wanted to do…buy a motorcycle.

"A friend I grew up with in Monticello, Kenny Frye, had a motorcycle that he rode everywhere when we were in high school," Kenny recalled. "I vowed that when I made enough money to buy one I would."

True to his word, when he received his first Converse check he bought "a small Honda motorcycle."

Several years later when Mike Calhoun, a former teammate at Georgetown, joined the basketball coaching staff at Eastern Kentucky, the two of them hooked up again. But this time on the back roads of Kentucky riding their motorcycles.

"Mike loved motorcycles," Davis said. "So both of us bought big bikes and traveled all over the south exploring all of the things you can never see unless you are on two wheels."

Rita remembers it well when Kenny bought his new motorcycle.

"The phone rang," she said. "When I answered, the guy calling said 'your fat-boy is in'. I said, excuse me, what did you say? 'Your fat-boy is in'. I said what's a fat-boy? 'A Harley', he said. When Kenny came home I said, by the way your fat-boy is in. He looked at me and said, 'Oh, I forgot to tell you.'"

Kenny still has a Vespa motorcycle stored in his garage, but now he puts more miles on his bike with pedals than the one with the motor.

Mike Pratt, the former U.K. all-SEC performer and Kentucky Colonel in the ABA, was another Joe Dean hire at Converse, and though he was there only two years before going into coaching, he has fond memories.

"My area was Kentucky and East Tennessee that included Nashville," Pratt said. "It kept me close to the coaches, and I still had the coaching bug in me."

Pratt, too, remembers some of those pick-up games with Kenny.

"Two guys that had gone to high school with me played with him at Georgetown, so we'd get together for some pick-up games in Georgetown when we couldn't get in Memorial Coliseum. If it weren't for Jimmy Reid playing with us, none of the others would have ever gotten any shots because Kenny didn't pass it," Pratt laughed.

Mike Pratt, in the winter of 1975, was Kenny's teammate on the Marathon Oil Team.

Chapter Twenty-Three

In 2001 Converse declared bankruptcy. They had become a victim of stiff competition from companies that produced sneakers for every facet of athletic footwear imaginable. Even though the finances had fallen on hard times, the brand name remained as identifiable as other heritage brands Levi's, Coca-Cola, or McDonalds. In other words, Converse still had value.

In 2003 Nike Inc. bought Converse from a holding group who had purchased the brand in 2001 on the courthouse steps in New York for $400 million. Converse is operated today as a subsidiary of Nike.

When David Allen, Vice President and General Manager of Converse North America came on board in 2008 it didn't take him long to know who Kenny Davis was. As a top executive with one of the world's top producers of athletic footwear, you better believe he knew the people he would be working with, especially those that had become the face of the company.

Allen had worked his way up the corporate ladder with Timberland, a company that produces outdoor footwear, and the move to Converse would mean he would be involved more with, not only sports teams, but individuals who were current stars, but also former athletes who had become part of the Converse team.

Kenny's four decades at Converse put him at an elite level on David's team. And within the company if Converse had a captain, surely he would be it.

"There's not anyone who doesn't like Kenny", offered Allen. "He woke up every day in his life to make a difference. And he did. His ethics, morals and self-motivation are an example to anyone who ever met him."

Allen knew there would be a day when Kenny would let it be known he was retiring. Although it was something he didn't want to think about, he was a realist, he knew it would come.

When Kenny came to him in 2011 with a proposal to do something that had never been done before, Allen was there to listen.

"He wanted Converse to be involved in a reunion of the 1972 Olympic basketball team," says Allen. "I remembered the game. Of course, who doesn't? I had heard the talk Kenny gives about Munich and what all went on. It's just amazing how he tells it."

Allen put his thinking cap on, too.

"We all knew he would be retiring from Converse soon, and all of us thought this would really be special if we could help Kenny pull a reunion off," he said. The entire team had never gotten together since the Olympics."

It would for sure be a major undertaking. Although Coaches Henry Iba and Don Haskins of the 1972 basketball team had died, all of the players were still alive. That, however, did not mean it would be an easy task to get twelve guys and an assistant coach together for four days.

With Converse on board, Georgetown College soon became a partner as well. Others, like coaches who had been involved at the 1972 Olympic Trials, were contacted. So, too were sportswriters, broadcasters, and even fans.

The reunion would be more than a few guys getting together for dinner and conversation.

The reunion had taken on a life of its own.

For well over a year sportswriter Billy Reed, then a part of Georgetown College's Academy of Character of Sports, had been working with Kenny and Converse to make the reunion a reality. Tirelessly Reed made phone calls, sent e-mails, and wrote letters, one of which went to President Barack Obama, inviting him to address the Olympians at the banquet on August 25. The letter was signed by Kenny Davis; Georgetown President, Dr. William H. Crouch, Jr.; and Billy Reed.

President Obama didn't show up but hundreds did in the ballroom at the Marriott Griffin Gate in Lexington.

"We felt it was a way to honor Kenny," said Allen. "He is one of our own and the reunion was a dream come true to bring the team back."

Allen admits to being as excited as Kenny about the event.

It made it easy because they all wore Converse back then, " he said. "Being involved in the 1972 reunion event is one of the highlights of my life."

Although Converse is still being produced in large numbers, it is not being done so as an athletic sneaker.

"Converse is now a lifestyle," Allen says.

Converse, the brand, still turns out the retro black with white soles, and an "all-stars" circle on the side. It is not, however, for serious sports, but rather casual wear.

Many have contributed to Converse's success over the years including Chuck Taylor, Joe Dean, Grady Lewis, and Gib Ford. Kenny Davis' name also tops that list.

"It would be impossible to calculate the number of hours I have spent listening to Chuck Taylor stories," said Kenny. "Clerks at hotels, airports, and restaurants, when they realized I worked for Converse, had a story of their favorite memory of this iconic product."

Chapter Twenty-Four

There had been several attempts to bring the '72 Olympic players and coaches together. Once in 1992, ten of them met in Washington, D.C.

"It was the 20th Anniversary," said Kenny. "And 'Sports Illustrated' organized it and paid for it all. We were put up at the Airport Marriott and that's where they did the interviews and photo shoot. We were all there except Mike Bantom and Jim Brewer.

But then in 2012, on the 40th anniversary of the never-forgotten loss to the Russians, all 12 teammates plus John Brown, and assistant coach John Bach gathered in Lexington, Kentucky. It was historic, emotional, and rolled into one wonderful weekend.

It only seemed right the reunion was spearheaded by team captain Kenny Davis, who was winding down a 40-year career with Converse.

It had been all these years since many had seen each other. Some came alone, while others brought their families.

There was nothing about their posh rooms at Marriott Griffin Gate that reminded them of their quarters at Colorado Springs, Pearl Harbor or even Olympic Village. For three days, the guys became boys again, reliving the good times, never dwelling on a single basketball game they lost, but actually won.

They golfed, dined at the Julep Cup Restaurant, and watched teammate Bobby Jones hurl a perfect strike while representing the Olympians in throwing out the first pitch at a local minor league baseball game.

"There was a reason his Olympic team named him captain," David Allen said at the reunion. "They listened to him. He herded them then and he herded them at the reunion."

At the seminar on the Georgetown College campus, one of the panel participants was Bob Hammel, a noted sportswriter from Bloomington, Indiana. He was in Munich.

"I've never bought into the fact we were robbed," he said. "I think it was a breakdown of a whole lot of people not knowing international rules and speaking different languages. It was wild."

Micki King was also a panelist. She had been the 1972 Olympic gold medal diving champion so she brought another perspective to the event.

"The athletes back then just didn't have a say in much of anything," she said. "Flying over to Munich all of the Olympic officials were in first class, wearing their suits, with plenty of room, while the athletes were in the back of the plane chewing on their knees. But, in the end, the Olympic basketball team had a say. And they said we will not accept those silver medals."

Jim Host, the sports marketing guru who changed the way colleges promoted their teams, also spoke at the Georgetown gathering.

"This reunion is one of the greatest events ever held in the state of Kentucky," he proclaimed.

Host pointed out that the NCAA finals from 1972 through 1976 had not been sellouts, and that's when he decided to take his radio background and turn it into a multi-media marketing blitz as his profession that became nationally known as Host Communication. It totally changed the landscape of sports marketing as it related to radio, television and print media in college athletic departments.

John Bach, the only surviving coach spoke. He talked about Iba and how he would eat bullion and crackers for lunch, how he referred to Kevin Joyce as a country kid who needed a lesson in defense. (Joyce played at South Carolina, but was from New York and spoke with an accent).

Bach recalled how "Mister Iba asked me to teach our Penn State zone defense to the team, and we practiced it a good five minutes."

Doug Collins emotionally talked about how the '72 Games was his "coming out" opportunity, and how when it was all over he only had $200 to his name. "It had to last me the entire year because I hadn't had a summer job. Now every player (in the Olympics) is a corporation."

Collins relived that military style, three-practices a day in Hawaii, and how tough it was. "But when I saw all those people waving the flags and cheering in Munich, it was all worth it. What happened happened. But we stood up for the truth…we won that game."

Jim Brewer recalled the turmoil in the country at the time that divided many Americans. He acknowledged U.K. Coach Joe B. Hall, his team coach at the Olympic Trials, for giving him confidence. He recalled how, at Pearl Harbor, the team practiced standing for the national anthem. He also talked about how the Cubans seemed to be enjoying their brief taste of freedom in Munich in spite of being closely watched to keep them from defecting.

Mike Vacarro, a writer with the *New York Post* told the group at Georgetown, "It's time to accept the medals. The team doesn't deserve to be looked upon the way the rest of the world looks at them…spoiled losers. End the boycott, call the I.O.C. and accept the medals."

Kevin Joyce didn't really know much about the Cold War and he didn't have anything against the Russians. 'We were basketball players," he said. "After the game we basically kicked the coaches out of the locker room when they came in and tried to get us to come out and accept the medals. We told them to file a protest. It was the wrong medal they wanted us to take and we didn't." Joyce, at the reunion was wearing a medallion his mother had made for him in honor of not getting the gold. "I wear it all the time," he said.

Ed Ratleff recalled that some of the other American athletes in the Olympic Village "agreed with us for not accepting the medals." It was so confusing to all of us…the referees…the clock…everything was a mess. We knew the rules of the game and we knew we won. Before that last game Doug (Collins) and I talked about how we were going to accept the gold and even what we were going to say."

National sports columnist Dave Kindred made a point that the '72 team had "taken a principal stand that's lasted 40 years, while a lot of us take stands that don't last 40 minutes."

Tom McMillen at one time offered a solution. "We would accept the medals, take the money for what the silver is worth and present it to a Russian orphanage. But this would only be possible if the Russians agreed to dual gold medals."

Tom Preston, a security expert, talked about the lax security at the Games, and the evolution of the Black September terrorist group. "They were a wing of Al Fatah, headed by Yasser Arafat. They were a part of the PLO (Palestine Liberation Organization) and their goal was to revenge Palestine's expulsion from Jordon in 1971. They also wanted to disrupt Germany. And by the way, Arafat later received the Nobel Peace Prize."

Preston offered that the total security cost in Munich was $2 million, whereas the 2012 Games in London cost $1.7 billion, and he added, "Security has to be right all the time…terrorist have to be right just once. In Munich they were right once."

Bobby Jones, the North Carolina player said, "I sometimes question the value of the Games. I didn't know anything about terrorism…I was a basketball player. In the Village I went to eat lunch and sat next to a Cuban. He looked at me with hate. When he saw my USA logo he got up and moved to another table."

Dwight Jones, after all of these years, has his take on the future of basketball in the Olympics. "The college players have been taken out of the Games because the "higher-ups" want to win so badly. And if they continue to take the $25 and $30 million players, it will increase the money needed for their security substantially."

Tom Burleson emotionally talked about how he had been teased and picked on in grade school because he was so tall. "I was different," he said. "My father was a Green Beret, but we lived on a farm and I milked cows. Being in the Olympics was the greatest of all-time for me."

Burleson, in 1974, was able to get some reprieve when his Norm Sloan-coached North Carolina State team won the NCAA, title defeating a Bill Walton-led UCLA team in the semis, before beating Marquette in the finals. Playing with Burleson on that team was David Thompson, the kid he had told his Olympian teammates about several years earlier.

Jim Forbes' father had served two tours in Vietnam, so he understood what patriotism was all about, "Coming into that Stadium, representing my country was the greatest feeling," he said. "I wouldn't trade that experience for anything. Nothing can take that away from me."

For Forbes the ill-fated gold medal game would be the last game he would play without an injury. "A few weeks after the Olympics I tore my knee up and was never the same. Jim Forbes has never accepted the loss. "It's hard for me to tell people we lost," he says. "It will always be 50-49, we win. Just before Coach Haskins died I told him maybe if we could have run. He looked at me and didn't say a word."

Kenny Davis and Jim Forbes were the only two U.S. Olympians who did not extend their basketball careers into either the NBA or ABA.

Over the years Tom Henderson has become philosophical about his

Olympic experience. "It's not hard for me to watch the Olympics anymore," he says. "The path to the Games is not straight, and in real life only one in a million might make it."

Henderson was Coach Iba's personal pick for the team, and looking back to that day in Colorado Springs stills stirs his memories. "I just had to make the team," he says. "But I couldn't believe it when my name was called…they had to call it three times. Henderson, after all these years, cut through the chase when talking about the U.S.-Russian game. "We never even scouted them. They had been together 12 years while we were three months. We went into the game blind, and in the bedlam on the court someone tried ripping my jersey off."

Henderson, who went on to a nine year NBA career, according to Iba was actually 18th in the voting by the selection committee. "It shows we do make mistakes," Iba said.

"We did worry a great deal about Russia," Iba said. "Regardless of what anyone says, Russia could beat one third of the pro teams. They had a veteran club and where we had played nine games before going to Munich, they had played 56."

Mike Bantom played at St. Joseph College, not one of the power schools for sure. He saw making the Olympic team the opportunity of a lifetime.

"I wanted to make myself known," he said. "Being on the team I hoped would at least give me a chance to play pro ball later." What we all went through with those three-a-day military-style practices and not being able to shoot the ball, made me question whether it was worth it. But when I saw all those people waving the flags and cheering…it was worth it."

Kenny Davis never dreamed not accepting those silver medals would bring so much publicity.

"It's taken on a life of its own," he says. "I know when we all left Munich we received over 100 telegrams and only one said we should accept them. But I've gotten a little criticism over the years from a few, so I've made an attempt to change one of the Olympic rules that pertains to medals to teams. It says if one refuses no one else can receive theirs. So if the others want their medals, I would support their wish."

When Swen Nater left the team in Hawaii and Tom McMillen came in to replace him, he roomed with Kenny at Pearl Harbor.

"Tom was studying to be a Rhodes Scholar," Kenny said. "He showed up with three suit cases. One had his clothes and two of them were filled with books. I looked at some of them and couldn't even read the titles."

The Reunion Weekend was capped off with an over-the-top banquet on Saturday, August 25, 2012, in the ballroom at the Marriott. With over 625 in attendance, the evening began with a video narrated by Lexington native and national sportscaster Tom Hammonds. Larry Conley served as MC. Kenny, along with Kentucky Governor Steve Beshear, featured speaker Doug Collins, and the other ten Olympians all spoke as well. A video tribute to the team by Coach Mike Krzyzewski was shown. It was a who's-who night when it came to Converse officials, former collegiate All-American, NBA players, coaches, and fans.

"It was a weekend of emotions," says Kenny. "There wasn't anyone who was there that didn't feel the raw emotions of what we all had experienced…not just in Munich, but in Colorado Springs and at Pearl Harbor in Hawaii.

"As much of a tragedy it was for us not being awarded what we had won, a gold medal, the real tragedy was the Israeli hostages that died at the hands of the terrorist. But we got to come home and they did not," said Kenny.

Chapter Twenty-Five

There are those who have said that Kenny Davis was an overachiever, but was he?

"From the standpoint of my rural background and limited opportunities to compete against the state's best, I suppose I did overachieve," he said. "But based on the amount of time I spent trying to develop my game, I sometime look back and feel I could have accomplished more. I strongly believe that whatever you achieve is in direct proportion to the amount of time spent reaching a goal. And from that standpoint, I don't feel I overachieved."

Kenny has always been a champion of the little guy, not because he is short in stature compared to his teammates, but because he showed that a player from a little high school and little college could make it all the way to the Olympics.

"I'm proud that I am the only player in U.S. basketball history to have played in the World Games, Pan American Games, and Olympic Games," he said. "It's not a distinction any NCAA player holds. I always thought of myself, not as a small college player, but instead, a basketball player who happened to play at a small college."

Early in 1996, the phone rang at the Davis home in Paint Lick. On the other end of the line was a representative of the United States Olympic Committee asking Kenny if he would be an Olympic torchbearer on June 6, as it passed through Kentucky on its way to light the flame at Olympic Stadium in Atlanta.

His portion of the run would be one kilometer just outside of Carrollton in northern Kentucky, and would be one phase of an 84-day relay to Atlanta involving former Olympians and celebrities.

"I was told to run slowly and savor the moment," he said. "Little kids were lined up along the road waving American flags, and all of the factories and businesses had let their people come out to see the torch pass by. I really felt a great pride in our country and the Olympics."

Kenny was dressed in all white, with a shirt saying, "The 1996 Olympic Torch Relay."

"Converse was coming out with a new shoe called the "All Star 2000," he said. "So they sent me a pre-sell edition for me to run in."

As a former Olympian and torchbearer he was permitted to keep the torch he carried, and now it is prominently displayed in his home.

The slow jog, carrying the torch, could not last long enough. Those almost unbearable practices, first with Coach Davis and then with Coach Iba, could not end soon enough. But now here he was, still representing his country in the Olympics. His mind raced as he tried to slow his legs. Rapid thoughts exploded in his mind…life is so short…sunrise…sunset. His mind drifted to his college coach, who was among the first to really believe in him. Other than his family, no one had done more for him than Coach Davis. To him this road in Carrolton was just as good as circling the track inside Olympic Stadium in Atlanta, or for that matter, Munich.

After all these years Kenny has had a lifetime to think about that gold medal game against the Russians, and all of the negative comments about Coach Iba and his style of play. And, too, he has thought about those Israelis who were murdered in what was supposed to be the safest place in the world.

"I'm not really sure now that we could have come that close to the Russians even if we had run with them," he said about that last basketball game.

During the 2012 Olympic Games in London, IOC President, Jacques Rogge, denied any recognition during the opening ceremonies for the 11 Israelis killed by Palestinian gunmen in Munich during the '72 Games.

NBC Sports anchor, Bob Costas, called the IOC's decision baffling, and decided to do his own on-air commemoration when the Israeli athletes marched into London's Olympic Stadium.

Costas called the denial not only puzzling, but insensitive, as Rogge said the opening ceremony "is an atmosphere that is not fit to remember such a tragic incident."

With mounting pressure, Rogge dedicated a moment of silence to the Israelis during an Olympic Village ceremony promoting a United

Nations initiative calling on nations to halt armed conflict during the Games. It drew about 100 people, while over 35 million in the U.S. alone saw NBC's telecast and heard Costas' comments.

For Kenny Davis, a life of playing basketball, and selling Converse shoes, has been a dream come true. What more could he wish for? A gold medal? Perhaps. A man of faith, his goals are set much higher than events that take place here on earth. The gold he is after paves the streets of his next home…and that gold cannot be taken away by an earthly judge. But what he has accomplished with his life of family, friends, and fans has turned out better than gold.

EPILOGUE

Today Kenny Davis might be considered a "gentleman farmer", as both words are accurate in describing him. He and Rita live in the house they built when they moved to Paint Lick in 1977.

He looks after a few head of cattle on his 135-acre farm, and spends a good deal of his time mending some of his three miles of fencing.

For the most part Kenny and Rita have accomplished in life what they set out to do together. First Kenny achieved his Olympic dreams, then they moved to Paint Lick where they wanted to raise their family, Jill and Bryan, and then Kenny enjoyed a 40-year career with Converse.

The landscape of college hoops and the Olympics has changed drastically since Kenny last bounced a basketball.

In 2012-13, Division I college rosters counted 333 foreign-born players. These figures dwarf the numbers from the early 1990's. The NCAA back then had rules involving international players who had played at foreign basketball academics, before there became a better understanding of what an amateur player is internationally. Once the NCAA developed academic evaluations throughout the world, there were hundreds of youngsters who met the requirements and made their way to college campuses in the United States. Today the process is so simple the only thing they have to worry about is grades.

By the time Kenny returned from Munich he was exhausted. Though he had played a career that spanned high school, college, post season all-star games, World Games, Pan-Am Games, Marathon Oil and the Olympics with virtually no injuries, he had had enough. The effort he would have to expend to play in the ABA or NBA at this point in his life was not an option. Make no mistake, he still loved the game, just short of worship. But now it was time to move on. Converse afforded him that opportunity. He could dabble a few more years with Marathon Oil enough to quench that thirst, and after that who knows, maybe some tennis, perhaps the motorcycle he had always wanted, and then bike riding, the kind you peddle.

When Kenny decides to do something, he's all in. Anyone who has ever known him at all knows that. He became a champion tennis player, then he started peddling his bicycle all over two or three states to the tune of 5,000 miles a year. Still, when it was all said and done, he had sold some eight million pairs of Converse tennis shoes. Say it again. Kenny and Rita's life is Better Than Gold.

About The Author

Gary P. West has simple criteria when it comes to writing books.

"I only take on a project that I will enjoy writing about and I only write about something I think people will enjoy reading," he says.

West grew up in Elizabethtown, Kentucky and attended Western Kentucky University before graduating from the University of Kentucky in 1967 with a journalism degree. At U.K. he was a daily sports editor for the *Kentucky Kernel.*

Later he served as editor for the nation's largest civilian enterprise military newspaper at Fort Bragg, North Carolina. From there he was employed in the corporate advertising office of one of the country's largest insurance companies, State Farm Insurance in Bloomington, Illinois, where he was a copywriter.

He returned to Kentucky in 1972 where he began an advertising and publishing business.

Along the way, for twelve years, he was the executive director of the Hilltopper Athletic Foundation at Western Kentucky University, and provided color commentary for Wes Strader on the Hilltopper Basketball Network.

In 1993, he became the executive director of the Bowling Green Area Convention and Visitors Bureau. He retired from there in 2006 to devote more time to his writing.

He is a freelance writer for several magazines in addition to writing a syndicated newspaper travel column, *Out & About...Kentucky Style*, for several papers across the state.

Gary is in demand as a speaker and for book signings throughout Kentucky.

This is his eighth book. Previous books are *King Kelley Coleman: Kentucky's Greatest Basketball Legend* (2005), *Eating Your Way Across Kentucky* (2006), *Eating Your Way Across Kentucky – The Recipes* (2007), *Shopping Your Way Across Kentucky* (2009), *101 Must Places to Visit in Kentucky Before You Die* (2009), *The Boys From Corbin: America's Greatest Little Sports Town* (2013) and co-authored *Kentucky Colonels of the American Basketball Association: The Real Story of a Team Left Behind.*

Gary and his wife, Deborah, live in Bowling Green, Kentucky.

INDEX

E

F

G

N

O

P

R

S

T

U

V